Protect Your Parents
and Their Financial Health...
Talk With Them Before It's Too Late

Susan C. Richards, CFP

Dearborn
Financial Publishing, Inc.®

This publication is designed to provide accurate and authoritative information in regard to the subject matter covered. It is sold with the understanding that the publisher is not engaged in rendering legal, accounting, or other professional service. If legal advice or other expert assistance is required, the services of a competent professional person should be sought.

Editorial Director: Cynthia A. Zigmund
Managing Editor: Jack Kiburz
Interior Design: Lucy Jenkins
Cover Design: S. Laird Jenkins Corporation
Typesetting: the dotted i

© 1999 by Susan C. Richards

Published by Dearborn Financial Publishing, Inc.®

Printed in the United States of America

99   00   01   10   9   8   7   6   5   4   3   2   1

Library of Congress Cataloging-in-Publication Data
Richards, Susan (Susan C.)
    Protect your parents and their financial health : talk with them
before it's too late / Susan Richards.
        p.   cm.
    Includes bibliographical references and index.
    ISBN 0-7931-2762-9 (pbk.)
    1. Aged—Finance, Personal.   2. Estate planning.   3. Aged—Care—
Finance.   I. Title.
HG179.R5154 1999
332.024′0565—dc21   98-36975
                                                                  CIP

Dearborn books are available at special quantity discounts to use as premiums and sales promotions, or for use in corporate training programs. For more information, please call the Special Sales Manager at 800-621-9621, ext. 4514, or write to Dearborn Financial Publishing, Inc., 155 North Wacker Drive, Chicago, IL 60606-1719.

Dedication

This book is lovingly dedicated to Bill and Rita.

Contents

Acknowledgments

My sincere thanks go to all those adult children who shared their sagas with me. "Their Stories" are a product of friends and colleagues, as well as strangers, all of whom wanted to share their anecdotes with others. I also want to thank those busy professionals who took time to speak with me or review my manuscript: Scott Blair, vice president of PaineWebber, and Thomas Drake, vice president of Sanford C. Bernstein and Co., both of whom spoke with me about affluent parents; David J. Levy, president of Adult Care Inc. (www.adultcare.com), who brought me up-to-date about the emerging world of corporate eldercare benefits; and Dr. Donna Wagner of Towson University and Dr. Neal Cutler of Widener University, who provided me with an academic perspective. My thanks also go to Gail Hunt, executive director of the National Alliance for Caregiving, who offered me needed direction through the complex maze of eldercare organizations, and Charles Mondin, director of communications and marketing at United Seniors Health Cooperative, who shared important information about health care programs for seniors. Carol Glisker, the Medicare education specialist at Empire Medicare Services was kind enough to read my health care chapter to ensure that it was technically correct given the current Medicare/Medicaid regulations; and attorney Peter O. Brown of Harter, Secrest & Emery provided a meticulous analysis of the legal aspects of aging. Paul Benjamin, CPA and a partner of Echales Benjamin & Co., examined the tax aspects of this book and corrected any misunderstandings. Dr. Patrick Arbore of the Goldman Institute on Aging offered a helpful perspective on mental health issues affecting aging parents and their adult children.

I'd also like to acknowledge the important role played by employees of Dearborn Financial Publishing, several of whom took time out from their busy work demands to share their personal stories with me. In addition, I'd like to thank both Anne Shropshire from Dearborn Financial Publishing and my editor, Cynthia Zigmund, for her support and insights. And special thanks go to Eric Kranke, president of Pension Actuaries, Lombard, Illinois, for his painstaking effort in determining how long your money will last.

Introduction

My Story

Because most baby boomers are manic about their financial future, people like me who are knowledgeable about personal finances are in great demand. This is unlike the old days when I could clear the crowd around the hors d'oeuvre table at a cocktail party by simply responding that I was a financial planner when asked about my profession. The other guests, fearful that I would try to sell them some wacky investment or, worse yet, an insurance product, would vacate the area. Their speedy departure allowed me unfettered access to the shrimp platter. I found the guests' rapid egress somewhat embarrassing but not so alarming that I lost my appetite. However, now things are, well, different.

Today at social gatherings, I never seem to be able to close in on the appetizers. Even if I could, shrimp is much more expensive now and seldom offered in large quantities. But more important, even before I get close to the food, I am repeatedly buttonholed with requests for information. These requests range from queries about what kind of pension plan would be best to questions about the long-term future of some well-known mutual fund or the tax status of Social Security income. Often, I am cornered by a financial news junkie inquiring about the condition of some esoteric new company after recently getting the nod to purchase its stock by an unknown but emphatic securities analyst. He wants my opinion. Sometimes all this activity is frustrating because it slows down my ability to consume the juicy appetizers I have been eagerly eyeing.

Unfortunately, the frequency with which people seek my advice has made me a bit complacent. So when it came to my own father's finances, I figured that I could handle whatever came my way. My dad is a widower; I am a long-distance only child. In spite of these impediments, I figured I could handle his affairs without too much trouble if and when the need arose. But I did have some lurking concerns. So I asked my dad to complete an inventory similar to the one that I prepared for you in Chapter 4. When I handed Dad the inventory, he responded by saying, "Everything is taken care of."

I was not prepared for his response. Even though I thought he would jump at the chance to get everything documented, I rationalized his reaction by saying to myself, "This is great." Deep down, I really didn't want to be dredging through Dad's personal financial affairs, so I never questioned him further. My reluctance was driven partly because I always held my dad in the highest regard. After all, I reasoned, Dad is smart, a successful entrepreneur, and financially savvy. If he says, "Everything is taken care of," what more could I need? Surely, together we were prepared for any contingency. I thought that whatever life could throw at us, we were ready. Besides, I was too chicken to press him for more information. What was I going to do if he told me something I didn't like or didn't agree with? After all, he is my father.

About six months after the infamous "everything is taken care of" conversation, Dad suffered a severe stroke and, with no warning, was suddenly unable to handle his own affairs. And there I was, trying to make informed decisions on his behalf when we had never really discussed his situation in detail. In spite of my education, training, and professional experiences, I was not so knowledgeable after all. I had to make crucial long-distance health care decisions without knowing what kind of supplemental health insurance Dad had. I had to take care of his car, which had been severely damaged when he suffered his stroke, without knowing the name of his insurance company or the location of his policy. I had to pay his bills without knowing where his checkbook was.

After flying home and visiting Dad, who was hospitalized, my next goal was to address the practical aspects. I confidently approached his desk, sure that the answers to all my questions would be quickly forthcoming. But they weren't. Dad had a system for organizing his records that I never did understand. He was a product of his generation's thinking. It wasn't that he resorted to animal skins, a quill pen, and an abacus; it's just that I couldn't fathom his methods. I am a child of the computer age who believes that adding and subtracting are tedious when you can easily create a spreadsheet with a few well-placed double clicks. Not to mention that my thinking is estrogen driven, while Dad's is totally testosterone based. I'm sure his records were fine. In fact, his accountant informed me that they were nothing short of spectacular even though they remained a mystery to me.

Eventually, Dad made a miraculous recovery. His determination and true grit were, and continue to be, a source of inspiration to me. But I will be forever humbled by the experience of his incapacitating illness. I was surprisingly ill equipped to handle my father's health crisis. I had not sat down with him and reviewed his records. I had never inquired about his supplementary medical coverage. I had only a vague notion about his investments and had never spoken with his broker. In short, I was not prepared. I thought that I could wing it. In hindsight our only savior was a power of attorney Dad had wisely signed several years ago enabling me to act as his agent. But other than that single document, we had no real plan.

Knowing how traumatic the experience was, I decided to write this book, the book I desperately wished I had *read* about five years ago. All the experts and pundits suggest that adult children talk to their parents about their finances and their emergency paperwork. And yet no one ever suggests how to go about it. The thought of chatting to Mom and Dad about these issues is daunting. Do you write a letter? Do you call a family meeting? What about your siblings? Do you call the family lawyer and tell her to do everything? So many questions and so few answers. Thus, this book is dedicated to helping you avoid the tumult of fumbling and groping on your own through all the important financial, emotional, and legal realities of your parents' aging. Our parents can't prevent the trauma that their aging brings, but working together we can minimize the problem with proper preparation.

How to Use This Book

Like most books, this one is designed to be read in its entirety. Because you may not have the time or the inclination to do this, however, for your convenience, I have outlined the top ten financial problems of the elderly and where to find the solutions for each.

1. The biggest impediment to getting our parents' finances squared away is the *low level of financial literacy* attained by Americans of all ages. Adult children may be reluctant to raise the issue of their parents' finances because they're afraid they won't be able to recognize potential problems. They fret that even if they *are* able to identify a predicament, they wouldn't know what to do next. Parents don't want to discuss their finances because they don't have enough financial knowledge to realize that they have a problem and/or they don't want to reveal their own financial ignorance. If you are hesitant to talk to your parents because you feel inept, you probably should take the time to read this book in its entirety.

2. Malcolm Boyd, an Episcopal priest and the author of many books on religion and spirituality, also writes an advice column in AARP's bimonthly magazine, *Modern Maturity*. In a recent issue he revealed that of the several thousand letters he has received from readers over the years, the vast majority of questions have focused on intergenerational issues: it's common for parents to fret about children and vice versa. If questions about intergenerational finances are a problem in your family, then join the majority of American families and forget the idea that you are alone in your plight. Financial issues are exacerbated by the fact that families seldom talk about money. We can speculate about the reasons for this silence 'til the cows come home. But what's more important is that parents and adult children begin to discuss the parents' financial and legal arrangements. In Chapters 1, 2, and 3 you'll find in-depth suggestions for both understanding and addressing your *parents' financial concerns* as well as your own.

3. Many of the elderly keep *poor records* that leave their adult children unprepared to handle a crisis. Work with your parents to complete the inventory found in Chapter 4 so you can locate that important name or piece of paper in an emergency.

4. Most of our parents never took paper and pencil in hand to plan their retirement years. They simply took the money available to them and created a lifestyle with the resources they had, coping as best they could. Would the money last as long as they would? Who knew? Their *lack of planning* is understandable, for no one can predict with certainty future inflation rates, longevity, or health problems. But the

real truth is that advance planning is the single most important factor for helping aging parents. If you want to learn how to help your parents plan for retirement costs, calculate annual income, and incorporate inflation into their forecasts, read Chapter 5.

5. Some parents don't want to bother with such paperwork details as wills, trusts, and powers of attorney, so *necessary paperwork* often is useless, nonexistent, out-of-date, improperly drafted, not signed, or, worse yet, current but impossible to locate. Check out Chapter 6 for suggestions on how to address this problem. Even if your parents have pristine paperwork, ask them to update everything every three years.

6. Many of the elderly are beset with *the problem of few assets* and yet fail to explore alternatives for solving the problem. Perhaps they are just old dogs having difficulty learning new tricks, or maybe it's just too hard for some of them to fathom the morass of eligibility rules and government regulations. Whatever the impediment, you probably need to buttress your parents' efforts by reading Chapter 7.

7. Children of parents who have money face different pressures than those experienced by parents with limited resources but pressures nevertheless. Some wealthy parents have overcomplicated their financial life, which makes trying to manage their affairs parent care hell. Others may allow their money to slip through their fingers because they don't work at managing their finances or they fail to correct their holdings to reflect a changing economy. Check out Chapter 8 to learn more about *coping with wealthy parents.*

8. Our parents are sure to run into *health problems* somewhere along the way, but are they prepared for the costs? Many parents depend solely on Medicare, assuming that it will cover all their medical bills. It won't. Others buy coverage that is either insufficient or just too darn expensive for what they are getting. Studies show that only a small minority of adult children understand how Medicare works, so read Chapter 9 to learn how to obtain the optimal health care insurance coverage for the least amount of money.

9. Many adult children operate in their own little universe and assume that their family is the only one that can't get its financial act together. Read all the vignettes entitled "Their Stories" to learn about

the prevalence of intergenerational financial issues, issues that are the norm, not the exception.

10. Finally, many of the elderly overpay their taxes or fail to incorporate *tax planning* into their financial decisions. This is not surprising given the inhumanly complex nature of our tax code, but it still costs the elderly money that they can ill afford to part with. To help you tackle this problem, tax planning suggestions are peppered throughout the book. Chapters 5, 7, and 8 offer specific suggestions.

CHAPTER 1

A Report Card on the American Family

"The more things change, the more they remain the same."

—Alphonse Karr (1849)

Before we get to the nitty-gritty issues—the issues that directly affect adult children, their parents, and their parents' finances—we should take a moment to consider the state of the family as we approach the millennium. The social, political, and economic environment has altered dramatically from 20 years ago. Some people feel that today's families face more difficult challenges. Others say that conditions impacting family life have changed for the better. The only certainty is that these shifts are having and will continue to have an enormous impact on both adult children and their parents.

The Good News

Our parents and we adult children are faced with an unparalleled rate of change. One of the most dramatic events reshaping the American family is lengthening life spans. It's no secret that currently we are in the midst of what some experts call a longevity revolution. When you consider the statistics, the demographic aspects of aging have been nothing short of stunning. At the beginning of this century, only 1 person in 25 reached age 65. Since that time, the average life expectancy has increased a whopping 28 years! A person born in 1900 could expect to live on average to the age of 47. Today, almost 100 years later, a male child can expect to live to 80 and a female child well into her eighth decade.

It comes as no surprise to learn that America ranks first in the world for its 80-plus-year-old population, a distinction all the more remarkable because we are by no means the most populous country. Pundits attribute the distinction to our advanced health care system and generous public and private programs that support our aging citizens. But as a nation we are just beginning to understand the ramifications of the aging phenomenon and how it will impact our daily lives. One thing is for sure—it's going to have profound consequences on how we work, play, and save for our later years.

By the time the baby boomers reach 65, they'll have lots of company. Around 2020, it's thought that more than 20 percent of all Americans will be 65 or over. The Census Bureau projects that 1 in 9 baby boomers, those children born between 1946 and 1964, will survive into their late 90s. A hundred years ago only 1 person in 500 lived to age 100; however, an increase to 1 in 26 is projected for the baby boom generation, allowing some people to have two or even three separate careers during their working lifetime.

Increased longevity will undoubtedly change the world as we know it. Author Gail Sheehy has even coined a new phrase to describe this change. She calls the ages from 45 to 65 second adulthood and suggests these years will be a time for baby boomers to reevaluate their lives. She predicts that during their second adulthood, boomers will attempt the challenges they always wanted to try but were too busy with first careers to even consider. This is a substantial change from a 100 years ago when few people lived long enough to make such choices. And if they were among the remarkable few who did live that long, they certainly did not consider this time of life as a rare opportunity to pursue their lifelong dreams.

The Bad News

Many experts argue that the impact of massive demographic and socioeconomic trends aren't as kind to the baby boom generation as would first appear. Most of the facts that buttress their universal concerns are indisputable. First, they point out that the trends have converged, noting that more and more adult children find themselves squeezed in the middle between their aging parents and their own children. Today's young adults are referred to as members of Generation X. Many boomers are finding that their Generation X children seem to need more and more time before they are prepared to launch themselves into the adult world. The other reason boomers find themselves in the middle is that the over-85 group comprises the fastest growing age segment in our society. Population studies suggest baby boomers may still have grown children at home while struggling to assist aging parents as well.

Second, like the rest of the industrialized world, the United States is experiencing a falling birthrate. Thus, our old people have far fewer children to help care for them. And because an increasing number of people are living long enough to require assistance with everyday chores, some adult children find themselves simultaneously helping both their parents and their grandparents. Further, many argue that the public and private systems of paid care tend to be costly, in short supply, undependable, and incompatible with adult children's time constraints posed by both paid employment and other family obligations.

The Special Case of Women

Concern has also been expressed for the well-being of the generation of women in the middle. Experts worry that these women have far too many simultaneous demands on their time. These pressures may stem from a challenging job or career in addition to children and a husband who require their attention. When these stresses are coupled with the responsibilities of caring for frail elderly parents and/or other elderly family members, the combined impact of all these obligations becomes difficult to manage.

Many of these women have chosen to have their children later in life so they could pursue a career. But they may discover that this strategy has backfired as they potentially could have the responsibility for both young children and old parents. And if these pressures aren't bad enough, many women may also be students preparing for a career or seeking career advancement. Many families today depend on a woman's income for their survival. Given the high divorce rate, it's likely that many working women with frail aging parents are single parents. If these daughters are the sole support and caregiver for a dependent child, their ability to help their parents is highly limited. Any one of these circumstances is difficult by itself, but can really wreak havoc on a woman's life when combined.

So now you know the drill. Long-term demographic trends are dire: the sons and daughters of aging parents may live far away, may be divorced or have never married at all, and must typically work long hours to get ahead in their chosen profession. In addition, these children, and especially the daughters who traditionally have cared for aging parents, have now taken on new roles. Experts worry that the new demands will make it all but impossible for these adult children to be concerned about their aging parents.

The "Sandwich Generation"

This view is so widely held that the current generation of adult children has its own moniker—the "sandwich generation"—for its position between aging parents and Generation X children. But is it true that adult children choose to be uninvolved with their parents, or is it just another prototype perpetuated by the media in their newspaper headlines and magazine stories?

In Truth: Who Needs Whom?

As early as 1993 some were beginning to question the purported demise of the concerned adult child. Carroll Estes and James Swan, in their book *The Long Term Care Crisis: Elders Trapped in the No-Care Zone,* noted that "the independence of family caregiving patterns from public policy is more impressive than the connections. While the demise of filial relations and responsibility has been reported and their survival regularly rediscovered, parents and children have conducted their affairs with each other without attention to either kind of news. Family life flows on, untroubled by scholars and columnists." So what's the real situation between today's parents and their adult children? Do the children continue to respect their parents or has that time-honored tradition been abandoned by the current crop of adult children?

First, we need to conduct a reality check. How much help do American seniors really need? We quickly discover that today's seniors are much healthier than you might expect. The conventional wisdom holds that older people are sickly, senile, and unproductive. If that's true, why is the senior golf circuit so popular? Look at the phenomenal careers of many older individuals who once were or still are healthy, vital, and productive well into their seventh, eighth, and even ninth decade. Many of these people—Bob Dole, Strom Thurmond, and the late George Burns and Grandma Moses—are household names. But there are literally thousands and thousands of other unsung seniors still going strong. Their vitality is supported by recent studies that show Americans 65 and older are averaging fewer than 15 days in bed a year as the result of illness, not so different from those under 65 who average 6 days a year. These data are even more remarkable given the fact that the numbers for the over-65 group are skewed to the upside by a small minority of the elderly who are bedridden year-round.

We often envision an elderly person as someone frail, usually a woman, who lives in an institution and spends her lonely days in the company of other frail women. That, however, is far from typical. The reality is that no more than 5 percent of the elderly live in a nursing home at any given time. Even after 85, when seniors are considered the frail elderly, the number rises only to 22 percent, suggesting that only one in five is institutionalized. Furthermore, a cure for Alzheimer's disease would empty about one-half of the country's nursing home beds, while a cure for arthritis would have a phenomenal effect on the mobility of the elderly, further reducing the nursing home population. Forget the notion that all of the elderly are frail. In fact, disability rates among people over 65 have fallen steadily since the early 1980s. Also, it's likely that our growing knowledge of the influence of proper diet and regular exercise will further improve the quality of the later years.

The notion that, as they age, your parents will inevitably become decrepit is no longer valid. According to a lengthy article in the June 30, 1997, issue of *Newsweek* magazine, "The good news is that even though people are living longer, studies show that every year more and more old people are able to take care of themselves. The percentage of people with crippling chronic diseases such as high blood pressure and arthritis has steadily declined. The care-giving industry is sure to boom with the sheer numbers of the elderly, but the predictions of overflowing nursing homes draining the nation's economic wealth now seems outdated."

Another equally unfortunate, but common, presumption about the parent generation that often goes unchallenged is that as parents age, they become increasingly dependent on their adult children. But when you ponder your own old age, do you see yourself depending on your children? You probably think that you can hold onto your independence. Your parents want to maintain their independence, too, for as long as they can. And they seem to be doing a surprisingly good job of it. To figure who is helping whom, in 1989 researchers in Albany, New York, interviewed 1,200 adults aged 40 and over chosen at random. The published study, entitled *Family Ties,* queried adults about how the family handled life's ordinary tasks and, more precisely, who did the handling.

This study differed from others in surveying a group of people chosen at random rather than researching the behavior of special groups. The chores evaluated by the study were the mundane tasks that bog us all down regardless of age. The researchers asked 1,200 people who cleaned the house, ran the errands, cared for the children, and handled the heavy chores such as yard work. The results were more than a little surprising: "The image of the frail elderly is misleading for intergenerational relationships: help (between adult children and their parents) is generally reciprocal, but more help is given to the child generation until the point when parents reach about seventy-five years of age."

The study showed that parents are twice as likely to be helping their adult children as they are to be receiving help from them!! The percentage of parents giving and receiving help finally levels out when parents are in their mid-70s and children are in their early 40s. Until then, parents spend more time, energy, and money helping their adult children than the other way around. The study illustrates that our parents are likely to continue the patterns of our childhood by providing more care for us than we provide for them. This behavior persists until our parents' physical limitations prohibit them from being equal partners, a finding that flies in the face of the widely held assumption that aging parents are dependent on others. The notion that older parents are a burden to their adult children is now being replaced with a more realistic view that most aging parents offer more help than they receive.

A number of recent caregiver studies have asked adult children about the type of help they extend to their parents. A surprisingly large percentage of adult children describe themselves as parental caregivers. Adult children indicate they assist by running errands or paying bills. But what is missing in many of these studies is the other side of the coin: What are these same children receiving in return? It's likely they are receiving reciprocal support from their parents. The parents may be pitching in and supplying child care so their adult children can hold down a full-time job. Or they may be giving their adult children money; financial assistance has a pattern similar to help with the practical side of life. Adult children, in sum, are more likely to be receiving than giving.

Family Ties demonstrates that parents not only help their adult children by giving of themselves as well as giving money, but many adult children move in with parents when it's convenient for the children. It was widely thought that an adult child moves in with Mom and Dad only when Mom and Dad require help with everyday activities. But adult children, at least according to the study, move in with parents when it fits their personal situation. The participants in the study indicated that moving in usually stemmed from a child's life event rather than a desire to help out the parent. It appears clear from this study that the older generation provides much-needed support to its harried adult children. The idea that our parents are just demanding older people who think only about themselves is not borne out by research. Nor is the idea that adult children simultaneously have responsibilities for both dependent parents and young children supported by the findings of this study.

Your parents will probably continue to be independent for longer than you ever imagined. It also appears that most parents pitch in and help their adult children to a degree that few researchers appreciated. Now let's look at the baby boomers to discover if they are holding up their end of the deal. This generation of adult children has been long scrutinized under the microscopes of sociologists and columnists. Their findings are often accompanied by frequent hues and cries about the "good old days." The think tank people first considered whether the boomers were leaving their own children in the lurch. Researchers worried that the burgeoning number of working mothers would spawn a large population of problem children. And yet, to date, all the studies on the impact of mothers' workforce participation have been inconclusive. The majority of these studies have failed to prove that employed mothers produce delinquent or troubled children at a faster rate than traditional intact one-income families.

The researchers then focused on the parents of working mothers. Again, no evidence exists to support the notion that the baby boom generation has abandoned its parents despite a shift in the way families operate. More and more family members work than ever before. The incidence of blended families has risen significantly, too. It was widely predicted that the boomers would desert their aging parents in droves. It turns out, though, that nothing could be further from the truth. Good news doesn't sell books, magazines, or newspapers, so we don't hear much about the positive side of this issue.

The following facts uncovered by researchers challenge much of the negative conjecture:

1. Despite the speculation, *families remain the main source of help for older people* who are unable to meet all their own needs. Almost all older people have at least one family member who is actively concerned about them. Family caregivers, in spite of the growing number of paid caregivers, still provide between 80 and 90 percent of the assistance needed by the frail elderly. Institutionalization is the last recourse for families and is chosen long after all other avenues of help have been exhausted. The old adage that the more things change, the more they stay the same, seems to be an apt interpretation of the effect of all the social and demographic changes on the parent-adult child relationship.

2. The notion that people can't cope with all the demands on their time has not been borne out by research. *Most families, it turns out, usually don't have to care for both young children and dependent parents simultaneously.* This situation, widely reported in the press, simply doesn't occur that often. Of course, it *is* traumatic for those families in which it does occur, but it is by no means a national phenomenon. According to researchers, it is unlikely that your teenage son will have to donate his bedroom to his aging grandmother.

3. *Parental caregiving has become a real family affair.* In previous decades it was traditional for one child to assume total responsibility for an infirm parent. There is evidence today that this model is changing. Constraints on adult childrens' available time have encouraged siblings to cooperate. According to a July 23, 1997, report in the *Wall Street Journal* ("More Family Members are Working Together to Care for Elders"), adult children are sharing parent care responsibilities. This new approach is applauded by many experts because it gives aging parents added vitality when all the children unite to provide joint parent care.

4. *The ties are still strong between the generations.* In spite of all the hot air, adult children have not abdicated their responsibilities. The Judeo-Christian admonishment to honor your father and mother still remains the unwritten law of the land. Continuing contact between parents and their adult children is the rule and not the exception. Even adult chil-

dren who work long hours or are single parents are no less involved with their parents than previous generations. Surprisingly, most older people live withing an hour's driving distance of at least one adult child. Besides, the fact that you chose to read this book speaks volumes in itself.

So despite all the hand-wringing to the contrary, adult children and their parents are doing quite well, thank you. Yes, there are some problems. Many adult children have too many demands on their time. Some parents are unhappy with their children's lifestyle choices. But from time immemorial, adult children and their parents have complained about each other. However, the relationships between this current generation of parents and adult children are for the most part intact, healthy, and happy. The notions that most members of the parent generation are sickly or that all adult children are self-absorbed don't hold water. Thus, I would give this current crop of parents and adult children a B+ for their continuing efforts to maintain a high degree of contact and mutual support. Still, diverse generational perspectives do exist, so in the next chapter we explore the unique financial outlooks of parents and their adult children.

CHAPTER 2

Why Is It So Hard to Talk to Your Parents about Their Finances?

"A mother can raise ten children but ten children can't raise a mother."

—Middle Eastern Proverb

Grown children often know all sorts of private things about their parents—the intimate details of their parents' childhood, including such minutia as the color of Mom's childhood bedroom, the names of their parents' little playmates, and even Dad's favorite childhood foods. They also know a lot of current details about their parents—whether Dad is a gourmet cook or if Mom can fix things. And they know plenty of family secrets, too, which can provide a bushel of ammunition in heated family discussions. But when it comes to conversations about the state of Mom and Dad's finances, the sounds of silence are nothing short of deafening.

In fact, it's so quiet you can hear a pin drop. Between the two generations, the conspiracy of silence that surrounds financial matters is standard behavior. It's the unusual family that talks freely and easily about its finances. Much of the resistance to talking about money is buried in strong cultural and generational barriers. The net result is that kids don't ask and parents don't tell, or perhaps it's vice versa. Both grown children as well as their parents tend to regard money as a private issue. Each group feels that sharing this special information could somehow make it vulnerable. And therein lies the paradox. We feel that if we remain silent, we are protecting our own emotional turf; in addition, we feel that silence on matters of money is a sign of respect. Yet we want to become closer to our parents. One way to do that is to understand their financial reality. But reaching that understanding demands we take an emotional risk.

The most important outcome of a discussion with our parents about the financial (or other) issues of old age often leads to both increased peace of mind and lessened emotional turmoil. Those people who talk to their parents openly and honestly about their concerns usually handle the problems that may be associated with their parents' aging better than those who remain uninvolved and silent. Such discussions are ticklish because they touch, at least tangentially, on the two most powerful taboos in our society—discussions of money and death. Underlying the need for your parents to get their finances in order is that someone else will have to take over the loose ends when parents become incompetent or die.

Dr. Mark Edinberg notes in his book *Talking with Your Aging Parents* that "your emotional responses and those of your elderly parents and the rest of the family to legal and financial issues are likely to be representative of every conflict, connection, norm, and value your family has. Money, assets, and control over decisions symbolize any and all of the following: power, control, identity, ability to influence others, dominance, the nature of relationships, and self-indulgence." In other words, in most families money represents much more than just the ability to buy things.

Two Types of Adult Children

My own research indicates that adult children are of two minds about the topic of their parents' money. The first, and larger, group does a lot of mental hand wringing about the unknown state of their parents' finances. But do they actually say anything? Nope, their lips don't move. In most cases adult children share their concerns with their spouse, friends, colleagues, and siblings. And yet, when it comes down to actually having "the conversation," most adult children find themselves at a loss for words. These same adult children may make frequent multimedia presentations at work, be corporate bigwigs, or have attained a highly regarded professional status.

In spite of their elevated position in society, these adult children nonetheless avoid having "the conversation"—the 1990's equivalent of the plague. Nobody in the family volunteers to talk with Mom and Dad about their finances because it's just too scary. Most adult kids are so intimidated about having "the conversation" that they fail to raise any questions at all. They feel unsure about choosing the optimal time to initiate a financial discussion. So they don't even bother starting the process. If you are among this group, take heart; you have lots and lots of company.

Then there is the second, and smaller, group of adult children, those who choose to assume that their parents have everything taken care of. Most children admire their parents during their growing-up years; and that admiration and respect tends to remain strong long after adult children have become established in their own right. Their long-held regard leads them to mistakenly determine that their parents' financial affairs must be in order—after all, we're talking about Mom and Dad here. As a result, this group rests easily within its own comfort zone and certainly doesn't want to upset the equilibrium by inquiring into parents' affairs. It would be much too inconvenient for children to learn that their parents' financial and legal affairs were not in tip-top shape. Nor do they want to discover that their parents are unknowingly running out of money.

The Problem with Ignoring the Problem

The hard truth is that sticking-your-head-in-the-sand thinking is delusional. If you are taking comfort in the mistaken notion that everything has been taken care of, I'd strongly encourage you to remove your parents from their financial pedestal. I know that a parental fall from grace isn't pretty, but it's necessary. The world is so complex today that you probably don't have a good handle on your own finances, so how can you rightly assume that your parents, who are at least 25 years your senior and probably less savvy about the realities of this rapidly changing world, would have their financial affairs in order?

Let's say that, in response to your questions, Mom and Dad give you the welcome information that they have executed both a power of attorney for property and one for health care. It appears, based on what they have chosen to tell you (and I use the word *chosen* carefully), that on the surface there is nothing for you to worry about. After all, it seems they have all the documentation that could possibly be required to meet any health care or financial crisis. Yet later you could discover, much to your horror, that the documents your parents had drafted in Massachusetts are not valid in Nevada, their current state of residence. I hate to be the one to break the bad news (remember the saying about killing the messenger), but the state of your parents' financial affairs is not an issue you can afford to ignore. Even if they have ample resources, your parents may require your involvement if and when they find it increasingly difficult to manage their own affairs. Or they may require your actual financial support at some future time.

Regardless of what Mom and Dad say or lead you to believe, you still need to get involved. Even if they read a daily financial publication, belong to an investment group, and meet with their lawyer religiously for the annual update ritual, you still need to become knowledgeable about their situation. Even if your parents' financial affairs are in top-notch shape, you can't afford the luxury of looking the other way. If a crisis develops, you certainly don't want

Their Stories
• • • • •

Ted, a successful small-town accountant, always thought that his dad was the greatest. Dad seemed so talented—after all, he knew how to make his own fishing lures and was considered a great real estate salesman. Even at 81, Dad was still working. Ted figured that his father was just working to keep his hand in and have something to do with his free time. But Ted figured wrong. After five years of giving a healthy monthly stipend to Mom and Dad to help them pay for their basic expenses, Ted's brother revealed that Dad and Mom were broke. Ted never knew until that moment that his parents were in any kind of financial trouble.

• • • • •

to be making critical decisions on your parents' behalf based strictly on conjecture. And therein lies the real issue.

When information is lacking, confusion ultimately results. If you are precluded from understanding your parents' financial affairs until the time they are no longer competent or they die, it's likely that you will have to deal with a jumble of papers and documents that can take months and months of hard work to square away. Your effort will inevitably lead to frustration if resolving your parents' financial situation consumes more and more of your time. At some point you will begin to wonder what went wrong. Then the blaming game commences. You'll start pondering the unavoidable question: Who is responsible for creating this mess? You can accept the responsibility yourself. Or you can place the blame directly on your parents' doorstep; but either way the emotional impact won't be good.

A True Story

The *New York Times* of August 10, 1997, carried a heartrending account of a freelance writer living in New York City who traveled to a small town in Georgia to help his ailing 94-year-old great uncle. Unfortunately, when he arrived he found his uncle in a very sad state. Formerly a meticulously groomed man, his uncle was now living in squalor with cockroaches and garbage as live-in companions. Piles of papers abounded. The uncle's final notice from the IRS lay in a foot-high stack of papers as federal and state tax returns had not been filed for years. In another pile, the writer located a moldy stock certificate later valued at more than $1 million. Uncle Joe also admitted to having 40 separate accounts spread over the southern half of the country.

The result of the uncle's lack of planning was as predictable as it was unfortunate, hurting everyone involved. The uncle wouldn't allow someone else to take over the management of his financial affairs or his personal care when he was no longer able to manage on his own. This situation left the family between a rock and a hard place, especially when the nephew became the target of his uncle's wrath. The only reasonable option was to petition the courts to declare the uncle incompetent. Like all competency hearings, this one was emotionally draining and expensive. The uncle was ultimately declared incompetent by the judge, a local man was named his personal guardian, and a local bank named to manage his financial affairs.

A competency hearing provides a mechanism for managing both a loved one's finances and health care under strict guidelines, but the price is usually the emotional scars. Even though no one wants strangers making crucial decisions for those who are near and dear, handing relatives over to strangers can be the result when prior arrangements have not been made. With his responsibilities concluded, the nephew reluctantly left his aged uncle living at his home with a qualified caregiver. The nephew was free to return to New York City and pursue his own life. And even though he had fulfilled his responsibilities, the nephew left with a heavy heart. The only bright spot was that his own father was motivated to supply the requisite paperwork to put his financial affairs in order, so at least the nephew was assured that he wouldn't have to go through a similar ordeal any time in the near future.

Truth or Consequences

The sad story of the Georgia uncle spawned a firestorm of responses from readers who had experienced similar situations with their own aging relatives. The reason this true story is so important is that you could easily be in the same situation as the nephew if you ignore the unfortunate ramifications of aging. Not every family will find itself in a similar situation, but some will be faced with similar consequences. Typically, at some point there will be a family crisis and you or an unlucky sibling will be madly scrambling in an all-out effort to untangle a relative's affairs. Such an unfortunate event usually occurs at the worst time—when the relative no longer has the capacity to unravel the routine mysteries associated with his or her personal finances.

If you don't have "the conversation," just when Mom or Dad is sick and both have a pressing need for your emotional support, you'll find yourself trying to juggle many demands. Instead of providing welcome moral support, you'll be busy discovering what, if any, supplemental medical insurance Mom and Dad have. You'll be dashing around trying to find the safe deposit box key in a vain effort to locate all those important papers that you can't lay your hands on. You'll be trying to organize your parents' records while simultaneously trying to make intelligent investment decisions on their behalf, paying their bills, and filing their taxes. At some point you'll need competent professional advisers who can assist you and your siblings. As you may have surmised, this task will be both daunting and time consuming if you are unprepared.

Trying to accomplish so many chores from a distance is even more difficult. If you have to gather loose ends from far away, your problems and your
resultant frustration will only mount, an unfortunate situation that can overwhelm your life and possibly derail your career. Like it or not, Mom and Dad
have to play along at least enough to get the big stuff out of the way. Items like
powers of attorney and living wills are a must for today's families. It's also critical to learn if your parents will have enough money to meet their basic needs.
Certainly you have the right to know if your parents are running out of money
because their needs will impact your own financial future.

The longer you delay, the more serious the problems can become. As your
parents age, it's likely that they will find it increasingly difficult to remember
the details of long-ago financial transactions. You'll need their help when you
try to untangle a web of securities discovered under the mattress or in the safe
deposit box. These items may include old bank books, deeds, or yellowing brokerage statements. Don't be surprised if you stumble across stock certificates
and insurance policies dating back perhaps to the 1930s, some of which are
valuable and others worthless. Most peoples' financial life takes years and
years to create. Over a lifetime, these choices evolve in a piecemeal fashion
and inevitably create a financial quagmire. Trying to figure out long-ago transactions without Mom and Dad's input can be a real challenge.

I hope I've made a compelling case for getting involved in your parents'
finances. It's in your own best interests to get at least the basic stuff squared
away. Now that you're convinced that you should have "the conversation," let's
roll up our selves and consider in-depth the reasons behind our universal resistance to talking to our parents about their money. What factors could possibly
foster our reluctance to involve ourselves in such important issues as whether
Mom and Dad's money will last as long as they will?

Different Generations, Different Perspectives

One major stumbling block is that Mom and Dad grew up under circumstances different from ours. As a result, our parents operate under their own
generational mind-set. The gap between the thinking of one generation compared with that of the next has always been a factor. But the thinking of these
two generations—ours and our parents'—about private financial matters seems

especially divergent. The generational perspectives may be so different that adult children are often afraid they just won't understand their parents' thinking. Adult children may fear that the differences, if aired, could somehow damage their cherished relationship with their parents. Given our fears, even if not well founded, we back away from a discussion about finances.

Our Parents' Reality

The generations part company on many issues, starting with the question of responsibility. Our parents' generation seems to be wedded to the concept that every person is responsible for himself or herself. Our parents' generation, which lived through the Great Depression and a major world war, is an independent group. Older people are less apt to support their own generation in potential conflicts over generational issues. Researchers note, for example, that parents are less likely than adult children to believe that the children should make room for them in their home if a parent becomes seriously ill or runs out of money. Aging parents are more likely to agree than are their children that providing care for older parents is too much of a burden for adult children. Many parents want the best possible future for their adult children, so they often minimize their expectations of support while emphasizing their own responsibilities.

This intense desire for independence was immortalized by 71-year-old Marian Juhl, who wrote in the October 13, 1997, issue of *Newsweek* that she wanted to have Do Not Resuscitate tattooed across her chest. She noted that all the Generation Xers were getting tattoos, so why not get on the bandwagon? She supported this desire by noting, "I do have a genuine fear of becoming incapacitated by a serious accident or illness. . . . I've always been fiercely independent. . . . What if I am treated by a doctor who believes that it is a physician's responsibility to apply all the heroic efforts available despite the patient's wishes? What if my paperwork gets lost? What if my paperwork is exactly where it is supposed to be, but no one stumbles across it until after I've been resuscitated and my oblivious body is kept alive by life support."

In the *Family Ties* study, which was conducted in Albany, New York, parents were asked if they should be able to depend on their adult children if they get into financial trouble. Of those between 40 and 50, 64 percent replied in the affirmative, whereas only 31 percent of those over age 80 did. The same results held on public policy issues too. Researchers asked people both over and under

65 their thoughts on the importance of affordable health care. Although the majority of adult children answered strongly in the affirmative, their parents, who were qualified to receive the benefits, were much less in favor of government-sponsored health care for the aged.

It's remarkable that adult children are willing to assume more responsibility for their aging parents than their parents themselves think is warranted. Part of the parents' resistance stems from their having come of age long before the inception of many public and private aid programs. The word *entitlement* is not likely to be part of our parents' vocabulary much less their mind-set. Most of our parents believe that they never got "something for nothing" in their entire life, and they aren't about to start now.

President Lyndon Johnson's vision of the Great Society represented a different way of thinking for our parents. Those who embraced this vision typically felt that the programs would benefit the unfortunate few. Certainly, our parents figured that these programs were not designed for hard-working people such as themselves. These entitlements were for other people—people willing to accept handouts. Thus, many seniors who are eligible for much-needed help fail to, or refuse to, consider the possibility of receiving outside help. Our generation was politically active, and we devoted much of our energies to helping those we felt were not getting their fair share. Adult children as a group tend to feel that it's the government's responsibility to help the less fortunate, unlike our parents who seldom see the world from the same vantage point.

Many of our parents feel that accepting help from strangers is not an option, nor do they want to address personal financial matters with others. They especially don't relish chatting about these matters with their adult children! A major part of the parent-child financial discussion dilemma is that our parents' generation was never part of the Jerry Springer era in which intimate family secrets are routinely displayed for the world's consumption. In our parents' time, family matters were kept private. It's almost a certainty that money was never part of dinner-table conversations when our parents were children. Nor did our parents routinely talk about their income or expenses with us while we were still living at home. As a result of these generational norms, therapists indicate that their depression-era clients are loathe to reveal the state of their finances, even in the context of private therapeutic relationships.

Our independent-minded parents usually don't want to talk about their finances. Period. But we need to view their reluctance from a broader perspective so that we can try to understand their thinking. Adult children should be sensitive to the fact that the importance of retirement planning is a fairly recent phenomenon. In earlier decades, worries about paying for one's retirement years were seldom an important consideration because few people lived long enough to actually retire. When our parents were growing up, it was the unusual individual who lived past 65. Besides, most people expected just to keep working until the end.

In those days, before the advent of public programs, if an individual could no longer work, family members would provide for him or her. The first public program furnishing an income for the aged was established in Germany about 80 years ago. The Germans selected 65 as the age when recipients could first qualify to receive benefits. And for some reason, the age of 65 has been the magic number for starting retirement ever since. In this country, the Social Security Retirement Income Program wasn't instituted until 1935 and was the first public program that addressed the need for retirement income. But even in 1935, it was designed only to augment personal retirement savings. Corporate pension plans didn't get their start until after World War II, when companies needed to attract scarce workers.

Members of our parents' generation have been pioneers as a profusion of events turned life upside down for them. Most of these events surprised both parents and their adult children, leaving everyone affected a bit off guard. Most of our parents never anticipated that they would live this long, so they couldn't foresee the amount of money that their retirement years would require. My own parents planned their financial and emotional lives around the certain fact that my mother would be a widow. It was taken as a given, based on family genetics, that my father would predecease her. Our family's entire retirement and estate plans were predicated on the unchallenged premise that Mom would outlive Dad by perhaps one or even two decades. And yet my dad, who is still going strong, is the first male in his family's recent memory to live past 65. In fact, happily, he has survived a decade longer than anyone dared hope.

This personal saga is only one of thousands and thousands in which a family member's life expectancy was far greater than anyone could have forecast. This longevity revolution has been spawned in very large part by vast improvements in the quality of medical care. Techniques such as heart transplants, which were avant-garde just a few years ago, are now fairly routine medical techniques, albeit expensive ones. These improvements like everything else, however, have come at a price. One unfortunate side effect of longevity is medical "sticker shock" when seniors are billed for newfangled medical treatments. It's often hard for them to accept that old low-tech methods for solving the typical medical problems of the elderly have been replaced by expensive high-tech options. In this era of high-tech everything, it's not only difficult for our parents to grasp how fast things are changing but they don't want to understand that technology will continue to have a profound impact on the financial aspects of aging.

Out with the old and in with the new may be an easy mantra for us to preach, but it leaves those who grew up before the advent of television, microwaves, and cellular phones longing for the days when things were much simpler. The unfortunate result of technology is that our parents often don't comprehend its enormous impact. They just don't realize why it's so important that they "get with the program." They often don't understand that devices such as medical directives and powers of attorney just make good sense today. It's difficult for them to realize that they need to implement legal techniques as protection against technology's dark side.

Another important distinction between you and your parents is that most of our parents worked during an unusual time in our country's history. Many members of our parents' generation could afford to be passive about their retirement planning because, during their working lives, both private industry and the government worked to create an acceptable retirement income for their constituents. These two powerful entities unwittingly cooperated to make it their collective responsiblity to provide for citizen/worker retirement. The average worker figured that everything would be taken care of; from medical care to day-to-day living expenses. Given the at-the-time public and private largess, it was only natural that many retirees also assumed that if they needed long-term nursing home care, the government would pick up the tab.

In my early days as a financial planner, I distinctly remember helping people plan for their retirement who, given their private pension combined with their Social Security income, were going to have more after-tax income as retirees than they earned while working. Our parents were lulled into thinking that they had everything squared away, assuming they would have plenty of money to provide for their basic needs. But assumptions often don't prove reliable for they are just that—assumptions. When retirees were making their retirement plans 15 years ago, they couldn't envision a time when the combined impact of inflation, spiraling health care costs, government cutbacks, and longevity could place so many in a precarious financial situation. Nor did our parents ever foresee that the financial issues of aging would become so complex.

Our Reality

Perhaps members of our parents' generation, then, didn't approach retirement planning with the appropriate zeal. This is not the case, however, with the current crop of adult children. We cut our teeth on the likes of *Money* magazine, which spawned a whole genre of personal finance magazines such as *Smart Money, Worth, Kiplinger's Personal Finance Magazine,* and more. The *Wall Street Journal* has evolved from a well-written newspaper favored by financial types to its current place as the most widely read and, some would argue, the most influential newspaper in the country. All of these publications urgently remind the baby boom generation that time is of the essence. Each day we are relentlessly bombarded with missives regarding our need to take immediate charge of our personal finances.

In addition to personal finance magazines, we now have other choices for receiving an accelerated stream of financial news. Just in case we feel that we are suffering from a lack of information, we can tune to television cable networks such as CNBC and MSNBC for receiving up-to-the-minute accounts of the financial markets. In many American cities, local independent stations also offer extensive financial programming. Even public television gives us the nationally televised *Nightly Business News,* while public radio presents us with the daily editions of *Market Place.* Just in case boomers aren't already suffering from an overload of information about their personal finances, they can also use computer programs to organize their bills and their investments, complete their tax returns, or plan for their retirement years. If they need still more information, they can hop on the World Wide Web and download their brokerage account information, which is updated daily. Or in their spare time they can receive stock quotes and place trades directly from their home computers.

We have so much information thrown at us, we are like the woman who lived in the shoe: we have so much input we don't know what to do. But in spite of the complexity inherent in today's financial arena, the predominant message is that today's workers must look to themselves to fund their retirement years. The baby boom generation has no illusions about this. We know

Figure

2.1 • • • • •
What Do Surveys Show about Americans of All Ages and Their Finances?

The Adult Children

The 1997 Phoenix Fiscal Fitness Survey sponsored by Phoenix Home Life was conducted by Yankelovich Partners, which interviewed 1,000 respondents aged 30 to 59 by telephone. The survey focused on households in which at least one adult earned more than $40,000 annually. In the 1997 survey, household income averaged $86,000 and showed some surprising results.

• Forty percent of those interviewed whose parents were living either provided for them currently or expected to sometime in the future. Ten percent provided or anticipated providing total support, while 19 percent contributed or anticipated contributing toward day-to-day expenses. This figure is nearly double the 1994 figure of 22 percent.

• The generational squeeze seems to be causing this generation of adult children to shift their financial focus from their young children to their parents. The results showed that adult children are planning to do less for their children in the future and more for their aging parents.

• Eighty-nine percent of those interviewed had started to plan for retirement, but only 17 percent expected to depend primarily on a traditional company pension plan for retirement income and 10 percent expected to keep working until they reached 70. According to the research, however, the amount the respondents had set aside wouldn't allow them to meet their retirement income goals.

• Some prefer getting financial advice from personal sources. Seventy-four percent indicated that they use a financial professional as a source of advice, but 22 percent depended mainly on friends and relatives, and 20 percent relied mainly on their own research. A similar study conducted by the Opinion Research Corporation revealed that 68 percent of investors seek financial advice from relatives and friends, but only about 20 percent indicated soliciting investment advice from a financial professional.

The Children

- College students understand the importance of financial planning but lack the basic tools; only 9 percent clearly understood compound interest and only 45 percent understood the term *budget*.

that we must be proactive. Unlike our parents, most of us adult children won't be entitled to receive a guaranteed lifetime retirement income. The day of the corporate handout is about over and the largesse of the government-sponsored retirement program seems doomed, too.

We boomers feel that we must take charge of our own personal finances as we rightfully realize that it would be foolhardy to depend on receiving much help from either our employer or our government. Besides, we are aware that we may live a long, long time. The prospect of increased longevity combined with little guaranteed retirement income is a sobering thought for most boomers. The quest for answers to the retirement planning quagmire has become a national mania. Unlike the more passive response of the depression-era generation to the financial concerns of old age, the current mantra of the baby boom generation has become retirement planning, retirement planning, retirement planning.

The Role of Emotions

Our Parents' Emotions

The outside world may influence our parents' reactions but, perhaps more important, so does their private inner world. The reluctance of many parents to reveal the intimate details of their finances is based on a variety of emotional factors. According to many, if not all, of the financial professionals I interviewed for this book, loss of control is probably the single most important fear for aging parents.

In his book *Talking With Your Aging Parents,* Dr. Mark Edinbery comments as follows:

> Loss of control is also one of the great unspoken fears of older persons who face giving up some decision-making power over their lives. Expect that your parents may have worries and concerns that existed before you began this discussion and that they are also as concerned as you are about how assets will be distributed and what happens if they become incapacitated. Be aware that control issues loom large in these discussions. Many of these discussions you will have will absolutely mean that your parents are giving some control over assets away. There may be grief, anger, frustration, and fear associated with these actions. To deny this reality will be destructive in the long run. It is also not useful to be falsely reassuring (such as saying, "Don't worry, Dad, you're still in control"), especially when your parents are feeling that control is lost. The reminder as to what they are in control of will be useful, but later, after the emotional reaction surfaces and is expressed.

The issue of control is a confusing one for children and parents alike. Parents who fear that their adult children may abandon them may use money to engineer their relationship. Parents who feel the most vulnerable hope that their money will give them considerable psychological power over their grown children. Even parents who have been the most self-reliant and the easiest to deal with may become surprisingly resistant. Unfortunately, some of our parents have suffered numerous age-related misfortunes. They may be in poor health and may have lost people near and dear to them. Their willingness to discuss their money may be one of the few things that they can still control, so they react to our questions with an angry silence.

Many children are reluctant to approach the control issue. They feel that making decisions on their parents' behalf doesn't feel right, and, let's face it, our parents probably aren't crazy about the arrangement either. The problem cuts both ways as parents worry about losing their independence and children worry about taking on new roles. You can avoid an exercise in financial arm wrestling by involving third-party professionals. In addition, as you'll learn in the following chapter, it's neither necessary nor even wise to try to wrest control from your parents while they are still competent to manage their own affairs. But you do want to be informed. It is reasonable that you know what may be expected of you in terms of management responsibilities or actual financial support because your life and your parents' are intertwined.

Your parents may resist your requests to learn more about their financial and legal arrangements because they're worried what you will do once you have the information. They fret that revealing pertinent facts and figures may lead to unpleasant consequences. As a result, they may become increasingly secretive in their attempts to keep information from you because they fear both your initial reaction and your subsequent actions. Your parents are worried about many issues. They want to avoid becoming dependent on their children for either financial advice or direct financial assistance. And sometimes they will go to surprising lengths to protect themselves.

Fathers in particular don't want to appear uninformed about financial matters. Dad may not know diddly about personal finances but he sure doesn't want his grown children to discover his lack of expertise. Loss of stature may be yet another in a growing string of losses for an aging father, and he may try to avoid this one at all costs. Fathers who have been successful in their line of work or have enjoyed an exulted position as the head of the family may find their adult children making unwanted inquiries especially difficult. When you start asking questions, Dad may assume that you are beginning to have doubts about his abilities. He may feel that your probing is a sure sign that you have lost respect, perhaps feeling that you are doubting his competence. An unsure father may not believe that his children are concerned; instead, he believes that his children doubt his mental and physical prowess.

Fathers also refuse to share information because they may feel a certain sense of shame about their finances. Some very successful fathers want to hide their accomplishment in a vain attempt to minimize their own efforts so that their children don't feel overshadowed. Others don't want their grown children to learn that Dad earned far less money than they will. A father doesn't want his children to discover that the money he did earn was badly managed. Nor does he want his adult children to learn that he has lots of money but has failed to share his wealth with other, less fortunate family members.

Many mothers and fathers actively collaborate to keep their wealth a secret. They fear that if their children know that they have ample resources, the children will criticize their frugal lifestyle. Many adult children cringe as they watch their parents scrimp on everyday expenses to save for their grandchildren's college education. Many adult children feel that their parents should enjoy their money and not try to enhance the lifestyle of future generations. Also, most parents want to avoid the censure of children they fear may be judgmental or those who will insist on a change in parental behavior.

Any conversation about money management and such things as powers of attorney quickly brings to mind the unpleasant concept that our parents may not always be able to manage on their own. This is a terribly unpleasant reality for anyone to consider. Avoidance is always a powerful motivator. But given our parents' tenacious desire for independence, it must be especially threatening for them to contemplate losing control. Their fears may cause them to fight this notion even harder than you thought possible.

Disclosure of closely held financial information comes in the context of the ongoing relationship you already enjoy with your parents. With any luck, you already have a good relationship with them and the conversation will go smoothly. Some parents will be among the minority who actually welcome a conversation about their finances and aren't threatened by the discussion. It's likely that these people are comfortable with their personal situation, their skills, and their degree of financial success. So it's likely that the more confident a parent feels about himself or herself, the more receptive that parent will be to having "the conversation."

People who are satisfied with themselves are typically relaxed when giving and receiving information. Some parents may be eager to talk about their finances as they think of their assets in terms of family money rather than as personal wealth. They may consider themselves merely a conduit, holding the funds in custody until they are passed on to their children. As a result, they want their children to be knowledgeable about their finances. They want their children to manage the money astutely when the time comes and, if possible, continue the tradition by passing money on to the grandchildren. Naturally, they welcome having "the conversation" as they want their children to be well prepared.

Unfortunately, though, you should be prepared for your parents to resist "the conversation" and question your motives. They may think you're raising financial issues in your own self-interest. They may think that your gentle

Mind over Money

• • • • •

The Women Cents Study, a survey conducted by the National Center for Women and Retirement Research (NCWRR), found a strong link between personality and financial behavior. *Working Woman* magazine of February 1995 reported that of the 4,200 women NCWRR studied, personality was a significant factor affecting financial decisions. Personality characteristics influence financial decision making more than do income, age, or marital or career status. If you are clashing with your mom about her financial decisions, perhaps each of you has a unique financial personality that makes it even more difficult than usual to reach a consensus. In such a case, it may be time to bring in a neutral third-party professional. Further, according to the NCWRR study, assertiveness, openness to change, an adventurous spirit, and an optimistic outlook are all qualities that lead to smart money choices.

• • • • •

questioning is nothing but a covert attempt to extract money from them either now or when they're gone. It's in the best interest of adult children to get their parents' finances squared away even though it's a loaded issue—but nonetheless one you *must* raise even if you don't want to.

Our Emotions

If discussing money is so important, why is it so difficult for adult children to share their concerns with their parents? Among the many reasons is children's apprehension about parental approval. As a result, most of us are loath to do something we fear our parents won't like. In addition, our parents hold what psychologists call positional power in our relationship. Most of us feel a debt of gratitude to our parents we feel we can never repay, and thus we have considerable emotional ambiguity about inquiring into their financial matters. On the one hand, they could perceive our questions as intrusive or, worse yet, disrespectful. But on the other, if we don't ask or we don't care what happens, then who will? Plus, few of us seek conflict with our parents. With a little luck and some hard work, you may finally have reached an acceptable relationship with your parents. Who wants to rock the boat now, especially if it has taken some effort on the part of both generations to reach this point?

Some children don't want to give up their cherished place in life as a child. Losing one's parents, no matter at what age, results in a loss of status as someone's child that many children fear. They associate a move toward discussing financial issues as a slow journey toward the beginning of that end. They worry about entering the phase in life when they start to lose their parents' emotional support—a very scary prospect for most adult children. Children fear a time when their parents no longer have the inclination to maintain their parental role. Thus, a discussion with parents about their money is viewed by many children as a watershed moment when their long-standing role with their parents slowly starts to disintegrate. Understandably, you'll want to prolong having "the conversation" if you see it as the end of a secure relationship and the beginning of a journey you want to avoid. However, try to avoid viewing it from this perspective. Another and equally important consideration is that your involvement provides you a rare opportunity to make a valuable contribution to your parents' golden years.

Then there is the general discomfort all children feel when trying to advise their parents. Some suggest that it is possible to parent your parents, but that's a difficult task. Adult children continue to be children and parents will always be the parents regardless of their respective ages, mental acuity, or physical prowess. There is an old saying that encapsulates this plight: A mother can raise ten children but ten children can't raise a mother. Trying to manage your parents is not part of the natural order of things. Role reversal is disturbing as it was never meant to be a regular part of our life. The way around this dilemma is to confine our mission to an educational capacity. We shouldn't attempt to solve our parents' problems but should limit our efforts whenever possible to offering information and suggestions. That way our relationship evolves into interdependence rather than one in which we try to become the parent, with the inevitable result that neither party is happy.

Parents Are from Pluto, Children from Neptune

• • • • •

You think that you have communication problems in your family? Join the crowd! In 1997, Elderplan, a division of the Metropolitan Jewish Health System (a Brooklyn-based health care organization), surveyed 500 adults to see how they viewed aging. The widely divergent generational perspectives strongly indicate that all families need to take a hard look at their communication patterns.

• Eighty percent of adult children said that their parents' health problems had affected the quality of their own life.

• Ninty-four percent of parents believed that their health status had little impact on their adult children.

• Fifty-three percent of adult children believed that eventually their parents would move in with them.

• Twenty-two percent of parents thought they would cohabit with their adult children.

• Thirty-one percent of adult children felt they would need to provide their parents with significant financial support.

• Eighteen percent of parents thought they would need extra help.

• • • • •

Getting Real

Another factor driving a reluctance to discuss money is that most adult children, regardless of how successful in their chosen field, are uneasy with their money management skills. The International Association for Financial Planning (IAFP) has discovered this trend in study after study. In 1993, the Equitable Insurance Company asked 900 baby boomers about their personal finances. Not surprisingly, the boomers noted that they were very worried about financing their children's college education and funding their own retirement. This finding was anticipated given results of numerous other studies. But it was surprising to learn that only 52 percent of the study participants had any kind of financial plan. Also, most baby boomers rated their money management skills as only average or below average. The findings were even more unexpected in light of the fact that the participants had above-average earnings (over $50,000 annually), leading us to conclude that most also had above-average education and talent.

Based on my years of experience as a financial planner, I would venture to predict that the vast majority of adult children don't have their own financial house in order. They don't have a power of attorney for property or one for health care; they don't have a living will covering life-threatening medical emergencies; and many don't have a will that directs the distribution of assets at their death. I would also venture to predict that less than 5 percent of adult children have an up-to-date personal inventory. I also know that many of these same talented and well-educated individuals have no idea how to undertake many of these tasks. Given the low level of financial expertise that exists among even highly educated people, I suspect that it is threatening to consider asking parents to undertake tasks that their adult children themselves are unsure how to execute.

Do as I Say, Do as I Do

I know that you will balk at the advice I am about to render, but I think it is very important that you get a handle on your own financial affairs before you ask your parents to do the same. This is important because much personal finance stuff is a learn-by-doing process. Hands-on experience is invaluable, and only if you first undertake these tasks yourself, are you in a position to guide your parents through the process. Reading and educating yourself is a good start, but rolling up your sleeves and getting personally involved is the best teacher of all. The knowledge you acquire as you go through the process of learning by doing will create an undeniable sense of personal power.

When you do your homework first, you will be more confident; you will know the ropes and you will have more practical information to offer. In addition, your requests will not create the impression that your parents are the only ones who are getting older and need to get their affairs in order. Getting financial tasks accomplished for yourself first moves you beyond the reach of the fairness argument: the one in which you suggest to your parents that it is important they draw up a power of attorney and they ask if you have enacted a will that names a guardian for your minor children. To avoid the fairness issue, you will want to complete the financial tasks for yourself before you ask your parents to tidy up their affairs. You want to put your own house in order before you ask your parents to do the same.

When to Have "the Conversation" and What to Ask

The best time for you to approach your parents is when they are in their early 60s. If you wait too long to encourage your parents to review their documents or change their tactics, there will be little if anything that you can do to help them rectify their situation. You want to start the process fairly early in their retirement while they are still young, vigorous, and willing to consider both new ideas and new approaches. The chances are good that your parents are running out of money and may not be aware that they have a problem. Their investments may be too conservative or too risky. They may not have tackled any estate planning or considered the cost of long-term care. In addition, most aging parents fail to regularly update their wills, trusts, and powers of attorney, which often causes unintended results.

First, you need to reassure your parents that your love and respect for them is not impacted by their financial success or failure. Your goal is to lessen the toll that aging takes on the whole family, rather than holding your parents to impossibly high standards. Don't pressure them to get everything resolved in one conversation. Tell your parents that if they get their affairs organized, they will make your life and that of your siblings much easier. Stick to raising only one issue at a time. As you will see in the next chapter, this process is best completed in a deliberate fashion in concert with your siblings, your parents, and your parents' advisers. Help is available from Children of Aging Parents (CAPS), which is a not-for-profit organization devoted to helping caregivers that can be reached at 800-227-7294.

Questions to Ask Your Parents

• • • • •

- Have you enacted any emergency paperwork? If yes, where are the originals and the copies located?

- Where are your financial records stored?

- Have you ever made a budget?

- What are your monthly expenses?

- How can I go about paying your routine bills, if necessary?

- Have you tried to project your financial situation over the next 20 years incorporating the impact of inflation?

- Do you have any ancillary medical insurance?

- Who are your doctors?

- What medications do you take?

- Have you thought about how you will handle the costs of an extended illness?

- Who are your advisers?

- What is your annual income?

- Where does your income come from?

- Have you prepared a net worth statement?

- Have you done any estate planning? If yes, have you used any advanced devices such as trusts that I should be aware of?

- If the house gets too big, what do you want to do?

- Have you written a letter of last instruction?

- When was the last time (or the first time) you looked at your asset allocations?

- Do you have any life insurance?

- Have you reviewed your property insurance limits within the last three years?

• • • • •

Why Is It So Hard?

• • • • •

- Money and death are taboo subjects in our culture.

- Most parents are unaware of potential problems.

- Many parents are embarrassed about their financial situation.

- Most adult children are afraid to confront their parents with questions about their finances.

- Most adult children lack adequate knowledge about the financial and legal aspects of aging.

• • • • •

CHAPTER 3

Breaking the Sound Barrier
A Step-by-Step Guide

"Well, it's one for the money, two for the show, three to get ready,
now go cat go. But don't you step on my blue suede shoes."

—Carl Perkins, "Blue Suede Shoes" (1956)

I know you really don't want to do this. I know you would prefer that your sister, the banker, handle this little chat with Mom and Dad. Alone. Or better yet, your spouse could talk with them. Then your parents can get mad at him or her, leaving you in the clear. I know that you would rather send a letter. Or preferably memorize a prepared script and then paraphrase its message to your parents. I'm not sure how persuasive you would be, though, as reciting a script in a believable fashion is difficult for even trained actors, who at times can be less than convincing. Nope, you can do a better job by having "the conversation" in your own words. Because you know your parents more intimately than any outsider possibly could, you are in the best position and should depend on your own thoughts and your own sense of timing.

Your fears about talking with your parents, while totally understandable, are probably overblown. Let's remember something very important—these people are your parents and they have a vested interest in maintaining a loving relationship with you. If you are a parent yourself, you know the parent-child bond is very strong. It will handle considerable generational push and pull before it starts to fray, let alone unravel. Besides, you are approaching this conversation with a mutual respect for both yourself and your parents. Your unwavering sense of fair play is a far better tool for achieving a successful outcome than relying on a rote conversation or sending a canned letter. These tools are appealing for reducing some of the emotional risk you fear. But, in truth, they will only compound the difficulty because props will make your interchange dry and lifeless.

If your parents are resistive, it's likely that part of their opposition is a product of their personal lack of financial confidence. Lets face it, in today's complex world no one feels entirely secure with his or her chosen course of action because the outcome is always unsure. Surprisingly, your parents may seem recalcitrant on the surface but may be more worried about their finances than you are. Their finances may be a matter they want to air, but they may feel uncomfortable initiating the discussion themselves as it seems a bit tacky, even to the most confident parent. Thus, it's possible that if you broach the topic with sensitivity, your parents may actually welcome a conversation about their finances. But the compelling question is, How do you achieve that highly desirable outcome?

Innovative solutions often flow when new thinking is applied to common problems. Employing some time-tested techniques can help you avoid an emotional blowup, the psychological equivalent of stepping on your parents' blue suede shoes, when you address the sensitive topic of money. Much leading-edge thinking was pioneered by the psychological community. The groundbreaking book by Roger Fisher and William Ury outlining successful negotiation techniques, *Getting to Yes,* was first published in 1981 and provided additional tools for conquering difficult discussions. These techniques work for solving nasty labor-management disputes and for bringing warring nations to agreement. This chapter will introduce you to these methods and will show you how to successfully break the conversational ice.

Preparation

The Make-or-Break Ingredient

Your success will depend on how much time and effort you put into preparing yourself. Don't even think about winging it; lack of preparation will be your single biggest handicap. Handing your parents an organizer and then going back to doing whatever it is that you do won't cut it. Your preparation should focus on six areas:

1. *Acquiring* enough information to both appear and feel knowledgeable

2. *Talking* with your siblings and achieving a meeting of the minds
3. *Devising* a plan of action
4. *Formulating* the actual conversation
5. *Thinking* about how you will handle your emotions
6. *Preparing* your response to negative remarks

The informational segment of the aging puzzle is usually the most straight-forward one. The rest of this book is devoted to the financial aspects of aging so that by the time you finish the book, you should have a good basis for under-standing. You may want to review additional materials before "the conversa-tion" because you don't want to grope for words in front of Mom and Dad or, worse yet, your siblings. You can order some of the supplemental publications or consult the Resources section at the end of this book if you want still more information. I would also suggest that when you come across articles of mu-tual interest, you clip them for future reference. You can set up an at-home file or hand over the information directly to your parents.

If you have friends, acquaintances, or colleagues who are struggling with some of the same concerns, talk with them. Find out what they did and, more important, find out what approaches were successful or—equally helpful—unsuccessful with their parents. Consult with your own advisers for individu-alized professional advice if you feel their input will be valuable. You may also want to seek advice from professionals who specialize in working with our aging population. These professionals may be able to guide you while respond-ing to some of your more involved questions and may also be able to make specific suggestions for helping you determine the best way to present your concerns with your parents.

Articles that authenticate your concerns are always helpful. The Ameri-can Association for Retired Persons (AARP) prints a free catalog describing its publications, which are aimed at the layperson, and offers material on a vari-ety of topics of interest to seniors and their adult children. Once you feel ade-quately educated, I suggest that you write down what you want to accomplish with your parents. A plan will provide you with a logical structure.

Avoiding the Lone Ranger Approach

After you feel comfortable with your practical knowledge, the next step is to consult with your siblings. You may want to avoid this additional hassle, perhaps saying to yourself that it would be best to just go ahead and handle it yourself. Going it alone is appealing on the surface by removing what seems just another layer of complexity. By dealing directly with your parents, you won't have to first thrash out all the issues with your siblings too. Somewhere down the line, however, you inevitably will encounter resistance from them if you don't confer with them first.

Your siblings will wonder why they were not consulted before you, on your own, encouraged Mom and Dad to take certain financial and legal steps. The realization that they were left out of the loop will probably come at a time when there is some sort of family crisis. You want to avoid having the effects of a family emergency further compounded by incurring the collective wrath of your siblings. You're going to have to deal with your siblings sooner or later about the financial issues. Why not do it now, when everyone is thinking clearly? The best way to avoid irreparable harm is to keep everyone informed. If you go it alone, you may create sibling strains that can never be repaired.

Besides, it's not in your best interests to saddle yourself with the idea that you are indispensable. Forget the notion that you are the only one in the family who is interested enough to spend the time and effort involved to help your parents prepare for the legal and financial aspects of old age. If you think that you are the only one capable of handling the problem, you will inadvertently telegraph that message to your siblings. When you do, it's likely you will wind up handling everything yourself. Then at some point in the future, your sibling support system will start fading away. You will become quickly frustrated if you end up assuming all the responsibility for your parents by default. Your angst will only be heightened if your siblings aren't doing what you deem to be their fair share.

Be proactive by involving your siblings from the very beginning. The only way to prevent yourself from becoming the designated child is to make sure that your siblings are included in the process. All of your brothers and sisters need to feel equally responsible and equally involved in your parents' life. Besides, including your siblings has its own rewards. Your collective brainstorming will probably elicit ideas that wouldn't have occurred to you if you tried to solve everything yourself. In addition, your siblings' emotional investment will give you peace of mind by knowing that Mom and Dad have more than one person who is concerned about them.

Having "the Conversation" within "the Conversation"

Before you chat with your siblings, though, take some time to consider everyone's interests. Not all the children will be affected the same way by your parents' financial situation. Some of the children may want to spend money to solve Mom and Dad's problems so they don't have to give up what little free time they have. Others, who have time but no money, may want to eliminate the need to shell out scarce funds. They may suggest that the children themselves take on any required work. Other siblings will act out their competitive instincts when they offer their solutions. Some of the children will want to get involved for all the wrong reasons, perhaps perceiving that involvement will give them more power with Mom and Dad. Some won't want to do the right thing for Mom or Dad because it will benefit someone else in the family. If the children are unable to agree on the best approach, seek third-party impartiality. Outside advice can reduce sibling friction and the likelihood down the road that one child will question the advisability of a decision made by another child.

If you decide that your family doesn't need outside advice at this early stage, pick a time when all the children can get together to discuss the best way to approach your parents. Ultimately, you and your siblings will need a plan of action. The meeting could be held in person or via a conference call with each child's concerns faxed or e-mailed to siblings before the discussion. Outlaw old family business and negative comments. Do brainstorm together to create as many good ideas as possible. Perhaps each child could have a follow-up assignment that would be completed before the next meeting when a plan is finalized. You may want to speak with others, such as a lawyer, accountant, gerontologist, psychologist or pastor, or rabbi or priest to garner additional advice. Not only are the best-laid plans those that have the support of all the children, but the importance of the children's collective influence on parents can't be underestimated.

Getting Yourself Together

Experts suggest that you must remove your own emotional baggage—easy to say but difficult to do. All parents and children continue to harbor issues that linger from remote events; some adult children have emotional wounds and scars from childhood that have never healed. Some adult children have disappointed their parents and don't know how to make up for past sins, and some still feel that a sibling will always be their parents' favorite. But as hard as it is to ignore these feelings, you need to move them aside for the moment. Simply put, for a successful outcome you must leave your personal emotional agenda as well as *all* your old parent-child issues somewhere else while you talk with your parents about their finances. This is not the time or place to worry about the fact that Dad didn't attend your Little League games or that Mom always mentions the petri dish phase when green stuff was growing rampantly on the unwashed dishes in your teenage bedroom.

Think about your real motivations. What you don't want to do is undertake a financial discussion for all the wrong reasons. The discussion is about helping your parents make good financial decisions. It is about protecting the people you love from harm. No one will benefit if this project becomes a contest of wills. It is supposed to be about preventing your parents from running out of money. It is supposed to be about protecting your interests too. You don't want to be stuck without the necessary mechanisms for handling your parents' affairs in the event of an emergency. And you don't want to be torn apart by an unwanted financial surprise. You don't want your life disrupted by the unexpected need to support your parents just when your first child is about to enter college. Because family is important, you want to ensure that everyone in your family is protected from unnecessary financial wear and tear—turmoil that can be mitigated or even eliminated by proper planning.

Going for the Gold

When you talk with your parents, you and your siblings want to pose your questions so the issue will appear to be what it is, a joint dilemma for you and your parents to resolve together. It's a problem for the whole family to consider rather than one caused by the parents or imposed by the children. You want to create a process whereby each of you can bring up potential predicaments, contribute ideas, or propose viable solutions. You'll want to involve your parents in the process immediately by eliciting their opinions. Ask what they don't like about your ideas too. Actively listen to your parents' concerns. Your parents must be made to feel they are an integral part of the process. They will see your efforts as patronizing if you talk down to them or try to impose your own agenda. Your goal is to educate your parents about the economic realities of aging. Although your parents may be the longevity pioneers, it's likely they are unaware of how much it costs to get old. You want to educate yourself about the issues while your parents are learning on their own too.

You're dealing with an invisible problem—a *complicated* invisible problem. Your parents may deny the economics of aging by arguing that your apprehensions are unwarranted and simply theoretical. But they aren't. If your concerns become a reality when your parents run out of money or can't afford necessary medical care, then it's just too late to take remedial action. You'll want to strengthen your hand by giving your parents real-life examples illustrating potential problems. Or you can bring in third-party professionals, who can support your position, if you aren't able to convince your parents about the importance of your concerns.

Focus your remarks on two main points: (1) the financial and legal realities and (2) your own feelings. You want to keep the discussion centered on the problem at hand while avoiding tangential issues that may cause hard feelings.

> **Do say:** "I read an article in the paper about the importance of having a power of attorney (POA). A POA is a legal document that allows a person to appoint another individual to handle his or her bills and other financial affairs in case the person becomes sick or disabled. I executed a power of attorney through the local bar association that complies with the requisite state laws. It only cost a few dollars. I named [Alice] to manage my affairs in the event of an emergency."

> **Do say:** "Mom, I worry that now that you are a widow, your bills could go unpaid if something were to happen to you. Perhaps a power of attorney would be helpful for you too. I know that you don't need any help with handling your affairs, but I worry about things that we can't control—bad things—that could make life difficult for our family. Perhaps I could go with you to visit your lawyer, Fran. I would like to meet her anyway if it's OK. I'm sure that she can give us good advice."

This approach sticks to the two main points: (1) today's legal realities and (2) your feelings.

Don't say: "Mom, I want you to see a lawyer and get your financial affairs taken care of. I wish you'd get organized—it would make life so much easier for me."

This type of dialogue doesn't tell Mom why she needs a power of attorney or why she should spend money for professional advice. It doesn't show her how she could benefit from getting her affairs in order. But it does tell her that she is a disappointment to her children. She may also infer that her children see her as a burden. I suspect that Mom will ignore this message. But she will hear its implications. The upshot will be that Mom will not see a lawyer, but she will feel that her children view her as incompetent.

If you start off on the wrong foot, there will be lingering hard feelings the next time the subject is broached. Mom will feel defensive; her negative feelings carried over from the previous discussion will only make future attempts to address the problem that much more difficult. If you usually have problems communicating with your parents, then you'll want to remember that old adage, "If you always do what you always did, then you will always get what you always got." So try to reconsider your tactics. Try to stop and think before you speak. Change your style by restating your comments in a positive way.

You want to frame your requests in such a way that your parents can imagine a positive result. You want to change their perception because their perception is also their reality. Present positive outcomes that focus on lessening potential problems for you and your siblings. Or present options for reducing their own difficulties. I would start by offering results that are commonalities, not differences. You want to show how your suggestions benefit everyone in the family. Here are some examples that can be tailored to your specific family situation:

Adult child: "Dad and Mom, I am concerned about managing your finances in the event that you wouldn't be able to write checks for a while. At this point, I wouldn't even know where to start. I don't know how to pay your mortgage or handle any of your affairs. I get scared when I think about it."

Adult child: "Dad and Mom, medical care is such a major expense these days. I caught a program on television last week that explained hip replacement procedures. These techniques look great, but they cost thousands and thousands of dollars. I got to thinking about my own insurance and decided to review the coverage I have through work. It appears I have excellent coverage, at least for now. But then I started to worry about your insurance as I keep reading and hearing that the politicians want to reduce Medicare benefits in order to balance the budget. So I got to thinking that supplemental medical insurance might be helpful. Maybe we should look into getting a supplemental insurance policy for you that will pay for medical procedures Medicare doesn't cover."

Adult child: "Mom and Dad, last week I was compiling a list of my emergency information for Ted. I wanted him to know the names of my advisers and where my emergency paperwork is located so he could handle my affairs in a crisis. When I was working on this project, I got to wondering if you have a list anywhere. It seems like a list would really help Betty and me if we needed to contact someone on your behalf. If you don't have a list, I'd like to show you my form so we can work together to compile one for you. Or if you already have one, I'd like to see yours so I can make sure that I have thought of everything I need to consider for myself."

Adult child: "Dad, I know that you have been buying stocks and bonds for years. But I don't really know much about all that type of stuff. I am concerned that if anything would happen to you, well, how would Mom manage, as handling money is so complicated today? Besides, even if you have selected good advisers, you know she doesn't feel comfortable with financial responsibilities. And I would feel bad if I couldn't help her out. Do you think that you could explain some of your affairs to me so I can advise Mom intelligently?"

Adult child: "Dad, did you know that Congress recently changed the estate tax laws. It's sure hard to keep up, isn't it? Over the next few years the government will be increasing the amount of money you can leave tax-free to your family. I am going to talk with my lawyer about what I can do to reduce my taxes. Would you like to join me? Or would it be better if we consulted together with your lawyer? I know how you hate paying any more taxes than you have to!"

Note that these questions are designed to be open ended. If Mom or Dad has the opportunity to answer simply yes or no, both will. A one-word answer won't give you enough information to help you determine what you need to say next. The conversation will stop abruptly; you will have succeeded in closing the conversational door rather than opening it.

At this point, I'd like you to just stop and consider your own feelings. If the very thought of asking your parents any of these questions causes your stomach to lurch, your body is telling you what your mind already knows. If your stomach is gyrating, your body is telling you that you are not the right person for the job. It's not that the task isn't important, but you don't feel comfortable getting the ball rolling. Perhaps your instincts are correct. Perhaps you shouldn't even think about approaching your parents with a discussion of their finances. Perhaps you should let your sister, the banker, handle everything. Perhaps you should simply turn your parents over to their advisers and wash your hands of the whole affair. But perhaps, after you read the rest of this chapter, you'll feel otherwise. So first consider some other ideas before you give up completely.

Preparing Your Plan

Decide what you want to accomplish. My suggestion is that you start with the emergency paperwork and then gently proceed to other items. Your parents may or may not be pleased with your involvement, and their reaction will dictate how fast and how far you can take this project. You are the best judge of where to start, but I would suggest the following five-step game plan:

1. *Get the emergency paperwork drafted, notarized, and signed in front of witnesses.* These documents include a power of attorney for property, a power of attorney for health care, a living will, and a regular will or living trust if your parents' situation is complex or they live in a high-cost probate state. Make sure that the documents have been updated in the last five years and that the documents were drafted in the state where your parents currently reside.

2. Financial literacy studies show that *most boomers are unfamiliar with the particulars of public and private reimbursement plans covering medical costs for seniors.* Because medical care is such an expensive item for aging parents, you'll need to understand your parents' medical coverage. (Read Chapter 10 which explains Medicare, Medicaid, and supplemental coverage.)

Discuss the coverage with your parents so that both you and they clearly understand what is covered and, more important, which medical services are not covered. If you feel that you can proceed further, I would also raise the issue of long-term care with your parents at this juncture. Many seniors think that Medicare will pay for an extended nursing home stay and thus are unprepared to handle these costs.

3. *Have your parents unravel the mysteries of their personal filing system with you or a sibling.* Learn how to pay their bills and deposit their checks. Have them show you how they go about preparing their tax returns and other complex transactions that you might need to oversee. Try to get as much information as possible that would help you run their household in their absence.

4. *The final must-do is completing the inventory presented in the next chapter.* If you don't like that inventory, make up one yourself or use one that you prefer. If you don't have an inventory to guide you, trying to manage Mom or Dad's affairs will be unbelievably difficult, especially if you're a long-distance child or are unfamiliar with the intricacies of your parents' affairs.

5. *Additional things to do include helping your parents prepare a budget, encouraging them to organize and streamline their investments, and helping them stretch scarce resources.* When you help them prepare a budget, you'll get a bird's eye view of their finances, information that will help you determine if they'll have enough money to finance their retirement. That same advice also holds for investments. Most seniors have overly complicated finances resulting from years of making individual financial decisions. It would be best if this task were undertaken by a knowledgeable, independent third-party professional who can advise your parents. In addition to gaining needed expertise, another benefit of this arrangement is that it will be the professional, not you, who bears the brunt of your parents' wrath if they don't like the advice or question its impact.

Reacting Appropriately

When you talk with your parents, it's difficult not to consider your own interests and stay focused on your parent's viewpoint. The best way to accomplish your goal is to stick to the golden rule—do to others as you would have them do to you. You will gain a lot of personal power by listening courteously to their thoughts. The best way to gain your parents' attention is to give them your attention first. If you want your parents to listen to you, you must listen to them. Go ahead and acknowledge their value, their authority, their knowledge, and, yes, their need for control. If you want them to agree with you, you must first agree with them.

Be prepared for them to react negatively at first. Nearly everyone is insecure to some extent. This is especially true when it comes to personal financial issues because few of us feel totally secure about our arrangements. Thus, when we feel threatened, hurt, or angry, we tend to blame others and be defensive rather than attempt to improve communication, according to Tom Rusk. It's tough to be objective when dealing with your parents, but you become part of the problem ratner than part of the solution if you lose your objectivity. Don't take their negative reaction personally. Remember that your parents probably view your requests in a different light than you do.

Just because their perception of the problem and yours are different doesn't mean that they've stopped loving you. It just means they don't see the world from the same perspective. Because their life experience has usually been so different from yours, you need to gain a clear understanding of their position. If they question your motives, it's a typical reaction and has more to do with the dynamics of the situation than with the dynamics of your relationship. Remember that feelings are facts to the person experiencing them. As Rusk has noted, rejecting a person's feelings makes the whole person feel rejected. Although it's tempting:

- Don't take it personally.
- Don't strike back.
- Don't give in.
- Don't break off the conversation.

Much of our parents' power is derived from getting us to react to old childhood themes. If they try to protect their turf by bringing up old stuff like your long hair, your childhood academic accomplishments, who you dated, or who you chose to marry, ignore it. Focus your thoughts on the end point. Visualize your possible reactions and be prepared for your parents' hitting your "hot buttons." You'll know you're there when your stomach churns and your heart starts to race. At that point, breathe slowly and focus on the reality that the only thing you can control is yourself. Besides, you want to be the one who initiates a turnaround in the discussion—an especially powerful move if you do this in spite of being the brunt of a personal attack. You'll gain personal power from being the positive force.

Getting Down to the Talking

What Are Your Parents Thinking?

Try to uncover your parents' underlying feelings and views about a discussion of their finances. Some parents will welcome the discussion. Others fear having "the conversation." For those parents who feel that a discussion of their finances is an intrusion into their private domain, they enter the discussion feeling they have everything to lose and nothing to gain. If your parents approach the issue with this unfortunate perspective, you'll face a difficult, but not insurmountable, obstacle. If they are resistant, your first goal is to envision how you can introduce managing intergenerational financial concerns as a shared objective.

> ***Adult child:*** "Mom and Dad, I understand from what I read and from talking with my friends and people at work that it's helpful for the whole family when parents explain their disability arrangements, such as power of attorney or living wills. How do you feel about talking about this?"

I hope they will level with you. You may discover that they feel a discussion of their finances is none of your affair. Or you may learn that they have concerns they want to share with their children. Your parents' reaction to discussing the topic will guide your strategy. They will let you know if you can plunge right in or need to take it slowly. Or, even at this early juncture, you may decide that you should turn your parents over to a third-party professional and assume an interested, but hands-off, role.

Formulating Your Response

The final part of the process involves your taking time to formulate, in your own mind, your rebuttals to your parents' replies. You want to be prepared for the conversational twists and turns well ahead of time. You may even want to make a conversational flow chart with potential responses to a variety of parental replies. Parents, like all of us, can be unpredictable at times but let's return to an earlier hypothetical conversation:

Adult child: "Dad and Mom, I'm concerned about managing your finances in the event that you wouldn't be able to write checks for a while. At this point, I wouldn't even know where to start. I don't know how to pay your mortgage or handle any of your affairs. I get scared when I think about it."

Dad: "What makes you think that I wouldn't be able to write checks at any time in the near future, young lady?"

Adult child: "Well, what made me think about all this was an article about disability that was in our local paper. Did you know that people of any age are much more likely to be disabled than die? I never realized that fact. So I started thinking about what I would do if you needed my help. I realized that I have no knowledge of your affairs. Then I suddenly realized that I wouldn't be able to help you. You and Mom have done so much for me, and I want to be able to assist you if I can."

Dad: "Well, what is it that you want to know exactly?"

And that's when you launch into a discussion of what you want to accomplish. I would strongly advise that you think about all your parents' potential responses and how you want to react well before the start of the actual conversation. You want to be well prepared so you don't have the pressure of constantly trying to think on your feet.

A few tips for getting your point across:

- Watch your body language: Make eye contact and don't roll your eyes.
- Don't try to push your own agenda too quickly.
- Don't say "yes but": "I know that you have always managed your own money, but now it's time to think about making other arrangements." Instead, say, "I know that it's difficult to think about turning this over to someone else when you have always handled your own finances."

- Make "I" statements: "I'm concerned about the quality of the advice you're getting." Or "I'm concerned what will happen to Mom if we don't make some plans now."
- Advocate your position: "It's important that you have a power of attorney, Dad. What if you can't make mortgage payments for several months? You could lose your house."
- Don't come on too strong because it makes it difficult for your parents to say yes when they do come to see your side of the problem. Don't say: "How can you say that you don't need a living will? You are so unreasonable!"
- Don't try to be the smartest person in the room. Don't say: "I *know* that a family partnership arrangement is the best way to proceed."
- Ask problem-solving questions: "I realize that you don't want to hire a money manager (lawyer, accountant, etc.), Dad, as you don't feel that you can trust anyone else to do a good job. I'm uncomfortable, though, because I don't have the knowledge, skills, or time to step in and help Mom if we no longer have the benefit of your advice. In order for both of us to stop worrying, we have to make some sort of plan. I don't want to make these decisions in the future without your insight—it scares me. What do you think would be an acceptable solution?"

Handling a Discussion That Goes Badly

The methods for lashing back are legendary. Mom and Dad may choose to

- play dumb;
- be rude;
- threaten you;
- try the good-cop, bad-cop routine; or
- use power plays.

Rather than responding in kind, I would recommending calling your parents on their specific behavior. In a situation in which we feel we are on our parents' personal turf, it usually seems as if our parents have more power than we do. This disparity is intimidating—and a common problem in difficult conversations. But the only effective way to react is to note and respond to what is going on in your discussion. Ignoring your parents' responses only validates their behavior.

If Dad is rude, you may want to say, "Dad, it sounds like you are having a bad day. Let's talk about this at another time." If Mom says that she won't come to visit if you mention her finances again, say, "Mom are you threatening me?" When Mom knows that you are onto her, she is less likely to repeat her behavior in the future. Mom may try to be the good cop to Dad's bad cop when she replies, "I think that this is a good idea, but you know Dad; he'll never go along." You don't want to be sucked into the middle, so the appropriate response may be, "The two of you seem to have a communication problem. One of you wants one thing while the other wants something else entirely. After you decide what's best, let me know how the two of you want to proceed." You want to put the problem back where it belongs—on your parents' shoulders. It's not the adult child's role to get involved in their parents' internal battles.

You may feel uncomfortable using the direct approach with your parents. It may be just too strong given the typical communication patterns in your family. A softer approach is to rely on the idea of fairness to persuade your parents. The trick is to be hard on the problem but soft on the people, according to Fisher and Ury. Encourage your parents to state their reasoning. Then base your requests on the merits of the issue: "Mom, I worry that if you get sick, no one has the legal authority to manage your affairs."

The more importance you can attach to the principle of your requests, the better off you'll be. It's difficult to argue with the truth, so gently stick to your guns. Your parents can refuse to go along, however. If they balk at having a discussion about finances, then I would recommend you continue to focus on the fact that their resistance creates a huge dilemma for the whole family. Don't push back too hard as it will force them to assert their position even more forcefully. If you can, offer them an attractive way to explain how they came to change their mind.

Finally, if all else fails, you may want to try the reality check. One of the most frustrating events is when Mom or Dad or both refuse to complete the most basic requirements—squaring away the emergency paperwork. Let's imagine a situation where Dad steadfastly refuses to sign both a power of attorney for property and one for health care. Let's also consider that his refusal comes under the worst possible circumstances: Dad is wealthy with complex business and investment arrangements in addition to being in very poor health. Perhaps he has to carry an oxygen tank around with him, but he still refuses to enact any emergency paperwork. Let's just say that his denial level is very high.

Don't say: "Dad, who in the hell do you think will make these important decisions if you are incapacitated? No one will be able to pull the plug and no one will be able to keep the business afloat."

This approach, while totally understandable on the part of an at-the-end-of-her-rope adult child who is frustrated beyond belief, will only make her father feel even more threatened and will contribute to his continuing refusal to cooperate.

Do say: "Dad, sometimes people get sick and can't make their own decisions. If that were to happen to you, a government agency would step in and handle your affairs and you would have no say over the outcome strangers would impose. I read an article and am appalled at how this process works."

At this point, you can launch into the nasty details. If you are really concerned about this issue, you may want to consult with a local elder law attorney to learn the specifics of what happens in a guardianship proceeding in your parents' jurisdiction. Perhaps the attorney will even tell you some war stories that you can share with your recalcitrant parent.

The Meeting Outside the Meeting

If your parents have advisers, you'll want to include them. The only question is when you should reach outside the family. If your parents' advisers have traditionally played an important role in their decisions, if you trust them, if you feel they are competent, and if they have a close personal relationship with your parents, include them early on. Sometimes, your best approach is to start with the advisers first because in some families the problem is better handled by outsiders who can contribute technical knowledge as well as impartiality. The advisers may have more clout because they aren't part of the generational politics that underlay many parent–adult child relationships. If your relationship with your parents has traditionally been troubled, then I would suggest getting the advisers involved from the very beginning. Ask your parents if you can meet their advisers the next time you talk or the next time you visit. If your parents don't have advisers or don't have advisers who are schooled in the legal and financial aspects of aging, you may need to help your parents locate knowledgeable advisers.

Remember that you are the employer in these arrangements. Too often, consumers are intimidated by professional advisers. If you are helping your parents hire a professional, do some comparison shopping. You want to understand the range of services as well as typical pricing arrangements. You can get names of prospective professionals by consulting with friends, reviewing professional directories available at public libraries, or asking for references from professional societies. During a phone interview you will want to inquire about the following:

- Is there a fee for the initial consultation?
- How many years have you practiced?
- Have you handled this type of situation before? If yes, is this the main focus of your practice?
- Do you sign written fee agreements?
- What are your usual rates?
- Can you provide me with references?
- Are your fees negotiable?

Select three professionals you wish to interview and then set up a time when you and your parents can meet with them. You will want to determine if they are experienced, willing, and able to assist your parents. They need to be knowledgeable about the legal and financial aspects of aging. Ask them about their areas of specialization. Ask them if they are familiar with how to plan for coping with the costs of long-term care and the minutia of the Medicare and Medicaid programs. You should also inquire as to what precisely will be done and how much it will cost for each of the services.

Try to determine the professionals' suggestions for dealing with your parents' specific situation and then compare their responses. You want to locate a professional whose training and experience are suitable and whose costs are in line with local fees. Depend on your comfort meter. If you aren't content with a specific professional, question your reaction and trust your own judgment. Also, I recommend that you schedule a face-to-face visit with each professional. Especially if you are a long-distance child, a personal interview will give you a certain peace of mind in knowing who is advising your parents. A personal meeting also tends to discourage professionals from thinking they can take advantage of your parents.

Breaking the Sound Barrier

• • • • •

- Get in touch with your own feelings.

- Talk with your siblings.

- Select which family member(s) will carry the ball, or together select a third-party professional to advise your parents.

- Decide exactly what you want to accomplish.

- Be prepared for an initial negative reaction.

- Move forward slowly but purposefully.

• • • • •

CHAPTER 4

A Word to the Wise
Documenting Your Parents' Affairs

"Oh dear! Oh dear! I shall be too late!"

—The Rabbit from *Alice in Wonderland,* by Lewis Carroll

A Word to the Wise

Imagine receiving a phone call in the next ten minutes requiring you to assume total responsibility for managing your parents' legal, financial, and personal affairs. You may be able to glide into this arrangement without a second thought. But for most adult children it would be a terrifying moment. If you try to engineer your parents' financial matters without a thorough inventory to guide you, especially from afar, you'll find yourself resembling those hapless newfangled-puzzle addicts who are devoted to jigsaw puzzles that eliminate the helpful picture on the front of the box. If you have to untangle the web of your parents' finances without an inventory or other indication of your parents' affairs, you won't be able to effectively piece together their situation. Without a signpost, your already considerable angst will be heightened by your ignorance of the financial and legal details of your parents' life. In short, you'll feel like the Rabbit in Wonderland.

If you'll be the primary person responsible for your parents' affairs, you can minimize your dilemma by taking a few simple steps now. Or, if a sibling plans to assume this important responsibility, you should give him or her a copy of the forms shown in Figures 4.1, 4.2, 4.3, 4.4, and 4.5. These are the instruments for documenting your parents' financial affairs. If this information is gathered together into one record, today's effort will prevent untold hours of future research and remorse. This information will help you and your siblings minimize the heartache that comes from not taking a few preventive steps. And it will help you and your loved ones avoid making costly mistakes.

There are several techniques for approaching your parents. Your options are:

- Make one copy of the forms and ask your parents to complete them together.
- Make two copies of the forms and ask your parents to complete them separately.
- Sit down with your parents and help them complete the forms, together or separately.

If you are involved in the process, it affords you the opportunity to make the task less daunting for your parents. You also can ask questions, which allows you the perfect opening to clarify any confusing points and will greatly enhance the odds that the forms will be completed instead of being shoved into the back of a drawer.

The following ten items can serve as your guide for gathering the necessary information about your parents' affairs *before* it's needed:

1. Make sure all emergency documents are dated within the last five years. If they have not been updated within the last five years, add a notarized page amending each document with a more current signature.
2. Make sure that documents have been executed in your parents' current state(s) of residence.
3. Make sure that any power of attorney (POA) is durable, meaning that it will not expire in the event of a disability. Also check if any POA is broad enough to give the agent the requisite authority to adequately manage your parents' affairs.
4. Check with financial institutions, including mutual fund companies, money managers, banks, brokerage firms, and retirement plan sponsors, to ensure they will accept such existing or proposed documents as a POA or trust agreement. You may also want to contact your parents' insurance carrier or the U.S. Postal Service, to ensure it will abide by the terms of the documents.

5. Ask your parents now, while they are still in good health, if you can meet their advisers. It will be much easier to work with advisers later if you already have an established personal relationship.

6. Gently encourage your parents to streamline their affairs wherever possible. Encourage them to have their Social Security checks, annuity and retirement plan distributions, stock dividends, and other payments automatically deposited into their checking or brokerage accounts. Urge them to hold their assets in a brokerage account rather than a safe deposit box or, heaven forbid, in a home file. Your parents may not be aware that today many financial institutions provide numerous ancillary services such as monthly accountings, automatic receipt of dividends and interest, immediate access to accounts through the World Wide Web, and year-end tax accounting statements. These services are often offered at no cost and can greatly minimize the need for time-consuming bookkeeping chores. Often, your parents can also place many of their mutual fund shares in the same account, thereby centralizing and streamlining their finances.

7. The sale of an appreciated asset, such as a stock, creates a potential tax liability just as the sale of a depreciated asset creates a potential deduction. One of the real headaches in managing someone else's finances is trying to locate the basis, or the amount they initially paid for a specific investment. Ask your parents to compile this information, update it regularly, and tell you where it's located. This attention to detail will be extraordinarily helpful.

8. Ask your parents to provide you with all the information you require if you ever need to sell their home. Have them explain where the deed or the mortgage papers are located. Ask them to identify their lender (if they still have one), what the house was worth when they bought it, what they think the house is currently worth, and who they would like to represent them in the sale.

9. If you can, ask your parents if the surviving spouse is entitled to receive a continuing payment from various sources of retirement income. This is a touchy, but important, question because it will have a big impact on the widow's or widower's future income. You will also want to establish that your parents are receiving all the money they are en-

titled to receive from entitlement programs, such as Social Security or the Department of Veterans Affairs.

10. It's easy to lose track of your individual assets if you move frequently. However, if your parents have assets scattered across the country from a former time when they lived elsewhere, remind them that they must include all those scattered assets in the inventory. Otherwise, missing assets will eventually be turned over to the state where they are held if any institution is unable to locate the rightful owner after seven years.

Figure 4.1

• • • • •
Documenting Your Parents' Affairs: Emergency Disability Paperwork

Personal Power of Attorney for Property

Date signed _____

State where drafted _____

Notarized   Yes _____   No _____

Witnesses _____
_____
_____

General	Yes _____	No _____
Limited	Yes _____	No _____
Durable	Yes _____	No _____
Springing	Yes _____	No _____

If springing, who will determine disability?

Name _____   Name _____
Address _____   Address _____
_____   _____
Phone _____   Phone _____

Agent _____   Phone _____
Successor agent _____   Phone _____

Location of original document _____

Location of copies _____
_____

Has document been accepted by financial institutions?   Yes _____   No _____

Names of institutions _____   Account# _____
                      _____   Account# _____
                      _____   Account# _____
                      _____   Account# _____

Institution-Specific POAs

Date signed _____

States where drafted _____
                     _____

Notarized   Yes _____   No _____

Witnesses _____
          _____
          _____

General   Yes _____   No _____
Limited   Yes _____   No _____
Durable   Yes _____   No _____
Springing   Yes _____   No _____

If springing, who will determine disability?

Name _____   Name _____
Address _____   Address _____
         _____   _____
Phone _____   Phone _____

Agent _____   Phone _____
Successor agent _____   Phone _____

Location of original document _____

Location of copies _____
                   _____

Has document been accepted by financial institutions?   Yes _____   No _____

Names of institutions _____ Account# _____

_____ Account# _____

_____ Account# _____

_____ Account# _____

Power of Attorney for Health Care

Date signed _____

State where drafted _____

Notarized   Yes _____   No_____

Witnesses _____

_____

_____

Agent _____   Phone _____
Successor agent _____   Phone _____

Location of original document _____

Location of copies _____

_____

_____

_____

Limitations or exclusions _____

_____

_____

_____

_____

_____

Special wishes _____

_____

_____

Organ Donor   Yes _____   No _____
   If yes, where is documentation? _____
   If yes, has physician been notified?   Yes _____   No _____

Living Will

Date signed _____

States where drafted _____

_____

Notarized   Yes _____   No_____

Witnesses _____

_____

_____

Attending physician   Name   _____
                       Address _____

                               _____

                               _____

                       Phone   _____

Location of original document _____

Location of copies _____

_____

_____

Have document provisions been discussed with physician? Yes ____ No ____

Has physician agreed to provisions?   Yes _____   No _____

Is a copy on file with physician?   Yes _____   No _____

Figure 4.2

• • • • •

Documenting Your Parents' Affairs: Estate-Planning Documents

Will or Living Trust

Name of trust _____

Date original signed _____

State where drafted _____

Codicils   Yes _____   No _____

Date #1 _____
      #2 _____
      #3 _____
      #4 _____

Attorney   Name _____
            Firm _____
            Address _____
            _____
            Phone _____
            _____

Notarized   Yes _____   No _____

Witnesses _____
          _____
          _____

Who determines disability?   Name _____
                              Address _____
                              _____
                              _____
                              Phone _____

Successor trustee (personal) _____

                    Address _____

                                    _____

                                      _____

                      Phone _____

Successor trustee (corporate)_____

                    Address _____

                                      _____

                                      _____

                      Phone _____

Executor _____ Phone _____

Location of original document _____

Location of copies _____

                                  _____

Figure 4.3

• • • • •
Documenting Your Parents' Affairs: Medical Information

General Medical Information

Primary care physician:

Name _____	Name _____
Name of practice_____	Name of practice _____
Address_____	Address _____
_____	_____
Phone _____	Phone_____

Specialists:

Type _____	Type _____
Name _____	Name _____
Name of practice_____	Name of practice _____
Address_____	Address _____
_____	_____
Phone _____	Phone_____

Type _____	Type _____
Name _____	Name _____
Name of practice_____	Name of practice _____
Address_____	Address _____
_____	_____
Phone _____	Phone_____

Pharmacy

Name _____	Name _____
Address_____	Address _____
_____	_____
Phone _____	Phone_____

Dentist

   Name _____   Name _____

   Name of practice_____   Name of practice _____

   Address_____   Address _____

           _____   _____

   Phone _____   Phone_____

Ambulance

   Firm _____

   Address_____

           _____

   Phone _____

Hospital   Hospital Emergency Room

   Name _____   Name _____

   Address_____   Address _____

           _____   _____

   Phone _____   Phone_____

Medicare identification number _____

Medicaid identification number _____

Supplemental insurance carrier   Yes _____   No _____

   Name _____

   Address _____

           _____

   Phone _____

   Contact person_____

   Policy number _____

   Precertification required   Yes _____   No _____

   If yes, phone number _____

   Location of claims forms _____

                                                 _____

Location of policy and explanatory information _____

_____

_____

Claims administration

    Address _____

    _____

        Phone _____

Policy type (A-J) _____

Premium _____

Qualify for Veterans Administration care   Yes _____   No _____

Long-term care insurance carrier   Yes _____   No _____

    Name _____

    Address _____

    _____

    Phone _____

    Contact person_____

    Policy number _____

    Precertification required   Yes _____   No _____

    If yes, phone number _____

    Location of claims forms _____

    Location of policy and explanatory information _____

    Daily maximum payment _____

    Maximum length of coverage _____

    Claims administration

        Address _____

        _____

        Phone _____

Number of activities of daily living (ADLs) required for coverage_____

Premium _____

Paid monthly, semiannually, or annually? _____

Address _____

Due date _____

Figure 4.4

• • • • •
Documenting Your Parents' Affairs: Inventory

Personal Information

Name _____

Place of birth _____

Date of birth _____

SS# _____

Resident of the state of _____

Citizenship _____

Maiden name _____

Advisers

Accountant

Name _____	Name _____
Firm _____	Firm _____
Address _____	Address _____
_____	_____
Phone _____	Phone _____

Attorney

Name _____	Name _____
Firm _____	Firm _____
Address _____	Address _____
_____	_____
Phone _____	Phone _____
Issues handled _____	Issues handled _____

Banker/Loan officer

Name _____	Name _____
Firm _____	Firm _____
Address _____	Address _____
_____	_____
Phone _____	Phone _____
Account # _____	Account # _____

Casualty Agent: Homeowners   Umbrella
    Name _____   Name _____
    Firm _____   Firm _____
    Address _____   Address _____
    _____   _____
    Phone _____   Phone _____
    Policy # _____   Policy # _____
    Policy limits _____   Policy limits _____

                Automobile   Automobile
    Name _____   Name _____
    Firm _____   Firm _____
    Address _____   Address _____
    _____   _____
    Phone _____   Phone _____

Deferred compensation
    Employer_____   Employer_____
    Address _____   Address _____
    _____   _____
    Phone _____   Phone _____
    Description_____   Description_____
    When benefit period   When benefit period
        begins _____   begins _____
    Benefit amount _____   Benefit amount _____

Employee benefits administrator
    Name _____   Name _____
    Firm _____   Firm _____
    Address _____   Address _____
    _____   _____
    Phone _____   Phone _____

Financial planner
    Firm _____
    Address_____
    _____
    Phone _____

    Firm _____
    Address _____
    _____
    Phone _____

Friends
    Name _____
    Address_____
    _____
    Phone _____
    E-mail_____

    Name _____
    Address _____
    _____
    Phone _____
    E-mail _____

Investment adviser
    Firm _____
    Address_____
    _____
    Phone _____

    Firm _____
    Address _____
    _____
    Phone _____

Life/Annuity agent:
    Firm _____
    Address_____
    _____
    Phone _____
    Policy #_____
    Beneficiary_____
    Face amount _____

    Firm _____
    Address _____
    _____
    Phone _____
    Policy #_____
    Beneficiary _____
    Face amount_____

    Firm _____
    Address_____
    _____
    Phone _____
    Policy #_____
    Beneficiary_____
    Face amount _____

    Firm _____
    Address _____
    _____
    Phone _____
    Policy #_____
    Beneficiary _____
    Face amount_____

Religious adviser
    Name _____
    Church/Synagogue_____
    Address_____

    _____
    Phone _____

    Name _____
    Church/Synagogue _____
    Address _____

    _____
    Phone_____

Retirement plan administrator
    Firm _____
    Address_____

    _____
    Phone _____
    Date of participation_____
    Payment option: Single ___ JS ___
    Monthly benefit_____

    Firm _____
    Address _____

    _____
    Phone_____
    Date of participation _____
    Payment option: Single ___ JS ____
    Monthly benefit _____

Safe-deposit box
    Box #1
    Institution_____
    Address_____

    _____
    Phone _____
    Authorized signers_____

    _____

    Location of key_____

    _____

    _____

    Box #2
    Institution _____
    Address _____

    _____
    Phone_____
    Authorized signers _____

    _____

    Location of key _____

    _____

    _____

Stock broker
    Firm_____

    Address _____

    _____
    Phone _____
    Web site _____

Location of Documents

Abstracts_____

Appraisals _____

Baptism certificate_____

Bank books _____

Bills of sale _____

Birth certificate _____

Bonds _____

Car title_____

Casualty insurance policies _____

Certificates of deposit_____

Copy of master list _____

Divorce papers _____

Death certificate _____

Deeds _____

Education reports/diplomas _____

Employee benefit statements_____

Employment history _____

Family tree_____

Financial records _____

Funeral instructions_____

Insurance records_____

Inventory of valuables _____

Legal agreements _____

Life insurance policies_____

Living trust_____

Living will_____

Marriage certificate_____

Medical records: (Mom) _____

_____(Dad) _____

Military service records_____

Mortgages _____

Naturalization papers _____

Passport _____

Partnership agreements _____

Power of attorney (property) _____

Power of attorney (health care)_____

Prenuptial agreements _____

Retirement plan information _____

Real estate surveys_____

Social Security card _____

Stock certificates _____

Tax records_____

Title to burial plot _____

Title policy _____

Trust agreements _____

Umbrella liability policy _____

Will _____

Burial Plot

Address_____

_____

Burial Instructions:_____

_____

_____

_____

_____

_____

List of Investments

Cash accounts

Institution	Account title	Ownership	Account #	Balance
			$	

Brokerage accounts

Institution   Account title   Ownership   Account #   Balance
_____$_____
_____
_____
_____
_____

Mutual fund investments

Institution   Account title   Ownership   Account #   Balance
_____$_____
_____
_____
_____
_____

Real estate

Description   Owner   Mortgage   Mortgage   Value
                                holder   balance
_____$_____
_____
_____
_____

Credit cards

Company and issuer   Card #   Balance owed
_____$_____
_____
_____
_____
_____

Ask your parents if they are eligible to receive benefits from:

Civil service job _____   Union employment _____

Railroad retirement _____   Disability or damage awards _____

Military _____   Lottery _____

State or local government _____

Pension benefits	Contact person	Issuer	Monthly payment
			$_____

Explanation of Ownership Designations

Sole ownership: Indicates an asset is owned by one individual. At death the asset is distributed through probate according to the individual's will or distributed according to state law if no will exists.

Tenancy in common: Indicates property is owned by two or more individuals in equal shares or sometimes in unequal shares. When one tenant dies, his or her portion of the property is distributed in probate court according to that tenant's wishes.

Joint tenancy: Indicates property is owned by two or more "tenants" in equal shares. When the first owner dies, his or her share automatically goes to the survivor and thus avoids probate.

Tenancy by entirety: Indicates a type of ownership available to married couples in some jurisdictions. Property is owned equally but cannot be sold without the permission of both owners. At the death of one spouse, the property automatically passes to the other owner.

Community property: Reflects the law in some states where assets and debts acquired by a married person are considered equal with that person's spouse regardless of title. If one spouse dies, his or her community property and separate property are distributed the same as with sole ownership—that is, the property does not automatically pass to the surviving spouse.

Figure
4.5

• • • • •
Documenting Your Parents' Affairs: Financial Statement

Net Worth

Assets

Liquid assets

Cash accounts	$_____
Certificates of deposit	_____
Savings bonds	_____
Cash value of life insurance	_____
Total value of mutual funds	_____
Total value of brokerage accounts	_____
Total value of investment management accounts	_____
Subtotal	$_____

Retirement accounts

Total value of IRA accounts	_____
Total value of Keogh plans	_____
Total value of other retirement plans	_____
Subtotal	$_____

Real estate

Primary home	_____
Secondary residence	_____
Other real estate	_____
Total assets	$_____

Liabilities

Real estate mortgages

Primary residence	_____
Secondary residence	_____
Other	_____

Other debt
    Credit card balances   _____
    Automobile loans   _____
    Bank loans   _____
    Personal loans   _____
    Other   _____
        Total liabilities $_____

Net worth = total assets − total liabilities $_____

Annual Cash Flow Statement

Cash income
    Earned income $_____
    Investment income   _____
    Rental income   _____
    Retirement income   _____
    Social Security benefits   _____
    Other   _____
        Total cash income $_____

Taxes
    Federal income taxes   _____
    Social Security taxes   _____
    State income taxes   _____
    Local income taxes   _____
    Local property taxes   _____
    Personal property taxes   _____
        Total taxes $_____

        Total after-tax income $_____

Expenses
    Mortgage/Rent $_____
    Utilities and upkeep   _____
    Debt repayment   _____

Transportation   _____
Vacation   _____
Medical out-of-pocket   _____
Food at home   _____
Restaurant meals   _____
Recreation   _____
Education and classes   _____
Gifts   _____
Contributions   _____
Clothing   _____
Holiday expenses   _____
Insurance   _____
Personal expenses   _____
Professional fees   _____
Other   _____

Total annual expenses $_____

Monthly Liabilities

Creditor	Address	Due Date	Amount

CHAPTER 5

A Reality Check

"Money does not make you happy but it quiets the nerves."

—Sean O'Casey

Making the Money Last

A wide range of life events causes people to retire. Sometimes people retire without any preparation as the result of an unexpected predicament so their retirement has a crash-and-burn quality. The predicament may be a termination, family caregiving demands, a corporate restructuring, vocational obsolescence, or a health crisis. If retirement comes unexpectedly, the retirees may not have given much thought to how they will finance their retirement years.

Some, on the other hand, may have happily anticipated retirement for years, adding to their retirement cache whenever possible or perhaps even purchasing some retirement-planning software to prepare for the inevitable economic realities. Typically, these folks saunter into retirement. But regardless of the journey or the degree of preparation, all retirees' paths converge. At some point each and every retiree, regardless of his or her readiness or station in life, faces the heart-stopping realization that it takes a wheelbarrow full of money to retire.

If your parents are just beginning to ponder the financial aspects of retirement, their first step is to obtain a Social Security Estimate of Benefits by calling 800-772-1213 and requesting Form SSA-7004 or by visiting the Social Security Web site at www.ssa.gov. If one or both of your parents are still working, they should also confer with their department of human resources representative to obtain comparable information about employer-provided benefits. Upon written request, employers must provide a benefit statement that outlines an employee's entitlements. Your parents want to learn about their employer's pension plan specifications as well as the scope of their other employer-provided retirement benefits. Among the questions they should ask are the following:

- At what age can I begin to draw benefits?
- How much will I be penalized if I take early retirement?
- Will I be allowed to take a lump sum distribution if I choose?
- Will the size of my retirement benefits be impacted by changes in my Social Security income?
- Will I continue to receive fringe benefits such as life or health insurance during retirement?
- If benefits continue, does my employer have the right to alter deductibles or copayments?
- How much notice will I receive regarding any changes?
- Can I work part-time for my current employer and still draw my full pension?
- Will my pension increase automatically based on a specific index or other factors?
- When I die, will my spouse receive a continuing benefit?

Assessing the Cost

The first step for anyone, whether retired or thinking about retiring in the near future, is to estimate postwork expenses and income. Before you blow this idea off as elementary, think again. I can state unequivocally that in the 25 years I have been helping individuals and families manage their personal finances, most people have only a vague notion about their personal finances; and even these nebulous ideas are usually off the mark. Most of us underestimate our expenses, our overall debt, and the amount we shell out for taxes. Almost everyone avoids compiling this information in the mistaken belief that somehow its absence will make the problem disappear. Our universal avoidance can be compared to the notion of dodging a regular physical exam and comes under the general umbrella of "what you don't know won't hurt you."

But what your parents don't know about their financial situation can and will hurt them. If they don't make the necessary effort to ascertain their expenses and income, how can they know what the future holds for them? How can your parents make good decisions without this information? The short answer is that they can't. Your parents may resist your idea, insisting that creating a cash flow ledger is a useless quest. Stick to your guns, however, for helping them with this basic exercise may be one of the best things you ever do for them. And even if you don't want to tackle this project either, remember that your parents' financial problems can quickly become your own financial problems—especially if you and they avoid facing the financial realities of aging. Also, there's always the chance that you may help your parents discover their financial situation is much more promising than they ever dreamed!

Ascertaining your parents' expenses and income entails gathering basic information and then using a spreadsheet computer program or the old-fashioned paper and pencil approach to calculate the numbers. Income information can be gleaned from prior tax returns, investment statements, the Social Security Administration, and benefit explanation statements from employers. If pension information is scarce, your parents are entitled to receive a copy of the *Summary Plan Description* from their respective former employers, who in turn are obligated by Department of Labor (DOL) regulations to provide that information.

Comparing What Comes In with What Goes Out

The Social Security Administration reports that a typical retiree's income comes from the following sources:

Source	Percentage
Social Security	40
Personal assets	21
Earnings from work	17
Private pension	10
Government pension	9
Other	3

Your parents' situation is, of course, different from these composite numbers, but aggregate statistics still provide a useful frame of reference. So let's start with the first step, compiling the income data. Income information is usually straightforward and easier to assemble than expenses because spending habits tend to be more fragmented than receipt of income. Your parents' sources of income may vary from the ones listed below, but the most common are shown in the following.

Sources of Income

Source	Annual Amount
Earned income from work	_____
Business income	_____
Pension distributions	_____
Social Security income	_____
IRA or 401(k) rollover or Keogh distributions	_____
Annuity payments	_____
Investment income from personal savings or inheritance	_____
Other	_____
Total Annual Retirement Income	_____

You can pull together expense information from a variety of sources such as tax returns, check-book registers, and charge card statements. An important caveat: **We all underestimate how much we spend.** This is especially true for nonreoccurring expenses such as major home repairs. Gifts comprise another area where most of us underestimate costs. They are typically underreported by doting parents, aunts and uncles, and especially grandparents, who deny to themselves as well as others just how much they spend.

Annual Retirement Expenses

Expense	Amount
Housing	_____
Auto	_____
Food	_____
Medical	_____
Leisure and vacations	_____
Personal care	_____
Clothing	_____
Gifts	_____
Education	_____
Other	_____
Total Retirement Expenses	_____

Reasons That Some Costs Escalate during Retirement

• • • • •

- Most retirees spend more on entertainment, travel, hobbies, and sports during their retirement years.

- Food costs may increase if eating at restaurants becomes a major form of recreation.

- Hiring household help or a home health care aide or paying nursing home bills will cause a retiree's budget to skyrocket.

- Medical expenses may increase for retirees, especially if your parents had extensive employer-paid medical insurance during their working years. The average retiree spends about 15 percent of their after-tax budget on medical care.

• • • • •

Compiling expense data can be tricky because of the many elements to consider. Let's look at the Jones family as an example. Bob and Ellen Jones are both 64, have two grown children, and live in a quiet suburb outside Boston. Currently, their $300,000 home carries a hefty mortgage; they both work and, as a result, require two cars. In conjunction with their financial adviser and their grown son, they are identifying their financial alternatives as they want to retire soon—very soon!

Their current expense projections, which they compiled by category from receipts and canceled check, indicate they spend about $5,600 each month, not including taxes. Concerned that they would not be able to afford the same lifestyle during retirement, they want to evaluate various alternatives and find out how much they could reduce their monthly expenses by making specific changes in their current lifestyle. Naturally, they want to weigh their opportu-

Reasons That Some Costs May Decrease during Retirement

• • • • •

- Work-related costs for commuting, clothing, lunches, and union or professional society dues are eliminated. For example, the Bureau of Labor Statistics reports that those under 65 spend about $6,700 on transportation, while those over 65 spend about $3,600 annually.

- Federal and state taxes may be lower as most retirees don't pay tax on their Social Security income. Seniors also are given a larger personal exemption on their federal taxes and may qualify for reduced local taxes as well.

- Insurance bills for disability and life policies often are eliminated or drastically curtailed.

- Most seniors benefit from a lifetime of personal acquisitions and aren't eager to collect more possessions.

- Seniors receive discounts on items ranging from airplane tickets to lawnmowers.

• • • • •

nities carefully and focus on making the most acceptable choices. With their adviser, they have given ample thought to their circumstances and have decided to explore the impact of the changes shown in the two scenarios seen in Figure 5.1.

Scenario #1

1. Eliminate debt/downsize by
   - selling the house and purchasing a condominium, and
   - selling both cars and buying one automobile.

2. Reduce expenses by
   - eliminating most restaurant meals and
   - spending less on clothing.
3. Increase expenses by
   - spending more on recreation and
   - purchasing long-term care insurance.

Scenario #2

1. Implement scenario #1 plus explore the financial impact of moving to a lower-cost area.

Jones Family's Projected Costs in Retirement

Jones Family	Actual Preretirement Budget	Projections Scenario #1	Projections Scenario #2
Situation	Current situation	1. Sell the house 2. Buy a condo 3. Eliminate one car	1. Also consider relocating to a lower-cost area
Housing			
Mortgage	$800	$0	$0
Assessment	0	220	150
Property tax	333	200	125
Homeowners insurance	65	50	40
Regular maintenance	60	50	40
Deferred maintenance	250	60	40
Utilities, telephone, and cable TV	400	150	125
Yard work, snow plowing	50	0	0
Household help	0	50	40
Replacing furniture and appliances	50	25	25
Auto			
Payment	$280	$0	$0
Gas	150	40	35

Maintenance	95	40	35
Insurance	200	100	40
Parking	125	0	0
Food			
At-home meals	$400	$460	$480
Restaurant meals	360	100	40
Medical			
Health insurance contribution	$160	$0	$0
Unreimbursed medical and eye care	250	25	25
Routine dental care	35	35	28
Prescriptions	75	75	75
Medicare Part B	0	62	62
Medicare supplement	0	300	300
Long-term care insurance	0	400	400
Personal Care			
Clothing and shoes	$400	$100	$75
Dry cleaning	75	15	10
Other personal care items	125	60	50
Travel and Leisure			
Travel	$250	$400	$400
Entertainment	125	220	150
Club memberships	50	50	25
Sports	100	100	50
Books and periodicals	30	60	60
Hobbies	25	125	125
Educational costs	0	100	75
Other	25	25	25
Gifts and Contributions	$150	$60	$50
Professional Services	$50	$50	$40
Other	$100	$50	$40
TOTAL COSTS BEFORE TAXES	$5,643	$3,807	$3,240
Taxes	$1,881	$952	$711
TOTAL COSTS INCLUDING TAXES	$7,524	$4,749	$3,951

The tax assumptions in our example were as follows:

- Preretirement: While working, the Joneses' overall tax rate is 25 percent because they have two incomes and pay Social Security taxes on their earned income.
- Scenario #1: Their retirement tax rate drops to 20 percent.
- Scenario #2: Their retirement tax rate would decline to 18 percent if they moved to a lower-cost area.

It was fortuitous that the Joneses decided to go through an evaluation process as they need to implement the options outlined in scenario #1 for their money to last as long as they will. If they want to save even more money by executing scenario #2, which requires relocating, they should research the total impact of their decision. Moving to a different location raises many tax and financial-planning questions that retirees must weigh. Important considerations include

Thinking about Relocating?
First Investigate These Tax Factors
• • • • •

- Taxes come at you from various directions, making it difficult to ascertain a tax-friendly state from one that reaches deeply into your pocket. But you want to be on the lookout for the following:

  – State income tax rates (flat or graduated tax)

  – Local income tax

  – Property tax

  – Additional fees for garbage removal and other municipal services

  – Personal property tax

– Sales tax

– Auto licensing fees (these can be surprisingly nasty)

– Intangibles tax (Florida, Georgia, Kentucky, Pennsylvania, and West Virginia)

- Little-known but important is that some states offer retirees exemptions and credits. Some states tax retirement income gently or exempt it entirely; others treat it the same as other income. Some localities offer retirees a break on their local property tax. If you want to check out an individual state, contact the state's revenue department for a copy of its tax form. Many states offer a Web page outlining their tax rules. An alternative, which is quicker (even if more expensive) is to purchase a couple of computerized state tax programs and play "what if" with your individual income numbers.

- A common misconception is that states with low or nonexistent state income taxes are tax-friendly places for retirees. Sometimes the states with no income tax compensate by imposing costly, but subtle, taxes that in combination result in high taxes.

- States that offer a tax heaven may also offer a cost-of-living hell. Anchorage and Honolulu are considered tax heavens but are very expensive places to live.

- When publications list the best places to live, be aware that those selections are based on specific criteria that may differ from your own. For example, *Money* magazine evaluates cities annually in an attempt to determine the best places to live, ranking them on the basis, in descending order, of low crime, clean water, availability of doctors, clean air, hospitals, schools, housing appreciation, low property tax, inexpensive living, and the area's resistance to recession. *Money* often ranks Madison, Wisconsin, as a desirable location. But *Tax Heaven or Hell* by Eve Evans and Alan Fox classifies Madison as a tax hell. So when it comes to the best place to live, beauty is indeed in the eye of the beholder.

• • • • •

the overall state income tax rate as well as how aggressively a specific state chooses to tax retirement income. Some states, such as Illinois, allow varying amounts of private pension income up to 100 percent, to be received tax-free, whereas others, such as New York, provide no state income tax exemptions on retirement income. In addition, some states give retirees a break on their property taxes and some exempt Social Security benefits from state income taxes. Local living costs are another important consideration. (See Figure 5.2 for the average dollar amount and percentage of expenditures for those over 65.)

One relocation firm has found that 80 percent of the difference in area living costs can be attributed to housing and taxes. The other 20 percent is found in the minutia of everyday life, according to David Savageau. More precise

What to Remind Parents on the Verge of Retiring to Do

• • • • •

1. Plan for the fact that your parents will have to pay income tax on all pension income they receive. All distributions based on before-tax contributions will be fully taxable regardless of whether the distribution is derived from a corporate plan or from a self-funded tax-deferred plan such as a 401(k). Their retirement income from pensions or from employer-sponsored annuity payments will be taxed at ordinary income tax rates rather than at the more favorable capital gains rate.

2. They may have to file and pay an estimated tax each quarter if some or all of their income is not subject to tax withholding. They need to have enough money in liquid assets to pay their estimated taxes quarterly because delaying payment until April 15 of the following year incurs underpayment penalties.

• • • • •

Figure **5.2**	. . . . . **Average Dollar Amount and Percentage of Annual Expenditures by Age**			

	Age 65–74	Percentage	Age 74+	Percentage
Food	$3,466	15%	$2,548	16%
Housing	6,849	30	5,871	37
Transportation	3,908	17	1,765	11
Apparel and services	1,270	6	638	4
Entertainment	871	4	444	3
Health care	2,300	10	2,197	14
Insurance	1,033	5	238	2
Other	2,897	13	2,050	13

Source: Bureau of Labor Statistics, *Consumer Expenditure Survey*, 1990.

cost-of-living information for specific areas of the country can be obtained from the most recent quarterly report of the American Chamber of Commerce Researchers Association (703-998-3540). The report costs about $60 so you may want to consult the local library or you may want to ask if your parents' local chamber of commerce will share past reports with nonmembers. Helpful publications that also compare tax costs are *Tax Heaven or Hell* mentioned above or *Retirement Places Rated* by David Savageau.

Estimating What Your Parents Can Afford

Now that we've taken a look at some of the Joneses' lifestyle options, the next question is to calculate their income from all sources. Let's assume, for our example, that Bob and Ellen can plan on receiving $1,200 a month from Social Security and another $1,200 a month from a corporate pension indexed for inflation, thus guaranteeing them an annual income of at least $28,800. In addition to their two regular sources of monthly retirement income, they also have a retirement fund of $450,000 accumulated from personal savings plus a small inheritance bequeathed by Bob's mother. The Joneses know that they can count on receiving $2,400 monthly matched for inflation, but they are unclear about how much they can comfortably remove from their retirement fund each year.

Knowing how much money to withdraw from savings is a problem that plagues most retirees. If you withdraw too little, you can shortchange your retirement lifestyle. But if you withdraw too much, you risk running out of money. What to do? Check Figure 5.3 for the answer based on various assumptions. Let's assume that at 64, Bob and Ellen expect to live another 20 years. Let's also assume that they believe they will earn 7 percent on their investments and feel that inflation will average 3 percent over the next 20 years. Given those assumptions, you can see from Figure 5.3 that they can withdraw 7.25 percent or $32,625 (the amount of their personal savings, $450,000, multiplied by 7.25 percent) the first year. Each year they can increase their withdrawal by 3 percent. Based on our assumptions, the Joneses' personal savings will be exhausted in 20 years. However, they will still continue to receive their Social Security and corporate pension distributions for their entire lifetime. Our estimate that Bob and Ellen will pay about 20 percent of their total income for federal and state income taxes creates a first-year spendable income of about $49,000. (See Figure 5.4.)

You can apply the same strategy to your parents' situation and do some "what ifs" for them as well. Our hypothetical family, the Joneses, found that they would have more money than they needed if they go with scenario #1 (they end up with an extra $300 a month) and even more if they choose scenario #2. If I were their financial planner, I would recommend that they add $100 a month to their travel fund and bank the rest. Why bank it? There are some nasty little details remaining, such as a replacement fund for the car, uncovered medical expenses, possible insurance deductibles incurred for an auto accident, and so on. It's not feasible or even recommended that you help your parents consider all the expense minutia. But in this hypothetical example where the Jones family has enough money, I would suggest banking the extra funds, which always creates a heightened sense of financial security.

The other idea the Jones family considered was relocating to a low-cost area. Their analysis shows that they do have a slight cushion of about $3,600 a year if they choose to stay put, but this isn't a large amount of money. Because the Joneses have enough money, at least for now, moving becomes more of a personal decision than a financial one. Resettling usually is a mixed bag for

Figure 5.3

**Estimating How Long
Your Parents' Money Will Last**

Number of Years	Interest Rate (%)	Inflation Rate (%)	Payout (%)	Number of Years	Interest Rate (%)	Inflation Rate (%)	Payout (%)
15	5	2	8.260	20	5	2	6.637
		3	7.710			3	6.065
		4	7.190			4	5.532
	6	3	8.270		6	3	6.641
		4	7.720			4	6.077
		5	7.720			5	5.549
	7	3	8.843		7	3	7.249
		4	8.275			4	6.653
		5	7.735			5	6.094
		6	7.222			6	5.569
	8	3	9.445		8	3	7.885
		4	8.852			4	7.260
		5	8.290			5	6.670
		6	7.753			6	6.115
		7	7.245			7	5.594
	9	3	10.066		9	3	8.551
		4	9.453			4	7.897
		5	8.887			5	7.277
		6	8.308			6	6.692
		7	7.776			7	6.141
		8	7.272			8	5.623
	10	3	10.713		10	3	9.244
		4	10.077			4	8.562
		5	9.467			5	7.914
		6	8.886			6	7.300
		7	8.332			7	6.720
		8	7.805			8	6.172
		9	7.303			9	5.657

Source: Pension Actuaries Inc., Lombard, Illinois.

Figure 5.4

• • • • •

The Joneses' Monthly Family Income

Pension and Social Security income	$28,800
plus	
Personal savings withdrawal ($450,000 × 7.25%)	+ 32,625
equals	
First-year cash flow	$61,425
minus	
Estimated federal and state income tax ($61,425 × 20%)	−$12,285
equals	
Annual after-tax income and	= $49,140
Monthly after-tax income	= 4,095

retirees. In this instance, the Jones family should base its choice on emotional as well as financial factors when they make the decision to move or not to, but the vast majority of retirees stay put, according to Savageau.

Example: A 65-year-old divorced woman has $150,000 in savings. She estimates that throughout her projected lifetime of 20 years her investments will earn 7 percent annually and inflation will average 3 percent. If those assumptions prove correct, she can deplete her savings by 7.25 percent or about $10,900 the first year, increasing the amount withdrawn each year by 3 percent to match inflation. Given that extraction rate, her savings will theoretically be depleted at the end of 20 years providing our assumptions prove on target.

• • • • •

Other Considerations

Investment Return

If the missing link in your parents' retirement planning is identifying how much income their personal investments will create, consider the following: Ibbotson Associates of Chicago has calculated investment returns and determined that over the last 30 years the return from short-term investments (certificates of deposit and Treasury bills) has averaged about 7 percent, the average return on corporate bonds has been about 8 percent, and the return on stocks 12 percent. Armed with this information, you can take a look at your parents' personal investments and help them determine a projected weighted return on their investments.

From the hypothetical investment allocation shown in Figure 5.5, we see that using the Ibbotson statistics, a weighted average of 9.3 percent ($41,850 ÷ $450,000) is the Joneses' return on their investments. As you can see, I was conservative when I used the 7 percent return numbers in computing the Joneses' annual withdrawal numbers in the previous example. But I would always recommend erring on the conservative side when making such projections as it is always difficult to factor in the precise impact of market fluctuations.

Figure 5.5

• • • • •

Projected Weighted Investment Returns for the Joneses

Asset Type	Percent Allocated	Amount Allocated	Historical Return	Expected Return
Treasury bills	30%	$135,000	7%	$ 9,450
Corporate bonds	30%	$135,000	8%	$10,800
Corporate stocks	40%	$180,000	12%	$21,600
Totals	100%	$450,000		$41,850

Inflation

Another consideration in retirement planning is the impact of inflation. Look at the table provided by T. Rowe Price at its Web site (www.troweprice.com) and you see that inflation can wreak havoc on the average retiree's budget. In our case study, the Jones family was protected against inflation by being one of the few American families whose private pension was indexed for inflation. But in the real world, in fact, only about 5 percent of all private pensions offer automatic inflation adjustments. And even those few companies that do provide automatic escalations, the amount is usually limited to a 3 percent maximum annual increase. Some pension plans offer ad hoc increases; that is, if the company has a great year, they may throw a few bones to retired employees. But the private pension system as a whole offers minimal protection against decreases in purchasing power for the vast majority of retirees. Most corporations pay their retired employees the same amount each month regardless of how much the retiree's living costs have increased. The fact that most pension distributions remain flat exposes the majority of retirees to the distinct possibility that they will experience a diminishing lifestyle as they age. (See Figure 5.6.)

Figure

5.6

• • • • •

Inflation and the Purchasing Power of One Dollar

Years	*Average Annual Rate of Inflation*		
	3%	*4%*	*5%*
0	$1.00	$1.00	$1.00
5	.86	.82	.78
15	.64	.55	.48
25	.48	.38	.30

Taxes

The U.S. tax code is inhumanly complex. Thus, it should not come as a surprise that nearly 50 percent of all elderly Americans overpay their federal income taxes, according to Ken Skala. This seems so unfair as senior citizens are among the poorest of all Americans and the least able to withstand inadvertent tax overpayments. You may want to remind your parents of the following:

- They may not be required to file a tax return if they meet income guidelines.
- At age 65 they are automatically granted a higher federal standard deduction and may also receive special tax treatment by state and city taxing bodies.
- They may be permitted to take a tax credit for the elderly if their income meets certain criteria.
- They may not have to pay tax on some retirement income, including Social Security benefits, if their gross income does not exceed the limitations.
- They may be missing out on itemized medical deductions; the average retiree spends 15 percent of his or her after-tax income on medical care. If medical expenses exceed 7.5 percent of adjusted gross income, which excludes tax-exempt income and often Social Security benefits, the taxpayer qualifies to take an itemized medical deduction.

The good news is that there are plenty of professional tax preparers who can help your parents complete their return. If your parents are not able to pay for professional help, then you may want to offer them the services of a CPA as a gift. Make sure that by hook or by crook your parents use a professional tax preparer once every five years at a minimum just to ensure they are getting all the deductions they are entitled to receive. Another idea is to seek free help from the Internal Revenue Service (IRS) volunteer program. The IRS Tax Counseling for the Elderly can be reached at 800-424-1040 to identify one of the 8,600 sites located closest to your parents. At each of these sites, well-trained volunteers will assist your parents, including even those who are shut-ins, and will prepare their returns on a no-cost basis providing they meet certain income limitations.

Longevity

No exercise in postretirement planning would be complete without considering how long your parents can be expected to live. Obviously this question can't be answered with certainty on an individual basis. But it is in your parents' best interests to review their respective family trees to identify longevity trends, to evaluate their individual health history, and to study actuarial tables. And when we do peek at our national statistics, the longevity of Americans is much greater than one would assume.

Actuaries estimate that an individual who lives to 65 has an average life expectancy of another 24 years. An individual who reaches 70 can be expected to live another 16 years on average. And believe it or not, an 80-year-old has an average life expectancy of 9.5 years, according to the U.S. Department of the Treasury. Further, according to Northwestern Mutual Life Insurance's (NML) Web site, there is a 92 percent chance that one of an average couple aged 65 in good health will live to 80 and a 55 percent chance that the other will live to 90.

The World Wide Web provides sites that guesstimate your longevity, if you answer questions about your family's health history, your regular health routine, and your day-to-day safety habits. These quizzes consistently predict that I will live to age 92—a staggering thought. I have been busily revising my own retirement plans by extending the time frame another ten years. In conjunction with ideas presented in this chapter, the Web can help your parents answer numerous questions about retirement planning without leaving home.

Many of the sites even provide interactive calculators to assist you in making "what if" assumptions. Most of the sites focus on helping people plan ahead for retirement, but some offer postretirement advice as well. Vanguard, the mutual fund company (at www.vanguard.com), continues to shine in this area—its interactive online program is terrific. If you prefer to take a more personal approach, T. Rowe Price sells inexpensive retirement planning software that allows the user to enter individualized information.

Helpful Web sites are too numerous to mention but can be easily located by asking your search engine to locate "retirement planning" sites. Just be aware that all sites are not created equal. Also keep in mind that financial planning is both complex and dynamic, creating an intricate interaction of tax, investment, and personal considerations that are unique to each individual. While you can get some worthwhile guesstimates from the World Wide Web, remember that all of these free sites have their limitations. The major drawback is that underlying assumptions supporting the calculations are not precisely tailored to your parents' situation. If your parents require a more intricate analysis, they should also plan to consult with a professional financial adviser. In most cases, consulting with a financial adviser is a worthwhile investment of both time and money.

After estimating how long your parents' money will last, you and your parents will know if they can be confident they have enough money to provide the lifestyle they envisioned. If their analysis shows that the money is insufficient, perhaps they will need to make some minor lifestyle changes or consider postretirement work for additional income. If your parents' financial future looks bleak, be sure to read Chapter 7, which is devoted to middle-income and low-income families that are unsure about their financial future. The chapter contains valuable suggestions for stretching scarce dollars. If your parents have ample resources, the issues are different but nevertheless compelling, so be sure to read Chapter 8 for beneficial tips on coping with wealthy parents.

The Financial Reality of Divorced Parents
• • • • •

- Compared to their married counterparts, divorced individuals are poorer, die sooner, and receive less help from their adult children, according to Vitt and Siegenthaler.

- Divorced women suffer more financial hardship than their former husbands, but divorced fathers usually form weaker emotional bonds with their children.

- Following a divorce, men usually regain their former financial status, but the vast majority of divorced women never recapture the economic well-being they enjoyed during their marriage.

- Some say that Social Security just adds to the problems of divorced women. Benefits for men are usually unaffected, but divorced women who were married for less than ten years are not entitled to receive any benefits based on their former husband's income. Individuals are entitled to 50 percent of their ex-spouse's benefits if the marriage lasted longer than ten years. But a 50 percent payment does not make them whole.

- Further compounding the problem, many women work in professions that traditionally do not offer an employer-sponsored pension plan.

If your mother is divorced. You need to be more concerned about your divorced mother's finances than your divorced father's. The amount you *can* help with obviously depends on your personal situation. The amount that you *want* to help with is an entirely other matter. If you yearn to help your divorced mom, you may want to inquire about the following:

- Ask your mother if she is entitled to receive part of your father's pension distribution at retirement. These arrangements are secured by a legal instrument entitled a Qualified Domestic Relations Order (QDRO). A QDRO is stipulated by a judge and must be agreed to by the administrator of your father's employer's pension plan. It is very important to have a written statement from the administrator indicating that he or she can and will abide by the terms stipulated in the QDRO. If your mother has not received such a written agreement, have her obtain one immediately.

- Encourage your mother to discuss her financial situation with you. She probably will need your help but is loath to bring up the topic, especially if she feels guilty about the divorce.

- Divorced or single daughters of divorced mothers often have the most difficult row to hoe. If you are a single daughter of a divorced mother, you may want to purchase a whole life insurance policy on your mother's life that names you as the beneficiary. If you need to support your mother during your working years, at least you can depend on receiving the proceeds of the policy at her death to provide income for yourself during your own old age.

• • • • •

To Do List

• • • • •

- Suggest to your parents that they base their retirement lifestyle decisions on facts and not on guesstimates.

- Help your parents calculate their expenses and their income. This is the only tried and true method for determining if they are overspending or underspending their retirement income.

- Don't neglect the impact of inflation. The average inflation rate over the past 30 years has been 5.4 percent. What it will average over the next 30 years is anybody's guess, but if inflation averaged 4 percent, a 60-year-old retired couple with an income of $2,500 a month would have their actual monthly purchasing power reduced to $1,388 by the time they are 75.

- Social Security keeps up with inflation, but remember that your parents' investment income needs to keep up too. Limiting investments to conservative fixed-income securities makes it difficult for retirees to maintain their standard of living. One of the biggest investment mistakes the elderly traditionally make is to focus on capital preservation at the expense of selecting assets offering growth potential.

- Budgetary pressures and rapidly rising health care costs are forcing the federal government to pass on more and more health care costs to retirees themselves. As a result, individual retirees can expect their personal health care costs to increase more than other expenses.

- Poorly performing financial markets have a way of disrupting even the best-laid retirement plans. Combat this problem with a diversified portfolio coupled with a conservative spending plan.

- Remember that underlying statistics change with time, and as a result inflation numbers, assumptions about investment returns, and life expectancy calculations should be updated every few years to reflect these changes.

• • • • •

CHAPTER 6

Getting Everything on Paper

"Experts can explain anything in the objective world to us, yet we understand our own lives less and less. We live in the postmodern world, where anything is possible and almost nothing is certain."

—Václav Havel, president, Czech Republic (1994)

As we approach the millennium, everything seems to have become increasingly complex. If it's getting hard to stay on top a of rapidly changing society when you're 45, try to imagine how it feels to be assaulted with so much change when you're 75. Aging usually makes it more difficult for most people to process new information quickly and accurately. As a result, our parents often feel overwhelmed by the swift transformation of the world swirling around them. When your parents seem to be resistant to your suggestions, they may not be exhibiting the orneriness we usually associate with old age. Perhaps, they are just reluctant to embrace fresh ideas when they prefer to depend on the information gleaned over a lifetime.

Resistance to change is understandable. Unfortunately, though, your parents' reluctance can cause very serious, but preventable, problems for them and for their entire family as well. Their opposition backfires when it involves executing critical legal documents covering emergency situations. These important documents are much more than just pesky forms your family lawyer mentions during each visit. They allow your parents to maintain their personal dignity and control their health care procedures, permit others to act on their behalf, and empower the people they designate, rather than the courts, to decide who will receive their assets after their death. These documents will ensure that your parents are able to move safely and surely into old age. Contrary to popular wisdom, instead of complicating matters, these crucial planning documents will help your parents reduce the trauma of disability and death. Having a valid, up-to-date power of attorney for property as well as one for health care plus a well-drafted will are a must. Other planning tools are valuable, but these three documents are imperative for everyone.

If you are having trouble getting your parents to agree to some of the suggestions in this book, you may just have to live with it. But some issues just can't be swept under the table. Regardless of their competence, training, or experience, no adult child wants to be forced to relinquish his or her parents' health care decisions to other people. Nor should any adult children be required to go into court to settle matters that could have been easily resolved by enacting a simple power of attorney or a living trust. *If you accomplish nothing else, at least ensure that your parents execute documents that name an agent(s) to represent them if they become incapacitated.* Legal experts will tell you that these documents are the most important pieces of paper your parents will ever sign. If you encounter resistance, it's important to emphasize that by signing these documents your parents are making a gift to the entire family.

Planning for Disability: Health Care Management

For years attorneys have emphasized the importance of wills. However, today with all the changes in medical technology, planning for incapacity has become an equally and perhaps even more pressing concern for most families than estate planning. Ignore the problem and you will find that

- doctors and other strangers will dictate the course of your parents' medical care;
- bills will go unpaid;
- tax returns will not be filed;
- no one will have the authority to manage your parents' financial, business, and personal affairs;
- court costs and administrative fees will decimate your parents' estate; and
- ultimately, the courts will control all financial and health care decisions.

Your parents can avoid these and other problems by executing durable powers of attorney for both property and for health care, as noted earlier. A power of attorney is a legal authorization made by a principal (your parent) to an agent, who is given authority to make certain decisions on behalf of the principal. In the old days, all powers of attorney expired when the principal became incapacitated. But today, you can and should make powers of attorney durable—that is, they stay in force when the principal becomes disabled. A power of attorney for property allows the agent to manage the principal's financial affairs; one for health care allows the agent to manage the principal's health care decisions. In addition, a living will provides instructions to the principal's physician regarding medical decisions that may artificially prolong life.

Durable powers of attorney for property and health care have legal force. They keep families out of court and ensure that the principal's wishes are fulfilled. It is very important to put these documents in place before illness becomes a factor as these types of decisions require mental acuity. Remember

Their Stories
• • • • •

Fred, a successful, big-city broker, was always quietly worried about the status of his father-in-law's emergency paperwork. Dad, 82, was a wealthy man but didn't like to waste money on such incidentals as legal fees. He always told Fred, "Those lawyers always want your money but don't care about you!" On the eve of his daughter's wedding, Fred received an ominous call from his father-in-law's doctor, indicating that Dad's death was imminent. The timing couldn't have been worse. Neither Fred nor his wife was able to attend the rehearsal dinner or other wedding festivities that evening because they were called to an emergency bedside meeting with the family lawyer. It seems that Fred's father-in-law had never bothered to draft a will even though he had been in poor health for years.

Moral: Don't let bad planning by your parents become your crisis. Insist that they have up-to-date paperwork enacted.

• • • • •

Their Stories

• • • • •

Stan, a successful dentist, knew that his father had drafted some type of legal instruments that would come into effect in the event he became disabled. But Stan wasn't exactly sure how it would work. Unfortunately, he found out. Dad, an attorney, was a secretive individual who didn't bother to seek outside counsel for a more informed opinion on the disability instruments he had taken on himself to draft. Unknown to the rest of the family, Dad had included a clause in his documents that mandated court approval before the legal instruments empowering others to act on his behalf in the event of his incompetency could go into effect. Not surprisingly, the children, who didn't enjoy the best of sibling relationships, ended up in court anyway, and the family squabbles that ensued were not pretty. It took much of Dad's remaining assets to get his affairs squared away.

Moral: Just because Dad or Mom is an attorney or other professional doesn't mean that he or she understands the esoteric points of disability planning. If you're not comfortable, ask your parents if you can have an outside professional review their legal instruments. They may be offended, but tell them that you need to understand the nature of their arrangements well *before* the crisis hits.

• • • • •

that 10 percent of those over 65 suffer from dementia, and that number rises to 25 percent in the over-85 population. Discuss the options with your parents. Encourage them to make the important decision to protect themselves. Explain that if they don't take these steps now, you won't be able to protect them later. Your hands will be tied just when they'll need you the most. Taking no actions allows government agencies and the courts to take charge, and the ensuing problems are only magnified if a parent is divorced or widowed.

Stress to your parents that if they fail to take the right measures, they are placing themselves and their whole family at risk. Your parents are creating a situation with the potential for imposing a tremendous emotional and financial burden on you and other family members. Assure your parents that they always have the right to change or revoke their directives. They should also know that their agent can only act with their consent and cannot override their wishes if they are competent. If their objection to creating documents is financial, you can easily obtain state-specific documents at the public library or from the World Wide Web at no charge. In addition, the local Area Agency on Aging may be able to suggest sources of low-cost legal assistance for creating legal documents.

Doing It Now

In the summer of 1997 the American Association of Retired Persons (AARP) sponsored an extensive phone survey of adult children to learn if the children had approached their aging parents about sensitive matters. The AARP discovered that two-thirds of the adult children surveyed had yet to talk to their parents about such touchy matters as continuing to live independently. This study authenticates what everyone already knows—adult children are understandably reluctant to get involved in their parents' affairs.

Most adult children just don't want to talk to their parents about a loss of independence or a terminal illness. In fact, they probably would prefer a prolonged case of flu than tackle difficult issues with their parents. The conspiracy of silence, fostered by both parents and children, is tempting to maintain but is very unwise, leaving the entire family completely unprepared to act if and when a disaster strikes. And, worse yet, it keeps family members in the dark about the individual's wishes. Talk to your parents at the first opportunity about how they want things to be handled in the event of a disability. To paraphrase a popular advertising slogan, "Just do it." (To review suggestions for approaching your parents about sensitive topics, see Chapter 3.)

Medical Directives

Advances in medical technology can keep terminally ill individuals alive indefinitely, which has caused anguish for more than one family. End-of-life issues create emotional turmoil as well as financial pain. Many of the elderly fret that a lifetime's worth of assets could be wiped out by unwanted medical treatment. Fortunately, for all of us who worry about the kind of medical care our loved ones will receive whether they want it or not, the legal tide has turned, giving patients back the right to control the course of their own medical treatment. The Supreme Court has ruled that a person's wishes, when expressed clearly and unambiguously, is consistent with the constitutionally guaranteed right to die and should be honored.

Health decisions are governed by state law. Some states have "family consent" laws permitting family members to make decisions for their loved ones under certain circumstances even if the loved one has failed to enact the necessary paperwork. But in the majority of states, no one, including a spouse, has the automatic right to make health care decisions if an individual becomes incapacitated. In many instances, a court proceeding may eventually be needed to sort things out if your parents haven't tended to these matters.

Fortunately, there are simple steps you and your parents can take to solve this problem. Even the federal government has gotten into the act on behalf of individual patients. The Patient Self-Determination Act (PSDA), which became effective in December 1991, requires that all hospitals who receive federal funds must inform patients of (1) their right to make their own health care decisions and (2) their right to execute medical directives. If the patient has executed an advance directive, that information must be noted in the patient's record. But, unfortunately, the law doesn't stipulate that a copy of the directive must be kept with the patient. Instead, it's legal to stash the document in a filing cabinet somewhere else in the building. So you may want to insist that a copy be added to your parent's bedside chart. The hospital and/or doctor must also inform the patient at admission about its policies regarding advance directives. Some institutions may not agree to abide by right-to-die provisions, so you need to pay attention to their policies before admission if possible.

Medical directives are subject to state, not federal, law, so the laws differ according to the jurisdiction. Meeting a state's basic legal requirements in your parents' directives is important. But even more important are the discussions you and your parents must have before signing the document. Advance directives were never meant to take the place of "the conversation"; instead, they are designed to document it. First, your parents should decide how they feel about a range of medical treatments. If they become gravely ill, do they want every possible measure taken to preserve their life? Or if it is determined that they have an irreversible medical condition, would they choose to implement minimal medical intervention?

It's very important for the adult child's mental health that the parents take responsibility for deciding what they want and not leave the task of making life-and-death decisions to others. Parents should be encouraged to communicate their thoughts clearly to their children and other family members. If an adult child is empowered to make decisions on behalf of an incapacitated parent, he or she needs a clear understanding of the parent's wishes. Imagine the mental anguish when a parent is in a life-threatening situation and the adult child must make a critical health care decision based on guesswork. Making medical decisions on behalf of your parents may be one of the most difficult things ever asked of you. But the fact that you have discussed the options with your parents is key. The emotional burden adult children bear is significantly lessened if they are acting on a parent's instructions rather than being forced to make their own decisions.

A family conference is a good way to discuss various treatment options because it gives all the members a forum for airing their thoughts and concerns. Use the medical directive as a focal point for the meeting. An open debate provides everyone the chance to be heard and provides the means for overcoming resistance. A group discussion can bring out conflict between family members over treatment issues—conflict that can be resolved when there is no immediate problem. Leaving these questions unresolved for later, when the family is in the midst of a medical crisis, is a sure recipe for disaster. Getting input from your family doctor is also important. A doctor's recommendations may shed a different light on the discussions and allow family members to resolve their differences.

If your family is ultimately unable to agree on an acceptable strategy, the differences of opinion should be addressed in the medical directive. Typically, medical directives don't require an attorney's assistance, but it is important to get a lawyer involved if there is considerable conflict among family members. An attorney can draft specialized language in health care documents that address differences of opinion and stipulate how parents want disagreements handled. This may seem like overkill, but your parents should endeavor to take all the necessary steps they can now so that the children don't end up fielding problems in a court of law.

Two types of medical directives. The living will, the original medical directive, was first introduced in California in 1976 and instructs the doctor about the type of medical procedures desired by an incompetent patient suffering from an irreversible medical condition. A living will usually details specific health therapies that the individual desires or specifically wants withheld in the event of a terminal illness. At present, 36 states allow an individual to refuse artificial nutrition and hydration as part of a living will. But implicit in all living wills is a serious limitation: a patient can't possibly address all eventualities in a single document.

Even the most complete document will become quickly outdated as medical technology evolves. The best approach is to include clear language unambiguously stating the patient's values about an acceptable quality of life. Another shortcoming of a living will is that it applies to terminal conditions only. The majority of health care decisions needed for incompetent patients involve less critical matters, such as day-to-day care decisions, treatment options, and placement alternatives, none of which is addressed in a living will.

Another serious drawback to living wills is that doctors often ignore them. A disturbing study published in the November 1995 issue of the *Journal of the American Medical Association (JAMA)* showed that many doctors and hospitals often disregarded patients' expressed wishes clearly outlined in living wills despite the fact that a living will is not just a wish but has the force of law. Often, the care that patients receive during their final hours and days doesn't reflect their personal wishes, a finding further corroborated by a 1997 study from the Dartmouth Medical School cited in "Why Having a Living Will Is Not Enough." Emphasize to your parents that a living will is not the only document they need because it is highly dependent on the ability and the willingness of their personal doctor to carry out their instructions.

Many states require a doctor to certify that Mom's or Dad's condition will not and cannot improve. Because the doctor's support is crucial to the successful implementation of the medical directive, your parents shouldn't drop the document in the mail along with a note explaining its importance. Suggest to your parents that they make a personal appointment with their physician to discuss their wishes. You may also want to recommend that they sign the document in their doctor's presence to give the instructions more weight. Ask your parents' physician to make the document part of their medical records. If the doctor doesn't want to comply with your parents' wishes, your parents may have no other choice but to select another physician.

In spite of their shortcomings, living wills are important directives for individuals who don't have family or who feel that their family will not act strongly on their behalf. Doctors and hospitals must abide by a living will, so it's an effective instrument even if it needs a little push from the family lawyer. Ensure that the document will be valid by carefully following the witnessing requirements. Remember, too, that medical directives are only as good as their availability. If no one knows about the existence of a directive, it's of little value. Your parents should keep a copy with their important papers in addition to giving a copy to their doctor, lawyer, and a family friend.

A second option, a durable power of attorney for health care (DPAHC), designates an agent to represent your parent. This document transfers legal authority to the agent if the principal (the person who signed the document) becomes unable to make his or her own medical decisions. The agent has the legal authority to speak for the principal in all medical matters. An important aspect of a DPAHC is that it resolves uncertainty by appointing a family representative. This one individual is given the authority to make decisions even if family members disagree among themselves or if the family disagrees with the physician. The agent acts as a spokesperson, investigator, examiner, explainer, and patient advocate.

An agent who has a firsthand relationship with the patient can act as a decision maker in responding to specific situations. This is important because no one can anticipate the unique and often complicated situations that may arise. If your family is large, your parents may have trouble deciding which child to designate as their agent. But a DPAHC is so important that family politics should never get in the way. The best agent is someone who is reliable, understands the issues, will follow your parents' desires, and is forceful enough to advocate your parents' position to the medical community. And most important of all, the agent must have the capacity to deal with difficult decisions.

Health care agents have significant powers. They can obtain and examine all medical records, receive information from doctors and other health care providers regarding proposed treatment strategies, consent or decline medical treatment, control disclosure of medical records, authorize admission to a nursing home, hire and discharge doctors, and make decisions regarding withholding or withdrawing medical treatment, including artificial nutrition and hydration. In short, an agent can do almost everything that a patient could do. Another argument for appointing an agent is that doctors prefer dealing with an agent. Physi-

Their Stories

• • • • •

Alicia, worried about her elderly aunts, finally decided to take matters into her own hands. After talking with the family attorney, she purchased inexpensive legal forms at a local stationery store; the durable power of attorney for health care and a durable power of attorney for property were happily executed by her aunts, who appreciated her concern. Their children, Alicia's cousins, later expressed their gratitude to Alicia for taking charge of the situation. They had wanted to do something but each felt that she shouldn't "upset Mother."

Moral: Don't assume that your parents want to avoid talking about powers of attorney. In fact, they probably are just as concerned as you are. As the adult child, it may just be your responsibility to find a good time to talk about these matters.

• • • • •

cians usually don't have the same level of concern about legal entanglements when an agent is involved as they do when they are required to execute the directives contained in a living will. Treating a patient without informed consent subjects a physician to a potential assault or battery charge. Because physicians fear being sued, they prefer that their patients have a health care agent. But reassure your parents that a health care agent doesn't have the authority to veto decisions made by a competent patient.

Naming an agent is not a foolproof solution, however, as an agent is *given* the power to act but is *not required* to. The durable power's effectiveness is totally dependent on the willingness of agents to carry out their responsibilities. An agent too overwrought to make decisions can't be forced to act. Address this potential problem by naming a successor agent. The selection of a health care agent is not a decision to be made lightly; it should be based on an individual's merits, not on love, guilt, or obligation.

Selecting the best directive for your parents. Should your parents use a living will or a DPAHC? Each document has its unique advantages and disadvantages. A durable power of attorney for health care appoints an agent who has wide latitude in all medical situations where the grantor is incapacitated. The obvious limitation is that the agent may not be capable of making a decision under the duress of a real situation. A living will is more narrow by being applicable in terminal situations only. But the advantage of a living will is that it is legally enforceable on the medical community. A conservative approach is to have your parents sign both documents, making sure that both documents are consistent with each other. Some states let you use a unified form—a

What Is an Elder Law Attorney?

• • • • •

Elder law attorneys are not only licensed to practice law but have additional proficiency in resolving problems that often result when the aged have to cope with state and federal agencies that serve the elderly, such as the Department of Veterans Affairs, the Health Care Financing Administration, and the Social Security Administration. Elder law focuses on a special population and "deals with legal and management problems that may result from aging, illness, or incapacity, reflecting the pace of change affecting older Americans," according to Strauss and Leiderman. An elder law attorney needs expertise in a variety of areas and may be familiar with such nonlegal problems as obtaining home care, remaining in the community, and obtaining a reverse mortgage. Elder law lawyers often specialize in conservatorship and retirement law and may have experience with estate, probate, and trust matters as well. When interviewing an elder law attorney, inquire about the specific issues the attorney has handled in the past. For a referral to a local elder law attorney, consult the information presented later in this chapter.

• • • • •

health care proxy—that combines a living will and a durable power for health care into one document.

Fortunately, you don't need a lawyer to help you draft an advance directive for your parents. First, get an official or generally accepted state-specific form. Try to locate at least one or two additional directives from other states to use as resource documents. Read all the forms and add additional language to your state-specific form if your parents want to replace it with alternative instructions. You can and should personalize the form (see the list of resources later in this chapter for places to locate free forms) and carefully follow the instructions for witnesses. Then talk with other family members, their doctor, and their friends informing them of their wishes. The portability of advance directives is always an issue, so your parents may need to sign more than one state-specific form.

Make sure that everyone in your family updates his or her health care directive every five years. Sometimes institutions object to "stale" documents, so it's always best to update frequently by adding a page that certifies the previously executed document. The new page can either be witnessed or notarized to show authenticity. Give both your physician and agent a copy of the updated document or documents. Agents also need to be able to locate the original document. It's critical that your parents take their directives to the hospital with them when they have elective procedures or that they are brought over later by a family member in an emergency. Also demand that a directive be kept with your parent's hospital chart and not filed out of sight.

Planning for Incapacity: Asset Management

As with medical directives, there are two planning alternatives to protect the property of incapacitated parents. The first, a power of attorney (POA), allows the principal to name an agent to handle his or her financial affairs. The other option, a living trust, is a more complex device that transfers ownership of a property asset from an individual or couple to a trust. A living trust offers more features and in some ways is more flexible than a POA. But the document usually requires the services of an estate planning attorney, which increases the cost substantially. A living trust is the top-of-the-line document, a great planning device whose use should be limited to situations in which the individual has substantial assets, needs special planning tools, or lives in a high-cost probate state (more details on living trusts are in a subsequent section of this chapter).

There are two types of powers of attorney for property; each is appropriate for specific circumstances. A *general* power names another party, an agent, to act on the principal's behalf immediately. This type of power is helpful for allowing another individual to pay your bills while you're on vacation, for example. Unfortunately, it is useless in planning for incapacity as a general power

Power of Attorney: A Very Essential Legal Document

• • • • •

- Every adult needs one.

- It should be prepared by an experienced attorney.

- It is governed by state law.

- Power needs to be durable to remain valid during an incapacity.

- Financial institutions should preapprove the document.

- The agent should have the right to hire outside professionals.

- The agent should have the right to establish and fund trusts.

- The agent should have the power to bestow gifts if gifting is a part of your parents' ongoing strategy.

- A POA terminates at the principal's death.

• • • • •

Alternatives to a Power of Attorney

• • • • •

- Joint accounts that allow adult children to pay bills

- Appointment of a *representative payee* to receive public benefits like Social Security

- Alternative signatory designations offered by many financial institutions

- Trusts

- A guardianship proceeding

• • • • •

ceases when the principal becomes disabled. A *durable* power of attorney (DPOA) is preferable in cases of disability because the document clearly states that the power continues in the event of incapacity; otherwise, the power would have no legal force if your parents became unable to make decisions on their own behalf. Such language as "This power of attorney shall not terminate on disability of the principal" indicates that the power is durable. If your parents create a DPOA, their agent can handle their affairs if they become incompetent, ill, disappear, or are even kidnapped! Remind Mom and Dad to update their respective POAs every five years, for a POA for property can become "stale" too.

POAs are flexible planning devices. An agent can be given narrow powers that are limited in scope, such as granting only the right to sell the family home. Or an agent can be given wide latitude that may include paying all the bills (including medical expenses), signing binding contracts, depositing checks and withdrawing funds, making investment decisions, handling tax matters, managing the family business, distributing funds to dependents, representing the principal in dealings with federal and state agencies, supervising the investments and distributions from a retirement plan, moving assets into a living trust, and any other duties the principal stipulates. If your parents don't have someone they trust or are worried about family politics, a better alternative is to use a professional fiduciary or the trust services of a local bank.

Mom or Dad may terminate the power of attorney at any time, and it is automatically terminated at death. If Mom is reluctant to create a POA that gives the agent authority immediately, one alternative is a "springing" power triggered by a disability. A parent might want to stipulate that the spouse receives agent status immediately and the children are given springing powers. The problem with springing power is agreeing on the definition of disability. If the document requires a court hearing to prove disability, the POA can cause the family more problems than it solves, so be very cautious if your parents decide to use a springing power. A better alternative is to base determination of disability on the opinion of two physicians not related by blood or marriage.

Incapacity without Advance Directives?

When parents become unable to write checks or manage their affairs for themselves, it's a real dilemma if they've failed to name an agent. During the initial phase, depending on the jurisdiction, your parent may find himself or herself in legal limbo with various public protective service agencies trying to oversee the situation with varying degrees of success. Your family may be forced to the wings, powerless to do much of anything. The advantage of guardianship proceedings (a long tradition in English common law) is that when individuals are no longer able to survive on their own, anyone may petition the court for a guardianship hearing. But the hearing may not be scheduled for several months and may be subject to frequent postponements and other legal delays. In the meantime, your parent's overall situation may become increasingly precarious. A guardianship proceeding is usually a prolonged process that includes

- defining the nature and extent of the disability;
- determining if the individual meets the definition of incompetent;
- determining the role of the guardian;
- selecting the guardian;
- the hearing process; and
- enforcement and monitoring.

The selection of the guardian is often determined by statute but can be overridden by a judge who feels an appointment of a guardian may not be in the best interests of the incompetent individual. It is the judge who, within specific state statutes, determines the role of the guardian. The unfortunate aspect of guardianship is that in some states this process entails the wholesale loss of basic rights normally guaranteed by the Fourteenth Amendment. Guardians have mandated reporting requirements and are compensated for their efforts by the incompetent individual. Usually, destitute individuals who are incompetent become the responsibility of public agencies.

It is a heartbreaking experience for most adult children to watch as a parent is judged incompetent in a court of law. And yet, if the parent is not able to cope and has not named anyone to act on his behalf, that may be the only viable alternative. In addition to the emotional toil, these proceedings usually cost between $10,000 and $30,000 depending on the nature of the situation and the jurisdiction. Ironically, a parent who is afraid of losing control and therefore refuses to sign enabling documents may later lose total control, including the right to vote and to marry, as a result of this refusal. A far better alternative is simple advance planning—combining a power of attorney for property and advance medical directives.

A Few Caveats

It goes without saying that your parents need to feel comfortable with their agent. Unfortunately, in the wrong hands, a POA is a recipe for disaster. One way to protect your siblings from serious infighting is to suggest to Mom and Dad that they authorize their agent, on request, to provide a detailed record of all financial transactions to the children. Further, the children may want to suggest that the agent receive modest compensation for his or her efforts if this bookkeeping chore is complex. If your parents want their agent to be able to make financial gifts to others, they should stipulate this specifically in the POA. Then there are those special planning needs for married couples. Vitt and Siegenthaler have noted: "Broad powers are often essential for married couples when preparing for the possibility of long-term illness or incapacity. A spouse, acting as an agent for an institutionalized spouse, needs a broad power of attorney in order to take advantage of laws permitting the transfer or sale of assets and protecting against impoverishment."

Agents are not subject to formal oversight but legally are liable for their decisions. Agents must put the principal's interests first and are accountable for their actions. But if an agent has already dissipated assets by the time anyone notices, the courts can do little to rectify the situation. It is hoped that agents will be trustworthy. If your parents choose one agent to manage their health care and an agent to oversee assets, make sure that the two agents can agree on cohesive strategy. Otherwise, the agent managing health care may find that the agent overseeing assets is refusing to pay for a medical treatment the financial overseer considers unnecessary. Also, designate a successor agent in the POA document(s) in the event that the first agent becomes incapacitated.

Major Limitations of POAs

POAs are used widely, but, unfortunately, several practical problems associated with them must be considered. An agent may find that it is difficult, if not impossible, to sell out-of-state real estate under a POA as a result of the legal limitations on an agent's powers. An even larger problem is dealing with third parties. Banks, brokerage firms, and title companies are notoriously finicky about accepting POAs. For example, my personal experience is that moving a financial asset from one institution to another with a POA may be a hair-raising experience requiring the completion of nine forms. A good way to circumvent this problem is to first contact your parents' financial institutions and inquire about their policies. Some financial institutions require that customers use special forms unique to the institution. Get a letter from each of your parents' institutions saying it will accept your parents' POA, just to be on the safe side even if using its form is not a requirement. You don't want to find out after the fact that your bank won't accept Mom's POA.

Living Trusts

A living trust is a legal mechanism for gathering assets under one umbrella as well as an important financial management tool. A living trust combines both incapacity planning and estate planning in one vehicle. It is usually revocable (you can change your mind) and, like all trusts, is considered a separate legal entity for legal and tax purposes, which provides additional advantages to the principal. A living trust is a handy device for eliminating many of the problems commonly encountered when using a power of attorney, especially when

Resources

• • • • •

If you have specific questions or are having a legal problem regarding some of the documents we have discussed in this chapter, you may want to contact some of the following associations:

Choice in Dying
1035 30th Street, NW
Washington, DC 20016
800-989-9455
Offers no-cost advice and state-specific directives at a nominal cost or you may download forms directly from its Web site at www.choices.org at no charge. Also offers DocuDIAL, a registry for advance directives for a one-time fee of $55.

Commission on Legal Problems of the Elderly
American Bar Association
740 15th Street, NW
Washington, DC 20005-1009
Offers booklets and will accept some individual cases. Its Web site is http://207.49.1.7/elderly

American Association of Retired Persons
601 E Street, NW
Washington, DC 20049
Planning for Incapacity: Self-Help Guide ($5) contains state-specific forms for living wills and powers of attorney for health care as well as an overall guide for using advance directives; also publishes *Organizing Your Future: A Guide to Decision Making in Your Later Years* ($5).

National Academy of Elder Law Attorneys
Tucson, Arizona
520-881-4005
Offers booklets and referrals to local attorneys who specialize in elder law; can be reached at its home page at www.naela.org

• • • • •

dealing with out-of-state assets. It is an excellent planning tool for future disability; compared with a POA, it offers more flexibility and greater authority. A living trust makes sense for people with substantial assets who require management expertise or who own property in several states.

A properly funded living trust provides the following benefits:

- Gathers assets in one place, which eliminates many management headaches for family members
- Names a trustee (family member or professional) who can manage all the trust's assets if the principal (the person who established the trust) becomes incapacitated
- Eliminates the need for a court-appointed guardian (important because anyone can petition the court to be appointed guardian for an older individual who has become senile)
- More readily accepted by financial institutions because the trust holds legal title to the assets
- Doesn't require special tax forms on April 15
- Makes it relatively simple to change beneficiary designations
- Avoids probate and keeps financial information private at death

A living trust, however, will not solve all incapacity and estate issues and is not the perfect instrument for everyone. It will *not*

- avoid probate for assets held outside the trust;
- provide income or estate tax savings;
- protect assets from creditors;
- be suitable for small estates;
- be inexpensive to implement or simple to use; or
- be effective unless each asset is placed within the trust and retitled.

A living trust is not necessary or even that helpful in situations where the portfolio consists entirely of insurance policies and retirement plans that already have beneficiary designations. If your parents are both living and have everything in their joint names, a living trust only helps in situations in which joint signatures are required for selling an asset such as a home or a car. If one or both of your parents are alone, however, a living trust will be especially helpful as each can name a trustee who can immediately take over managing the assets in the event of a disability. The benefits of a living trust vary dramatically from one situation to another, so sheer asset size alone is not the best criterion for determining when a living will is indicated, but, in general, it is best confined to estates of $500,000 or more or in high-probate-cost states such as California.

A living trust may slightly complicate everyday money management for your parents. But on the whole, a living trust will greatly simplify life for those around them and may save money in the long run if they have an involved financial situation. If the estate is large and the trust fully funded—that is, all assets have been retitled and placed in the trust—these assets are kept out of probate. Probate, the legal process of transferring assets at death, has gotten a bad reputation because in some states it may devour as much as 7 percent of an estate. If your parents are living in a high-probate-cost state, a living trust can pass on more money to the beneficiaries and less to state or attorneys' coffers.

Estate Planning

The purpose of estate planning is to ensure that your parents wishes are carried out when they die. Good estate planning reduces court costs and administrative delays, and minimizes conflicts within the family. Volumes have been written about estate planning, so I won't attempt to tell you everything you need to know about estate planning but instead will offer four important tips.

1. *Make sure that your parents write a will.* Over half the people in the United States die without a will. Dying intestate, or without a will, causes lots of problems for heirs. Writing a simple will is not a big undertaking nor an expensive one; it's just an unpleasant task.

2. *Check to see how your parents have titled their assets.* Property ownership designations determine how assets will be transferred and thus are very important. In fact, they are so important that designations override will provisions. For example, let's say that your mother has named your brother as the beneficiary of her huge life insurance policy and has made you the beneficiary of her small IRA account. She subsequently writes a will declaring that her assets should be divided equally between her two children. She is now proud of herself, mistakenly thinking that she has done right by both of her children. Unfortunately for you, however, the assets will not be divided equally but will instead be distributed according to the beneficiary designations. Ouch!

The inventory form in Chapter 4 accompanied by a sidebar showing ownership designations can be used for collecting this information.

3. *Consider using trusts in your parents' estate plan.* Too many people think that trusts are just for the wealthy. But in truth they are good for any far-thinking individual who wants professional management or to provide for beneficiaries with special circumstances. And unlike living trusts, which are primarily a management tool, many types of trusts can be drafted to minimize estate tax and income tax obligations as well.

4. *Be supercautious if parents want property held in joint tenancy with anyone but a spouse.* It is the most overused and abused ownership tool around. Many people think of it as the poor man's will because the property automatically reverts to the survivor at the first owner's death. But there are many hidden problems to consider. Let's say that your mom decides to put your brother's name on her house as a joint owner because he's living with her and helping her with the day-to-day management chores. This joint tenancy seems like a good idea as your brother is close to the situation and can make informed decisions about the house and/or Mom in the event of an emergency. When Mom signed over half of the house to your brother, she unwittingly made a gift of one-half the value of the house. Because she is allowed to give away only $10,000 a year to any one person, a gift tax form must be filed and taxes may be due.

Second, she creates a situation in which a simple idea may become an expensive mistake. When Mom dies, according to tax law, the value of her house "steps up" to reflect its current market value. Accordingly, if Mom bought the house for $45,000 and it is now worth $245,000, there would be no tax due if the heirs want to sell the house the next day. But because Mom has already given away half of the house to your brother, in most states his half of the house, his joint tenancy, will not "step up" and may cost Mom's heirs additional taxes when they attempt to sell the home.

To make matters even more interesting, let's say that Mom gets mad at your brother and decides she no longer wants him to inherit the house. If she wants to change the ownership designation, the only way she will be able to effect that change is with your brother's written agreement. Or consider your Mom's plight if your brother gets into financial difficulty and his creditors take the family house to satisfy their claims. Suffice it to say, joint tenancy is appropriate for some married couples. It's also acceptable to designate joint owners of a small checking account so a family member can pay immediate bills, but for the most part joint tenancy can cause a lot of unintended repercussions. Check with a lawyer familiar with state law before your parents make titling decisions, for different states have local rules with important consequences.

Their Stories

• • • • •

Fred, a seemingly organized individual who had been divorced for over 30 years, was asked by his two adult daughters and his sister if his will and other important papers were up-to-date. He always protested that "everything was taken care of," and there was no reason to doubt it. Besides, no one wanted to raise questions as that surely would rock the boat. Unfortunately, his oldest daughter discovered, when Fred was diagnosed with a terminal illness, that his 35-year-old-will left everything to his now deceased ex-wife. In addition, Fred had failed to sign both medical directives and a power of attorney for property. Fred's oldest daughter, at the worst possible time when she was understandably distraught, was forced to get her father's affairs in order.

Moral: When your parents tell you that "everything has been taken care of," don't accept the remark at face value. Gently probe to determine what documents have been drafted, when the documents were originally drafted, and ask if they have been updated within the last ten or preferably five years.

• • • • •

The Pros and Cons of Joint Tenancy

• • • • •

Advantages

- Easy and inexpensive to establish

- Requires no special documentation or court orders

- Offers a simple tool for managing your parents' affairs

- Creates automatic inheritability

- Eliminates the need for probate

Disadvantages

- Can't sell jointly owned real estate without both signatures

- Gives each party total ownership of some types of assets

- One joint owner's creditors can seize the entire property for nonpayment

- Creates an immediate gift to a nonspousal joint owner

- May trigger a gift tax obligation

- May create an unintended tax obligation

- Will or trust provisions do not override joint ownership designation

- Inflexible tool as it's difficult to change the ownership designation without selling part or all of the asset

• • • • •

To Do List

• • • • •

- Establish your own medical directives; have a will and power of attorney or living trust drafted too.

- Discuss your parents' financial and medical situation with your siblings.

- Broach the topic of advance planning with your parents, beginning with a discussion of how you have handled your own situation.

- Encourage your parents, with the help of your siblings, to get the necessary paperwork drafted or revised to reflect a changed family situation.

- Ask your parents if you can read their documents.

- If children are named as agents, ask to retain the original copies.

- If there is disagreement among family members, have a third-party professional mediate a family meeting.

- Health care directives apply to institutional settings only. If your parents' state permits it and if your parents are serious about preventing certain life-saving techniques, they can obtain a nonhospital Do Not Resuscitate (DNR) power that should be kept in one's possession at all times.

- Don't accept the answer that "everything has been taken care of" to mean that everything *has* been taken care of. Find out exactly what that statement means. If arrangements are not specified, children are unprepared to take over.

• • • • •

CHAPTER 7

Ideas for Helping Parents Who Have Some Money, Little Money, or No Money

"I've got enough money for the rest of my life unless I want to buy something."

—Comedian Milton Berle

Ever watch television and wonder about those handsome oldsters hawking various products? Seniors are often featured swallowing vitamins guaranteed to make them young and vigorous, cruising away the nights while enjoying a romantic moment dressed in their finery, playing a leisurely game of golf or tennis, or, my personal favorite, using a special shampoo that makes grey hair appear lustrous. It seems that most senior citizens don't have a care in the world. But, unfortunately, that's just another misguided perception created by advertising.

Some Americans have money, but the majority of older Americans don't have a lot of money. In fact, some senior citizens have darn little. For starters, more than 12 percent of the elderly can be considered poor and another 2 million are considered near-poor. However, compared with prior decades, most of the elderly aren't dirt poor or filthy rich, but most of them are somewhere in the middle range. This is especially applicable if your parents have other resources such as a home, a paid-up life insurance policy, personal savings, or Individual Retirement Account (IRA) to cushion the financial bumps associated with aging.

Although old age was not too long ago the preserve of the few and wealthy, we have recently begun to experience what Robert Butler, founding director of the National Institute on Aging (NIA), has called "the democratization of old age." To this we would add that so too we see the expanding distribution of a comfortable retirement income to a larger number of men and women in the form of pensions, individual retirement arrangements, Social Security, home equity and investment assets (Cutler, Gregg, & Lawton).

If your parents find themselves in a similar situation, they enjoy the enviable position of having additional assets that could be tapped if necessary. Many of our parents are in a far better financial position than they ever expected to be during their sunset years as most have, much to their surprise, accumulated their wealth slowly, almost without realizing it. As a result, many seniors are unaware of the resources at their disposal and the tactics for making these resources work to their advantage. Thus, in both this chapter and the next, we will explore a variety of strategies you can recommend to your parents for improving their lifestyle by wielding often untapped assets.

You can assist your parents more than you realize by acting as both their eyes and ears. They need your energy and your resourcefulness to help them explore various alternatives. Unfortunately, several studies and surveys agree that the majority of older Americans remain woefully unaware of most of the options for improving their lot. Another startling problem is that over one-half of all seniors overpay their taxes. These findings strongly suggest that many seniors need to improve their financial acumen. Their collective low level of financial literacy is certainly understandable given an increasingly complex tax system and aid programs; but it also is terribly unfortunate. Let's start this process for helping your parents create a better lifestyle by examining three possibilities: the old-fashioned notion of increasing income, reducing outgo, or a combination of both.

Increasing Income

How Much Money Your Parents Will Need

A surprising number of people sit around wearing green eyeshades, using calculators and computers, trying to determine the impossible—that is, how much money it takes to replace a worker's lifestyle after retirement. Thanks to the American Society of Pension Actuaries (ASPA), we have some idea of the percentage of preretirement income needed. ASPA's findings are a helpful benchmark for people approaching retirement or for those who are still in the process of deciding whether they want to continue working. ASPA looked at the work of several researchers who employed the basic premise that "income from all sources throughout retirement should provide the same standard of living as that enjoyed in the later years of full-time employment."

In their quest to determine how much it costs to maintain the same lifestyle during retirement, the researchers eliminated work-related costs and retirement savings. They also considered the progressive nature of our tax system. They agreed that because retirees would no longer have to pay Social Security tax on earned income, the replacement ratio for all workers would be less than 100 percent. The ASPA study concluded that if your parents earn $40,000 or less, they will need about 80 percent of their preretirement income to maintain their lifestyle. Thus, if your parents earned $35,000 during their last year of paid employment, they will need about $28,000 to stay even during their first year of retirement. If their earned income was between $40,000 and $100,000, they will require a 75 percent replacement ratio. However, 70 percent of preretirement income will suffice for high-income wage earners whose earnings exceed $100,000 annually.

The researchers, however, did not consider three factors:

1. Many families voluntarily change their consumption patterns at retirement.
2. Inflation has a profound impact on retirees.
3. Escalating health care expenses often place huge unexpected financial pressures on retirees.

Thus, I would caution the reader to use the replacement ratios presented here conservatively as they don't factor into their calculations the impact of inflation nor the high cost of mandatory medical care or hands-on assistance to those elderly who become sick or feeble.

What Social Security Provides

A compelling unknown for retirees who are not entitled to receive a private pension is the type of lifestyle they can expect to attain living solely on the proceeds from their Social Security checks. The amount a worker ultimately receives from Social Security at retirement is a function of the number of years worked, annual earnings, and marital status. Single workers who have no other source of retirement income and who earned less than $30,000 annually will find Social Security replaces about 42 percent of working income. A one-income couple makes out a bit better; married workers who earn less than $30,000 annually will learn that Social Security replaces about 63 percent of working income. Social Security provides the least help for single high-income workers. High-earning singles will discover that Social Security only replaces about 14 percent of their former income.

These differences are driven by three events. First, the Social Security contribution level phases out at around $70,000 so high-income wage earners contribute less to the system on a percentage basis. Second, the calculation of the Social Security retirement benefit is based on a decreasing percentage as average indexed monthly earnings increase. In other words, the Social Security system helps those who earn less more than it helps high-income wage earners. Third, the system favors one-income families. So a word to the wise: the more money your parents are earning or have earned from work, or if they are divorced or widowed, the less help they will receive from Social Security. High-income parents need to have significant personal savings, a big pension, plans to continue working, or accept that there is little chance their retirement lifestyle will mirror the life they enjoyed during their preretirement years.

Deciding How Long to Work

If your parents are now just beginning to contemplate their retirement options, there are several angles they should explore, especially if they are thinking about taking early retirement. If your parents are entitled to receive a private pension that pays a regular benefit for life, the plan probably uses a benefit formula based on employee tenure and average wages. If your parents are considering early retirement, they should know it can cost them dearly.

The price for taking early retirement is high. Most employers reduce employees' lifelong annual benefit by 6 percent for each year that an employee retires before age 65. If your father, for example, retires at age 60, he may receive only 70 percent of what he would have otherwise collected had he continued working until 65. However, if your father decides to continue working past 65 for the same employer, the federal government does protect his future pension income to a certain extent. If he continues toiling, he is entitled to receive an increased benefit based on federal guidelines or a benefit based on the pension plan's formula, whichever is greater. Another approach is for a parent to quit the current job at age 65, draw the pension, and then go to work for another company.

Deciding When Your Parents Should Draw Social Security Benefits

Many people wonder if they should start claiming Social Security benefits at 62 or wait until 65? If your parents start drawing their benefits at 62, the benefit will be 20 percent smaller. If they start receiving benefits at 62 and die before 77, the early choice will create more income. If your parents are in poor health, the best option is to start drawing benefits early at age 62. The break-even point is age 77; so if your mother, for example, waits to draw benefits until age 65 but lives to 77, she'll be in the same overall economic position as someone who drew the smaller benefit starting at 62. But if your mother lives past 77, she will receive more money if she waits because the benefit she draws at 65 is larger. In a nut shell—suggest starting to draw early if you think your parents will have a short lifespan, but your parents should wait until 65 if they feel they will outlive most of their peers.

Social Security also has a quirky, little-known special rule that your parents can take advantage of for one year while working and drawing benefits. Under this rule, a parent can receive a full Social Security check for any one month regardless of yearly earnings as long as *monthly* earnings remain under a specific limit. For recipients under 65, this earnings limit is $690 a month and increases to $960 if your parent is between 65 and 69. Social Security recipients over 70 can earn as much as they want from work without experiencing a penalty. Thus, if Dad at age 68 earns $18,000 from self-employment, the first year he draws Social Security, he can still receive his full benefit without a penalty for 11 months if he refrains from paying himself more than the monthly limit. Then, when he pays himself the remainder of his income in one month, he only loses the benefit from that specific month rather than being penalized for making too much money during the entire year.

There are special rules for spouses. A spouse can choose to receive a benefit based on her own work record or she may collect one-half of her spouse's benefit as long as he has started to draw his benefit, whichever is larger, up to the family maximum. If one of your parents is divorced but the marriage lasted at least ten years and the parent has been divorced at least two years and is not currently married, the divorced spouse can claim benefits based on a former husband's or wife's earnings record. If you have a divorced parent, remind him or her to consider this alternative before he makes final benefit arrangements with the Social Security Administration.

Other Aspects

Naturally, sufficient cash flow is a pressing concern for most retirees. But choosing when to leave work should incorporate other considerations too. Employee benefits are an important factor for many workers, especially medical and dental benefits. If your parents select early retirement, the cost of health insurance until they qualify to receive Medicare at age 65 can require an outlay of hundreds of dollars a month. Other considerations include access to a cafeteria plan and the loss of disability and life insurance coverage. Of course, work enjoyment is a huge factor. If your Dad loves his work, there is little motivation to take early retirement. On the other hand, if he had been miserable for years, perhaps early retirement combined with after-retirement employment may be the best overall solution. Income is an important element but certainly not the sole driving factor for many people who are trying to decide how long to continue working.

Making the Money Last

Most companies that pay their employees a monthly pension contract with an insurance company that agrees to pay the employees a fixed monthly income in the form of an annuity featuring a payment the employees can't outlive. The exact amount of the monthly payment depends on years of service and final average salary. The insurance company will offer retirees options for receiving the guaranteed payment—(1) life only, which is paid over an employee's life alone with no beneficiary options, (2) term certain, which is paid for life with a guaranteed minimum number of years either for a single individual or for a couple, or (3) a joint and survivor annuity for a married couple that distributes the funds over the couple's joint life span.

Since the Retirement Equity Act was passed in 1985, an employer must provide income for a couple based on their joint life expectancy unless the nonemployee spouse agrees to waive this arrangement. If the nonemployee spouse signs a notarized statement, the employee may choose a life-only option that will provide a higher benefit over his or her single lifetime. But this decision leaves the surviving spouse in the unenviable position of losing both spouse and monthly income simultaneously. Generally speaking, for most couples a life-only option is not a good choice as it exposes the remaining spouse to a sudden and precipitous loss of income.

Elderly women are the poorest group in the country and the life-only option, which was routinely selected before 1985, contributed significantly to this problem. Some retirees who choose the life annuity option circumvent the problem of a sudden loss of income for a spouse by purchasing life insurance to provide continuing income. If the amount of income the policy provides is adequate, this approach may be a worthwhile alternative for some couples. However, this is a complex decision and one best made with the help of an impartial adviser.

Most couples should select a joint life option that pays a monthly income to the retired employee for life with a percentage of that benefit (50 percent, 75 percent, or 100 percent) paid to the surviving spouse. The percentage varies, but usually a joint life option with a 50 percent benefit pays a monthly benefit that is about 20 percent smaller than the life-only option. The larger the continuing percentage for the surviving spouse, the smaller the initial benefit. Part of the annuity selection process should be based on the ratio of pension income to the couple's overall income. If the pension income represents 50 percent or more of total income, then a large percentage of the pension must be maintained for the survivor to remain solvent. But if the ratio is small, say 25 percent or less, the remaining spouse may be able to manage with a smaller monthly benefit.

In some instances your parents may be offered a lump sum option. This alternative allows the employee to receive the money that has been accumulated on his or her behalf in one large payment. This sum, which was set aside for the employee by his employer or was accumulated by the employee himself, is handed directly over to the retiree. Instead of receiving a monthly check, the recipient manages the funds himself or herself. As a result, the retiree can control the investment strategy as well as decide how much and how often disbursements are made from the account.

A retiree receiving a lump sum distribution usually transfers the money into a rollover Individual Retirement Account (IRA), allowing the money to maintain its tax-sheltered status. A big part of deciding whether your parents will benefit from a lump sum arrangement rests on when the retirement funds will be needed—the later the better. If the employee plans to work or has enough investment income so the money can compound untaxed for several additional years, the more attractive a lump sum distribution becomes. Tax and estate laws are complex, so check with a financial adviser before making any final decisions.

An annuity only benefits those retirees who live longer than their life expectancy, as their long stream of payments total more than the amount projected. This phenomenon makes a lump sum settlement attractive for retirees who currently are not in good health or for some other reason believe that they will experience a less-than-normal life expectancy. A lump sum distribution is most suited to someone who is knowledgeable about investments and has the personal fortitude to assume the risk of outliving the money. This option is not an appropriate choice for the fainthearted. But it's a good arrangement for an individual who likes to play with his money or for a retiree who has the discipline to time his disbursements so he or she can take a big trip one year and live frugally the next.

401(k) plans that are funded by employees themselves have come of age during the last decade; thus, the chances are fairly good that the amount your parents have contributed to such a plan is small compared to their other sources of retirement income. If your parents have an employee contribution plan, they can continue making contributions as long as they are employed. If your mother works at a university where a 401(k) plan is offered, for example, and wants to work past age 65, she can still make a tax-deductible, tax-deferred contribution as long as she is employed, regardless of age. If she wants to contribute to a regular IRA, she can continue as long as she has earned income until age 70. However, the new Roth IRA has no age limits; the only requirement for making a contribution is having earned income.

The secret to making these tax-deferred accounts work hard is to keep the deferred money intact for as long as possible. You always want to spend your personal money first as this allows the deferred account to continue compounding. Let's look at an example. Our hypothetical couple retires at age 65 with $300,000 in a tax-deferred annuity and another $300,000 in a regular taxable account. And for the purpose of our illustration, we will assume that both accounts grow 8 percent annually. If the couple decides to withdraw $40,000 a year by first tapping their tax-deferred account, and then after it is depleted they spend the taxable funds, they run out of money in 20 years when they are both 85. However, if they spend the taxable money first while allowing the tax-deferred account to compound, even at the same withdrawal rate the money lasts—another 17 years to age 97!

Money left in a regular IRA or a Keogh must be distributed starting at age 70½ or a 50 percent late-withdrawal penalty is assessed. At age 70½ the IRS requires recipients to withdraw at least enough money each year to exhaust the tax-deferred account over the recipient's lifetime. Your parents must abide by the IRS withdrawal schedule or suffer the consequences. Your parents can remove a smaller amount each year penalty-free if they wish, though, by naming a younger joint beneficiary. This approach allows the IRA to compound to an even greater sum by keeping those tax-deferred dollars growing. But that strategy has its limitations: If the joint beneficiary is not your parent's spouse, then the lifespan difference is held to a ten-year-maximum regardless of the joint beneficiary's actual age. If you feel inquisitive about how all this works, you can check out the IRS withdrawal requirements at www.irs.ustreas.gov. Or you can pick up a copy of *Maximize Your IRA* by Neil Downing.

Considering Postretirement Work

Lots of retirees, about one-third, continue to work after they retire from their lifelong occupation or job. Many retirees want to earn some extra money from part-time employment to augment their retirement income or they want to work full-time at something they enjoy but couldn't afford before they amassed a retirement nest egg. Anecdotal evidence also suggests that many retirees work not just for the money but also for the opportunity to stay involved, to continue to develop professionally, or just for something to occupy their time.

Before you suggest to Mom or Dad that they start slinging burgers, you may want to help them evaluate the financial aspects of postretirement work. For starters, earned income has a dramatic impact on the amount of Social Security they are entitled to keep, as shown in Figure 7.1. At year-end, your parents will receive a Form 1099-SSA from Social Security showing the benefits collected during the prior year. If your parents are between 62 and 65 and they both work and draw Social Security benefits, they will each lose $1 in Social Security benefits for every $2 that they earned from paid work in excess of

---

Figure

7.1

• • • • •

The Skinny on Social Security

What's considered work? Wages, net earnings from self-employment, bonuses, commissions, fees, vacation pay, severance pay, cash tips, and director's fees

Loss of Benefits from Work

Age	Consequences
62–65	Loses $1 in Social Security for every $2 earned over $9,140 (1998)
65–69	Loses $1 in Social Security for every $3 earned over $14,500 (1998)
Over 70	No reduction in Social Security regardless of earnings

What's not considered work? All forms of investment income, Social Security benefits, pensions and other retirement pay, VA benefits, annuity payments, gifts or inheritances, rental income, royalties, and some partnership income

---

$9,120 (1998). Between 65 and 69, they will lose $1 in Social Security benefits for every $3 they earn above $14,500 (1998). The good news is that for workers over 65, the earnings limitation is ratcheting upward and will increase from its current level to $30,000 by 2002.

Working impacts not only the individual who draws the benefit but others as well. The deduction for excess earnings is subtracted from the total family benefit. If other family members receive benefits based on the retiree's earnings record, additional earnings will not only offset the wage earner's benefits but also those payable to other family members. However, divorced spouses receiving a benefit based on their ex-spouse's income will not be impacted. But after age 70, there is no loss in Social Security benefits for any family members as a result of work. It just puts your mind at rest knowing that Arnold Palmer and a host of other high-earning seniors don't have to worry about the consequences of racking in big money while also drawing Social Security benefits.

Even if your parents don't suffer a direct reduction in the size of their Social Security benefits, an increase in their overall income could cause them to join the ranks of the 20 percent of all retirees—one in five—who pay tax on their Social Security benefits. If your parents' taxable income plus any tax-exempt interest and one-half of their Social Security totals less than $25,000 for singles or $32,000 for couples, no income tax need be paid on their Social Security income. The tax impact changes dramatically, though, if your single or widowed parent has more than $34,000 of income a year or your married parents receive more than $44,000 annually. (See Figure 7.2.)

The bottom line is that earning money from work while collecting Social Security benefits can have a major impact on your parents' financial situation. Given the increased income tax burden that can result from work, plus the need

---

Figure

7.2 • • • • •
Taxation of Social Security Benefits

Adjusted gross income $_____   Adjusted gross income $_____

Plus tax-exempt income _____   Plus tax-exempt income _____

Plus ½ of Social Security   Plus ½ of Social Security
  benefits _____   benefits _____

Total $_____   Total $_____

Single Individuals   *Married Individuals*

Must include 50% of Social   Must include 50% of Social
Security benefits in taxable   Security benefits in taxable
income if the amount of total   income if the total income
income computed above is   computed above is between
between $25,000 and $34,000 $32,000 and $44,000

Must include 85% of Social   Must include 85% of Social
Security benefits in taxable   Security benefits in taxable
income if the amount of total   income if the amount of total
income computed above is over   income computed above is over
$34,000 $44,000

to pay Social Security taxes on earned income and the work-related costs associated with commuting, buying a restaurant meal at lunch, and maintaining a presentable appearance, working may not provide the economic benefit that would be expected at first glance. Your parents should do some "what ifs" with a tax preparation computer program or consult with a tax expert before they make a decision on postretirement work. And perusing Figure 7.3, "Figuring the Financial Implications of Working Past 65," should also be useful.

Figure
7.3
• • • • •
Figuring the Financial Implications of Working Past 65

Annual Cost of Working

Lost pension benefits	$_____
Reduction or loss of Social Security benefits	_____
Additional federal income tax	_____
Additional state and local income tax	_____
Additional Social Security taxes	_____
Loss of the credit for the elderly	_____
Potential loss of medical expense deduction	_____
Loss of means-tested benefits	_____
Total work related costs (travel, uniforms, etc.)	_____
Total Costs	$_____

Annual Income from Work

Earned income	$_____
Increase in future Social Security benefits	_____
Increase in future pension benefits	_____
Value of other employee benefits	_____
Total Extra Income	$_____

If it turns out that drawing Social Security benefits while working does not make economic sense, there is a bright side. If one of your parents forgoes the benefit after age 65 and keeps working and contributing to the Social Security system, that parent's Social Security check will be larger when finally collected. It's estimated that those who put off drawing Social Security until age 70 will get a 25 percent increase in their monthly benefit, according to an article in the May 6, 1997, *Wall Street Journal* by Jonathan Clements. People

Their Stories

• • • • •

John, a college professor who earns $72,000 annually, decides to continue working for the same university beyond age 65. We aren't privy to every financial detail entailed in this decision, such as his deductible mortgage interest, the amount he pays in local property taxes, the size of his personal investment income, or the amount of his wife's earnings, so we can't calculate the impact of his continued work down to the exact penny. But we do know that if he continues to draw his full-time salary, he will have to relinquish both his university pension and his Social Security benefits. He will also have to pay federal and state income taxes as well as Social Security taxes on his earned income. His work-related expenses, such as commuting costs, meals, and a work-appropriate wardrobe, will continue too. On the plus side, his current earnings are greater than his retirement benefits. Also, his future Social Security and pension benefits will increase. If John and his wife Emma are concerned about the financial impact of continued work, they could use a computer program or hire a financial planner to assist them.

• • • • •

born before 1940 receive a 4 percent annual increase for each year they delay receiving their Social Security. In addition, each year your parents work, they add another year of earnings to their respective work record. For more specific information about the impact of work, order the booklet *How Work Affects Your Social Security Benefits* from the Social Security Administration.

Finding Hidden Assets

If your parents can't pull together enough money from their private pension, Social Security, and personal investments to make ends meet, it's time to start looking around for extra sources of income.

Reverse Mortgage

One of the very best places to create additional money can be found right in your parents' own home in the form of a reverse mortgage. Reverse mortgages have been around for more than 25 years. About 75 percent of seniors own their own home, making a reverse mortgage a terrific idea for many seniors 62 (including coborrowers) and older, who are house-rich but cash-poor. Seniors can use a reverse mortgage to convert the accumulated equity in their principal residence into spendable cash regardless of the amount or size of their other assets. They can do this without having to meet financial suitability requirements, giving up title to their home, selling or moving out of their house, or even making traditional loan repayments.

A reverse mortgage, as its name implies, operates exactly the opposite from a traditional mortgage. A regular mortgage is characterized by falling debt and rising equity, whereas a reverse mortgage is distinguished by rising debt and falling equity. A reverse mortgage is only available for owner-occupied properties that are incumbered with a small mortgage or preferably none at all. The amount owed at the end of the term includes loan advances, fees, and interest. Under most arrangements, even if the value of the home is less than the loan, no additional money is due when the owner dies or moves. However, if the heirs wish to retain the home, they must pay the money owed by refinancing the debt or by paying off the reverse mortgage. If the home has appreciated considerably in value, your parents or their heirs may be required to pay back only the outstanding balance. The remaining equity, if any, may be due to the owner or heirs depending on the terms of the reverse mortgage.

Some lenders limit the amount borrowed to between 50 and 75 percent of the appraised value. Still, a paid-up house is an excellent way for many seniors to enhance the quality of life in their later years. A typical client for a reverse mortgage is a 73-year-old widow who owns a $120,000 home with no mortgage debt. Using the Federal Housing Administration (FHA) formula that incorporates the value of the home, the borrower's age, and the geographic lending limit, the widow would be entitled to receive about $56,000 from a reverse mortgage. This amount could be paid out in several ways: as a lump sum, as a line of credit for the full amount, or as a lifetime payment of $420 a month. Or the widow could get $10,000 in up-front cash plus a $46,000 line of credit, or a $344 monthly payment for life. But most retirees opt for the line of credit as it provides the greatest flexibility. The funds are not subject to income tax nor do they require monthly repayments. The money can be put to a variety of uses, from making needed household repairs to paying overdue bills and enhancing everyday life. But these loans carry considerable up-front costs that may run as high as $4,000 or $5,000, according to an article by Jonathan Clements in the May 6, 1997, issue of the *Wall Street Journal*. Therefore, they may not be appropriate for everyone. Also, because no current payments are made, interest costs compound on prior interest costs, which causes the amount owed to increase rapidly.

Reverse mortgages are not suitable for homeowners who are in poor health because their high initial costs make them prohibitively expensive in the short term. As with most mortgages, the up-front costs include origination fees, an appraisal fee, and miscellaneous closing costs. One reason that reverse mortgages carry high costs is that lenders run the risk that the value of the house when the mortgage is terminated will not equal the investment. In order to protect the risks, most lenders charge an additional amount for "insurance," which covers the repayment exposure and adds 2 percent or more to the other costs. In addition, some lenders charge a monthly servicing fee which adds another .5 percent to the interest rate charged on the outstanding balance. A new truth in lending rule requires lenders to provide cost estimates for three time periods—short term, life expectancy, and long term (greater than life expectancy), according to a standard formula.

How Much Can Seniors Borrow from the Federal Housing Administration (FHA)?

• • • • •

The amount homeowners can borrow is a function of their life expectancy, the value of their home, the lender's loan policies, total loan costs, and local conditions. "The maximum amount varies per locality, [currently] from $67,500 in low-cost rural areas to $151,725 in costlier housing markets," say Strauss and Lederman. Payments are also based on actuarial tables. If interest rates and other costs are low, the amount borrowers who are old and have an expensive home can borrow is high compared with what younger borrowers with a less expensive home can borrow. A 75-year-old with a $100,000 home would typically receive a credit line equaling $39,116, but an 85-year-old owning a $150,000 home would qualify for $86,380. In the case of joint borrowers, the age of the youngest borrower determines the amount of the loan advance. The insurance premium is paid as follows: 2 percent at closing and .05 percent monthly on the outstanding balance. In most cases, a reverse mortgage is best suited to a low-income retiree who owns a house that has greatly appreciated in value.

• • • • •

Unfortunately, reverse mortgages can be hard to locate because they are offered sparingly by public, private, and federally insured lenders. The largest number is available from public agencies, including the Federal Housing Administration (FHA), which is authorized to offer up to 50,000 reverse mortgages until September 2000 in conjunction with the Department of Housing and Urban Development (HUD). The government-insured Home Equity Conversion Mortgage (HEMC), which at present is the most popular and the least costly reverse mortgage, is currently being offered under a national pilot program. A list of HUD-approved lenders can be obtained by calling 800-466-3480.

The amount borrowed through a reverse mortgage has a ceiling based on appraised value, location, and maximum claim amount, which currently limits loans to a maximum of around $155,000. Based on recent loan rates, a 65-year-old could borrow up to 26 percent of a home's value or the maximum claim amount, whichever is less, a 75-year-old 39 percent, and an 85-year-old up to 56 percent (www.hud.gov). In addition, the Federal National Mortgage Association (Fannie Mae), which has 2,000 lenders and can be reached at 800-732-6643, offers a so-called Homekeeping program that allows a higher dollar limit and grants lending limits up to $207,000. Fannie Mae also provides an option that entitles borrowers to give up 10 percent of the equity in their home in exchange for additional funds.

Risks of Reverse Mortgages

• • • • •

• The fixed monthly benefit may not be adequate in the future.

• Interest costs are not deductible until the year the loan is paid.

• Plans that require relinquishing part of the home's future value are unpredictable.

• A borrower may be forced to repay the loan if the property is not well maintained, the insurance lapses, or property taxes become delinquent.

• If the homeowners leave their home for an extended period, repayment demands could be triggered.

• Reverse mortgages using taxable annuity payments from private lenders can reduce or eliminate cash benefits from means-tested government programs such as Medicaid.

• • • • •

Important Questions to Ask about a Reverse Mortgage

● ● ● ● ●

1. What are the up-front costs?

2. What will be the total costs ?

3. What are the distribution options?

4. How much income will your parents be entitled to receive under the various payment options?

5. Does the loan contract have a nonrecourse provision?

6. Is it possible to change payment options after the loan commences?

7. Will there be penalties if the property is not repaired?

8. How much money will be left at the end of the reverse mortgage, including any appreciation that may be owed the lender?

9. Is the mortgage covered by federal insurance?

10. What are the equity limits on the loan, if any?

● ● ● ● ●

All federally sponsored programs mandate that borrowers attend a seminar explaining the details of their reverse mortgage program. In addition, they offer trained third-party counselors who can explain the details of government loan programs and those available privately as well as the financial impact of these loans on other sources of help for seniors such as Medicaid or meals-on-wheels. This information is important for deciding which programs offer a less expensive or a more appropriate solution in your parents' personal situation. Never, never, never suggest to your parents they work with a firm that charges fees for advice on reverse mortgages as the same information is available at no charge from the government.

Self-insured reverse mortgages are available from private lenders such as Transamerica or Household Senior Services. Private lenders offer higher loan limits and are a better source of cash for individuals who have considerable home equity. Private reverse mortgages often are combined with lifetime annuities, which continue to pay a monthly benefit even if the home is sold and the loan is repaid. But under these arrangements, usually the money is considered taxable income and makes your parents ineligible to receive assistance from means-tested programs. If your parents contract with a private lender that does not sell the reverse loan to an outside insurance company, there is no guarantee other than the good faith of the mortgage company itself. Unless your parents receive an up-front lump sum distribution, they could be at substantial risk. A safer choice is an FHA mortgage, which is backed by the full faith and credit of the U.S. government but carries high insurance costs. Shop carefully for these mortgages and be on the lookout for different fee structures as well as the total amount your parents are permitted to borrow.

It's very important to deal with a reputable lender because, unfortunately, numerous reverse mortgage scams have been perpetrated against the elderly. The better business bureau warns seniors to be particularly cautious when approached by a telemarketer that encourages them to get a lump sum reverse mortgage and use the proceeds to purchase a monthly income annuity. Purchasing an annuity on top of the already high costs of receiving a reverse mortgage can add another 8 percent to the cost of the entire reverse mortgage transaction. In addition, sometimes scam artists charge thousands of dollars for advice that is available for free from government-trained counselors.

Sale-Leasebacks

Other homeowner ideas for creating income include a sale-leaseback, an arrangement that allows homeowners to sell their home, usually at a discounted price, to an outside investor that in turn immediately agrees to rent the home back to the original homeowners with a life-long lease. Sellers usually receive a small initial down payment plus a monthly disbursement secured through a land contract or deed of trust. The purpose is to provide sellers with more monthly income than they owe for rent. Usually, new owners pay the taxes, repairs, and insurance, and often deduct these costs on their income taxes as a business expense. A sale-leaseback transaction usually does not include a financial institution but is conducted between private parties such as aging parents and their adult children.

This arrangement eliminates home ownership costs for parents while providing them a monthly income. But sale-leaseback transactions must be formalized and handled by a lawyer who is knowledgeable about the tax and estate implications of such transactions. Sample sale-leaseback documents are available from the not-for-profit National Center for Home Equity Conversion 612-953-4474 for $39. Another possibility is to use a legal device, a retained life estate, which allows a parent to sell the rights to his or her home at death. This strategy provides the proceeds immediately but permits the parent to maintain ownership rights (and responsibilities) until death.

Life Insurance

If using the family home as a source of extra cash for your parents' later years sounds too risky, then a paid-up life insurance policy is another option. Several ways to squeeze money out of a cash value life insurance policy are available. One is to *borrow the cash value* of the policy, using the policy itself as collateral. Usually, the insurance company will offer an attractive rate of interest to the borrower. The amount borrowed reduces the value of the policy at death, so this strategy is not a free ride. If the loan proceeds don't exceed the total premiums paid, the funds generally are not considered taxable income, but, unfortunately, the interest paid on the loan is not usually tax deductible either. A distinct disadvantage to this approach, though, is that the borrower must continue making the premium payments. Borrowing cash from the policy may not be practical if your parents are really strapped for money.

Another tactic is to *surrender the life insurance policy* for its cash value and terminate the insurance contract. Your parents can use the proceeds for anything they wish, but they may want to consider purchasing a paid-up policy, which will keep some insurance in force but eliminates annual premiums. Or they may want to use the proceeds to fund an income-producing investment that will not only eliminate the ongoing cost of paying premiums but also create a stream of current income.

You can ask your parents' insurance agent to prepare some proposals, but remember that the agent probably will advise your parents to retain their insurance contract as it is never in the agent's best interest for a client to surrender a policy. Unfortunately, then, you can't depend on receiving unbiased advice from the agent. A strategy that may be even better for most seniors is to convert their policy to an insurance annuity. This process is called a *1035 exchange,* named after the relevant IRS regulation, and allows your parents to purchase an annuity that guarantees a lifetime income. From a pure dollar perspective, this is not a perfect arrangement as the insurance salesman earns a big commission when your parents purchase the annuity, although you may be able to purchase it from a no-load provider. But if that's not practical, the peace of mind provided by a guaranteed monthly check for life has significant appeal.

A terminally ill parent can arrange for a *viatical settlement,* the term stemming from the Latin word for provision for a journey. A viatical settlement is designed to be a source of immediate cash for the terminally ill. The company that purchases the policy continues to pay the premiums and also names itself as the beneficiary of the policy. More than 70 companies today buy over $500 million of life insurance policies annually. The best way to begin the process is to contact the Viatical Association of American, a not-for-profit organization at 800-842-9811 to get a free list of its member companies.

You will find it's to your ill parent's advantage to shop around; what you ultimately want to create is a bidding war between companies. A couple of caveats: Unfortunately, most viatical companies don't have their own source of funds. Rather, they use a broker whose commission reduces the amount of money your parent receives. Thus, it is worth the time involved to search for a company that has money on hand. It's imperative that the viatical organization establish an escrow account in your parent's name. You want the funds to be available immediately because the whole point is that your parent doesn't have time to wait around for the money. You also want to be wary of health care providers who steer your parent toward a specific vendor—they may be swayed by the fact that they are receiving a commission.

Another alternative, if your parent is ill, is to inquire about receiving an *accelerated death benefit* (ADB). ADB provisions allow the owner of the policy to receive a portion of the death benefit when a critical event that triggers the ADB occurs. A critical event may include a terminal medical diagnosis or lifelong confinement to a nursing care facility. Not all insurance contracts offer ADBs and the precise terms hinge on the specific insurer. "Depending on policy terms and state laws, the maximum amount that can be accelerated ranges from 25 to 100 percent of a policy's face value," according to Vitt & Siegenthaler.

Be aware that receipt of money from an ADB may make your parent ineligible to receive Medicaid and the other array of government-sponsored means-tested programs. Then there is the question of whether the money will be subject to federal and state income taxes. The IRS initially considered funds received from viatical settlements and accelerated benefits to be taxable, but recently changed its mind. Thus, it's important that your parents consult a financial professional before making any final decisions about using insurance to raise cash.

Saving Money

Spending less money doesn't have the same allure as creating more income, but if your parents are able to spend less money while still enjoying the same lifestyle, they end up in the same place. It takes time, effort, and diligence to save money on many items so it's most time-effective to go after big ticket items first. A large savings may be realized immediately if the amount your parents have to pay federal, state, and local government is dramatically reduced. I noted earlier that seniors have the highest rate of IRS overpayment in the country. Encourage your parents to consult with the AARP-sponsored Tax-Aide Program. This program has been praised by the IRS for its low rate of error and could uncover some important savings such as missed exemptions, deductions, or credits. Many states also offer income tax relief for low-income seniors, but to qualify, your parents will first have to complete the requisite paperwork.

In addition, you may want to suggest that your parents look into various local programs that offer deductions, exemptions, or deferrals on local property taxes. A property tax deferral program, now available in 17 states, allows seniors to delay paying their local property taxes until they move or die; some locales even charge a below-market rate of interest on this loan program. Some communities offer a form of tax relief, a "circuit breaker," whereby the amount of the tax reduction is based on need by comparing taxpayers' income with their property tax liability. In other communities, an extra homeowners exemption is granted to seniors regardless of their financial situation. Some local governments also offer deferred-payment loans for the repair or improvement of seniors' homes. Usually, the borrowing costs on these loans are modest and repayment is due only when the homeowner moves or dies. For more information on these programs, you can contact your local government representative or your parents' local tax collector.

It's well known that many businesses offer discounts to seniors. Many seniors are reluctant to request these discounts, but gently encourage your parents to be more assertive if they're hesitant to find and request discounts available for the asking but not automatically offered. Seniors should always carry their identification (ID) and ask about a discount before a transaction takes place. Discounts for seniors are numerous and include the following:

- Local stores that have senior discount days
- Most movie theaters and recreational facilities
- Banks that waive monthly service charges on checking accounts
- Communities that offer reduced rates on local phone, gas, and electric charges
- Fares on public transportation
- Classes at local high schools, technical schools, colleges, and universities
- Airline fares, club memberships, and hotel and restaurant charges
- Golden Age Passports that allow all U.S. residents 62 or older and their companions to obtain a lifetime entrance permit to federal areas that charge fees
- Senior centers that offer no-cost or inexpensive recreational activities
- Off-peak activities

Seniors spend lots of money on medical care so savings in this area are especially important. Most seniors are covered by Medicare and indigent seniors are covered by Medicaid as well, which usually pays 100 percent of a senior's medical costs. For those who are not covered by Medicaid, a Medicare HMO may be especially helpful because HMOs, unlike most supplemental policies, usually cover the cost of routine medical care. Your parents may also be able to get a less expensive supplemental policy if they are members of a fraternal, alumni, or religious group that offers this type of policy. Or if they are having trouble qualifying for supplemental coverage, they may be able to obtain a supplemental policy when their local Blue Cross/Blue Shield offers an open enrollment period for seniors who are otherwise uninsurable. They may also be able to purchase drugs from a mail-order source or substitute generic versions of their prescriptions.

Taking Advantage of Private and Public Resources

Most seniors have survived a major economic depression and a major world war. As a result, many take tremendous pride in their independence and typically are reluctant to accept help from many of the resources designed specifically to aid them. More than 75 percent of seniors never look for any outside assistance and less than one-half of qualified seniors receive supplemental security income (SSI) or food stamps. Only a minority of those who qualify receive help through the Qualified Medicare Beneficiary (QMB) program, which pays their Medicare Part B monthly premiums, or for very low-income individuals, Medicare Part A and Part B deductibles, copayments, and other out-of-pocket expenses. Over 4 million seniors are thought to be eligible to receive help from QMB, which is administered by state and local Medicaid offices. Less than 30 percent of all eligible seniors receive any help from Medicaid, so you may want to contact your parents' local or state insurance senior hotline, to get additional information on these programs. It may be difficult to persuade your parents to accept help, but it may become necessary to minimize the potentially overwhelming financial pressures on you and your siblings.

The first place to start is with the local Area Agency on Aging, which may be found by calling the ElderCare locator at 800-677-1116. Seniors who meet the requirements are entitled to receive a variety of services from home-delivered meals to personal care, rehabilitation, transportation, case management services, and government housing alternatives. Not all services are available in all jurisdictions and many services are tricky to obtain, but with enough persistence, it can be done.

Surprisingly, only about one-third of all veterans are aware of the many health, pension, and burial benefits that they and their dependents may be entitled to receive. Eligible veterans must have had service during active combat and received an honorable or general discharge, or suffer from a service-related disability, and/or must meet specific income requirements to receive free health care benefits. Mandatory recipients are those who have a service-connected disability, are former prisoners of war, and are low-income individuals who qualify for Medicaid, or those who receive a VA pension. Care is offered on a space-available basis for other low-income veterans. But even if eligible veterans don't meet all the income restrictions or suffer from a non-service-connected disability, they are eligible to receive some care at reduced charges. The health services provided for veterans include hospitalization, outpatient and nursing home care, rehabilitation programs, dental services, and prosthetic appliances. Your parent will need a copy of his or her discharge and separation papers in order to qualify. If you can't locate the requisite paperwork, contact National Personnel Records Center; Attn: [Applicable Service Branch]; 9700 Page Avenue; St. Louis, MO 63132.

Other free or low-cost services for seniors include the federal Low-Income Home Energy Assistance Program, which is administered by state and local governments to provide low-income households with financial assistance for utilities or weatherization services. The Senior Community Service Employment Program is administered by the federal government and extends part-time community service employment for unemployed low-income seniors who are 55 and older with poor employment prospects.

Arranging for any of these benefits can be both time consuming and frustrating as the array and complexity of these programs is daunting. Don't try to go it alone. You'll benefit from getting advice from knowledgeable professionals such as a geriatric care manager, a hospital outpatient specialist, or an elder law practitioner. Because all federal and state benefit programs for the needy allow administrative appeals, these hearings provide an opportunity to challenge decisions made by agencies that administer benefit programs. For example, if your parent is receiving treatment that is considered experimental by the government, Medicare may refuse to pay for the medical care; or the Veterans Administration may refuse care for a parent you feel is a qualified recipient. In these circumstances, it pays to hire an elder law attorney to represent your parent's interests.

Their Stories

• • • • •

Hilda, age 62, enjoyed working but wanted to retire and join her already retired husband, but she couldn't. Hilda had a little problem. Her aging parents who lived in Florida were financially dependent on her. Hilda used her entire salary to support her parents. She struggled with this until one day, in desperation, she consulted with some knowledgeable professionals. She learned that her parents qualified to receive Medicaid. She was able to locate a competent nursing home that would accept both her parents. She wondered, after she was through completing the arrangements, why it had taken her so long to make this difficult but necessary step.

• • • • •

Tax Incentives

If all else fails and adult children become financially responsible for a parent, there are some tax advantages that should be weighed as parents and children review their options. Tax planning is secondary to other issues but should be considered nonetheless. You may be able to claim a parent as a dependent for tax purposes, but the restrictions are very stringent: To make such a claim,

- a parent's gross income must be less than the personal exemption amount ($2,700 in 1998);
- your parent must not file a joint income tax return;
- your parent must be a citizen;
- you must provide at least one-half of his or her support (although there is a complex multiple support arrangement that you may claim if you share support with your siblings); and

- You may be able to claim a dependent care tax credit reimbursing you for the cost of an aid or adult day care if your parent qualifies as a dependent. The value of the credit will range from $720 to $2,400 depending on your specific circumstances.

It's tough to meet all these requirements, especially those that mandate that your parent's income is less than the personal exemption. But there are some other approaches that can help you reduce costs. You may choose to pay your parent's medical care directly to the provider. The amount you can pay on his or her behalf is unlimited and not subject to any gift tax restrictions. If you provide over one-half of your parent's support and are entitled to claim the medical deduction based on your own expenses, you may add the costs you paid for your parent to your own. You can then claim the entire deduction based on both your and your parent's combined expenses to the extent that these expenses exceed 7.5 percent of your adjusted gross income. Other children have been able to take advantage of their flexible spending account up to $5,000 to defray the costs of dependent parent care, allowing these adult children the opportunity to pay for care with before-tax dollars, which helps them save a few bucks.

Sibling discord can be a real issue for children when their parents have few assets. One child may be able to contribute generously to the parents' support while another is just getting by and is unable to help out. These differences can cause hard feelings. If this becomes an issue in your family, you may want to consider the support provided by the financially able child a loan against an illiquid asset such as the family home. When the parents die, the child who has provided an inordinate amount of support would be entitled to be reimbursed from the estate, thus eliminating the problem of penalizing the generous child at the expense of siblings. This strategy also allows parents to retain their pride by knowing they are paying their own way.

Making the Wisest Choices

Trying to judge the best course of action is difficult. Let's consider a hypothetical situation in which your 63-year-old divorced mother, who has worked for the same company for several years, becomes disabled. Her assets are limited to a mortgage-free small home worth about $100,000 and a tiny savings account with a balance of about $5,000. This seems like a straightforward situation, and yet your mother has the following options to weigh:

- She can draw her Social Security retirement benefits, but the amount she receives will be reduced by early retirement.
- She could apply for retirement benefits under her own account or under her husband's work record because they were married for more than ten years.
- She could try to claim Social Security disability benefits, which may be larger than her early retirement benefits.
- She may be entitled to receive a workers' compensation award for her disability claim.
- She could sell her house and move in with her daughter.
- If her income is low enough, she may qualify for supplemental security income (SSI) benefits. SSI eligibility usually allows her to qualify for Medicaid benefits too.
- She may be entitled to receive continuing health insurance coverage from her employer.
- She may be entitled to receive disability income from her employer.
- She could apply for a reverse mortgage.
- Part-time employment will create needed income, but it may also reduce or eliminate her eligibility for many of the assistance programs.
- Each of these decisions has tax implications that must be considered.

As you already realize, deciding the best course of action for your parents is complex. In this case, as in any elder care decision, there are personal aspects that figure heavily into making the best decision for the entire family. Determining what to do is perplexing given the intricate details of entitlement programs, incapacity arrangements, and estate planning. But if the above example applied to your own mother, you might want to include a third-party professional to help you determine the best course of action after you, your siblings, and your mother discussed the situation.

For those whose parents don't have money, the following list includes many of the suggestions in this chapter and provides a summary of issues for consideration.

To Do List

• • • • •

- Ask your parents to weigh their options carefully before they choose to take early retirement.

- If they plan to receive their retirement funds in one lump sum amount or they select a life-only retirement distribution option, they should always consult with a professional financial adviser.

- Because postretirement work has a significant impact on your parents' financial situation, encourage them to consider its overall implications before they jump headlong into a new job.

- Try to motivate parents who are struggling to make ends meet to think about tapping their home equity or assets hidden away in a cash value life insurance policy. Perhaps they are holding out, thinking they should save their money for their children, when the children want them to spend the money on themselves.

- Help is out there for the asking. A good place to begin inquiring about eligibility requirements is with your parents' local office of Area Agency on Aging. Your parents' state insurance department hot line may also be able to offer information on state-sponsored programs such as Medicaid and QMB. If a senior center is in your parents' town, the resident counselor may be able to point your parents in the right direction.

- A host of questions swirl around income taxes, such as when Social Security income is subject to taxation, eligibility for reverse mortgages, long-term care insurance reimbursements, life insurance accelerated benefits, and viatical settlements. It's important to consider tax implications within the context of your parents' financial situation. Order Publication #554, *The Older Americans' Tax Guide*, from the IRS for a more detailed explanation.

- If your parents are reluctant to accept help, perhaps a family friend or religious adviser can persuade them.

• • • • •

CHAPTER 8

Helping Parents with Substantial Assets

"The use of money is all the advantage there is in having money."

—Benjamin Franklin

Because the vast majority of people over 65 just don't have enough money to ski, surf, take up expensive hobbies, and travel to exotic places, many retirees aren't able to enjoy the lifestyle they had envisioned during their working years. If your parents are among the minority of retirees who have a few bucks, count your blessings. Certain responsibilities, however, accompany wealth—making good use of it and investing it wisely so income is provided well into the future. But certainly the burdens inherent in managing money pale in comparison with watching your parents cope with the rigors of living a Spartan lifestyle.

The benefits of having money are numerous, but first and foremost it allows your parents the chance to live the good life, although the likelihood of living the good life is based on your parents' continued ability to manage their money wisely. Just because your parents have money now or they had money in the recent past, you can't assume they will remain financially independent forever. Unfortunately, money tends to be a bit like sand; it has a way of slipping through your fingers. Given today's complex and volatile financial markets combined with a labyrinth of gyrating income and estate tax laws along with the exorbitant costs often associated with growing old, professional guidance is crucial. If your parents were good at making money but not skilled at managing it, it's hoped they had the good sense to seek and follow knowledgeable advice.

As an adult child you probably assume that your parents are surrounded by a bevy of astute professionals. Unfortunately, though, the idea that wealthy

153

people have everything squared away is just another myth. Perform some detective work to determine just how savvy many rich and famous people have been when it comes to managing their money. Read about the lives and finances of wealthy people and be prepared for a surprise. You'll quickly discover that many have made serious mistakes—mistakes that cost them the lifestyle they worked so hard to create. Let's face it, it's often easier to amass money than it is to manage it.

The Wrigley family, for example, those people who provide us with endless flavors of gum, were notoriously bad planners. At the death of the senior Wrigleys, the heirs found that the parents had left a huge fortune, which was tied up in numerous illiquid but profitable holdings. Normally, this isn't a problem as smart business owners purchase very large insurance policies that create the cash heirs need to pay estate taxes. Not the Wrigleys! Perhaps they had a "thing" about insurance. Perhaps they didn't get good advice. Perhaps they didn't care, figuring the children could straighten out the mess. But in the end, the heirs had to jury-rig the family fortune at a cost of millions of dollars by selling off various assets (such as the Chicago Cubs) just to keep the gum company afloat. All of this heartache could have been easily avoided with proper planning. I suspect that the Wrigley children were like the rest of us unsuspecting adult children; they probably figured Mom and Dad had gotten and followed good advice. I bet they were surprised!

Some parents do indeed have all their finances squared away. But with all the complexities inherent in today's financial arena and like the majority of Americans in all age groups, such parents tend to be the exception rather than the rule. Let's look at some of the various types of money management personalities that cause adult children to pull out their hair.

The Assortment of Financial Personalities

First is the *I already took care of it* school of parental financial management. This school insists that a financial review every 20 years or so is more than adequate. Of course, in the last 20 years financial markets have soared, substantial changes have been made in the tax laws, new financial instruments have evolved, and innovative planning tools such as living trusts have emerged. There may have been substantial alterations in your parents' personal situation as well. Perhaps your father was widowered and has since remarried. Even more likely is that Dad has an expanded family circle that now includes sons-in-law and daughters-in-law and all those special grandchildren. Dad needs to update his financial plans to reflect these changes. He should tackle this project at least every five years or whenever his personal or financial circumstances alter substantially.

Then there is the depression-era school of *I don't trust anyone with my money.* These parents, who are notoriously independent, may have children who are financial professionals themselves, yet distrust all financial institutions. They refuse to reveal their total financial picture to anyone. They won't even share financial and net worth information with their own trusted advisers such as their lawyer or the CPA who has been preparing their tax return for more than 30 years. And even if they did acquiesce and seek advice, the advice was sought in such a piecemeal fashion it was of questionable value. Some of these depression-era parents still don't trust banks and, as a result, keep money hidden around the house. Others, who may be millionaires, sit around in dark, cold houses unwilling to turn on the heat or lights because that costs money.

The *who me?* school includes parents who were of ordinary means all of their lives but who almost by chance purchased some stellar corporate stocks or mutual funds over the last ten years. Now, much to their surprise, these parents find themselves among the new wealthy created by years of burgeoning stock markets. Their money appeared quickly after a lifetime of having to pinch pennies. Most likely the *who me?* parents find the idea that they are wealthy a foreign concept. Consequently, the notion they need sophisticated financial and estate planning advice feels weird. This is a difficult situation as most people, especially at this point in life, are resistant to change.

The *money is my life* school consists of those retirees who, instead of going to work, spend their days glued to the front of their computers or television screens, following the financial markets. They fill their time frantically buying and selling securities. This activity keeps them occupied and makes them feel as if they are creating value. Just because their trading costs are prohibitive and their profits nonexistent shouldn't be a concern, right? This obsession with money can also cause considerable tension in their marriage. Often, the *money is my life* parents are so preoccupied with the incessant wheeling and dealing that they may refuse to travel or join their spouse in other leisure activities, fearing what will happen when they are whisked away from their money management duties.

Finally there is the *I don't understand anything about money* group. These individuals usually had a spouse, recently deceased, who managed the family's assets without consulting their partners. The surviving partner, who didn't concern themselves with the financial end of things, now find themselves completely in the dark. They don't know what their monthly income or expenses are or how much money they have, let alone where the money is invested. And coping with taxes is a terrifying prospect. This lack of knowledge leaves them uncertain about how they will be able to survive, much less thrive. Unfortunately, the current state of bereavement and loss is further compounded by overwhelming financial anxiety.

Common Financial Problems of the Elderly

All age groups, from 16 to 116, find it difficult to manage their money wisely. And the elderly are no exception. Aside from specific personality profiles, an assortment of financial misjudgments are frequently made by the over-65 age group. For example, older individuals often have portfolios that are inappropriate for their situation. Consider the 92-year-old former college professor who has a $1.5 million estate comprised entirely of individual stocks with a low cost basis. The professor never bothered to manage his portfolio because most of the stocks were acquired during the late 1940s as payment for consulting services. As a result, his potential tax liability is huge as he paid nothing for the stocks when they were acquired over 50 years ago. And yet, unfortunately, his portfolio is invested in a manner that doesn't generate enough cash flow to pay his expenses, which have risen dramatically as of late to include the costs of maintaining a full-time caregiver.

Then there is the high-powered corporate manager who went into his retirement with a fistful of company stock. As a loyal former employee, he decided against selling any of his holdings because he felt such a strong emotional attachment to his lifelong employer. His reluctance to sell, unfortunately, left him with a one-stock portfolio, setting him up for a potentially disastrous all-your-eggs-in-one-basket investment strategy. Other older individuals who are very risk averse invest solely in certificates of deposit. Avoiding risks has its own costs, however, as certificates over time, when incorporating the impact of taxes and inflation, tend to grow at a negative rate. Their dismal earnings in turn creates a diminishing lifestyle for their owners.

Other nasty financial situations are created by years of neglect, misunderstanding, or procrastination. Most investors make their investment decisions piecemeal. Many don't take an overall view and consequently end up with a portfolio that features a jumble of investments badly out-of-whack. As a result, losers need to be weeded out and the portfolio rebalanced to reflect the investor's current goals and needs.

Many wealthy seniors have lost their handle on their investments by allowing them to become far too complicated. Your parents should be able to describe in detail the investments they own and the overall purpose of each investment. However, by the time many people have retired, they have invested in numerous issues spread over multiple accounts at both brokerage firms and mutual fund companies. In addition, Mom or Dad may have 100 or so individual stock and bond certificates tucked into a crevice of their safe deposit box, creating a situation in which it becomes a formidable task for adult children to step in and effectively manage their parents' portfolio if the need ever arose.

Resolving the Problems

First and foremost, you want to help your parents ensure that their money will last as long as they do. Even if they have substantial assets, they still need to act prudently. It's a touchy situation when savvy parents, who have been successful during their working life, start to make poor financial decisions either by commission or omission. How should children respond to situations where it becomes obvious that parents could use some professional guidance?

Scott Blair, a vice president of PaineWebber, acknowledges generational issues: "They [the parents] think that the kids are trying to shake them down. Even if the kids are successful, the parents still feel that the kids want their money." He goes on to explain that the parents routinely cancel the first two meetings with him. But by the time the parents do show up, they have read enough articles and spoken to enough of their friends to realize that it's now time to take action. According to Tom Drake, a vice president at the money management firm Sanford Bernstein: "The kids are the catalyst in these situations to start the process [of getting the problem solved]. One child usually takes the lead and then the rest of the kids try to get the parents to buy in. But the parents usually question the children's motivation behind all this."

In addition, Drake often sees a dual objective: parents who want to invest their assets in a manner that will support their current lifestyle without subjecting their portfolio to any investment risk. In contrast, adult children are interested in structuring a medium-risk portfolio whose investments offer the opportunity for future growth. This dichotomy causes problems as each group has its own agenda. For starters, the siblings must discuss the issues together as a group and come to some kind of consensus. An individual child is just asking for problems if he or she decides to go it alone. Certainly, the ugly question of motivation will be raised not only by the parents but by siblings as well if one child tries to push too hard.

Failure on the part of parents to get their financial house in order often precipitates a crisis for their adult children. This is especially true if mental or physical disabilities arise. A parent historically reluctant to seek professional

Keep It Simple

• • • • •

If your parents have substantial assets, their holdings probably have gotten much too complicated over the years. When you and your parents complete an inventory of their assets, keep an eye out for areas where you can help your parents streamline their affairs.

• Usually, the more money your parents have, the more complicated their situation. Ask your parents to pare their account relationships down to one; that means one banker, one broker, and, if they use a variety of mutual funds, one account at an institution that will accept all the funds and provide a consolidated statement. If they use several advisers, ask them to appoint a team leader who will be responsible for coordinating the advisers' joint efforts.

- If your parents have different retirement accounts—an IRA here, a 401(k) there, and a simplified employee pension (SEP) tucked away somewhere else—see if it would be possible to consolidate them in one location. This will simplify matters and encourage your parents to take a global view of their investments.

- Ask your parents to go through their files and their safe deposit box to make sure they don't have securities lying around in the box or a file where no one would ever find them. All securities should be placed in a brokerage account where a trusted individual has the authority to make financial decisions for your parents if the need arises.

- Try to encourage your parents to eliminate their individual securities and purchase mutual funds. A fund will provide professional management as well as diversification and simplified recordkeeping services. But too many funds is a problem too. Financial experts advise that 3 funds is a minimum and 12 a maximum. In its spring 1998 issue of *Perspective,* Fidelity Investments recommends paring those funds with overlapping investment styles and objectives.

- Get your parents to donate to just a couple of charities, thus eliminating the need to document all those small contributions.

- If your parents own property in more than one state, encourage them to place the property in a living trust so the heirs won't have to go through probate in more than one state.

- Make sure that your parents complete the financial inventory in Chapter 4, update it when their situation changes, and keep good records establishing their asset basis information.

- While they're at it, ask your parents to locate all their insurance policies and place them in a central location. The policies should also be reviewed and their beneficiary designations updated to reflect current circumstances.

• • • • •

advice may become even more reluctant to proceed if his or her mental acuity becomes impaired. Again and again it's important to stress that adult children must tackle these discussions sooner rather than later. By the time a parent loses the ability to understand the world around him or her, it's then almost impossible for the parent to feel comfortable with change.

Comfort seems to be key in this situation. In order to be successful, children must operate within the context of their parents' comfort zone; they must obtain a green light from their parents before proceeding. The key to bridging the gap between parents who aren't receptive to advice and children who welcome a professional strategy is keeping the parent involved at every juncture. Even if your parents give you the go-ahead to bring in a professional, they will probably balk if you move too quickly. Drake suggests that, ultimately, parents resistant to professional advice should be exposed to the complexities of today's technology-driven markets. That exposure may convince your parents, much like it has convinced most Americans, that given the current pace of the fast-moving global financial markets, managing your own assets may be equated to representing yourself in court—you end up with a fool for a client.

Hiring a Professional

Hiring a professional to guide your parents may be a rite of passage that many, if not most, children resist. If you or your siblings are not especially comfortable making your own financial decisions, how can you be expected to help someone else? Begin what may first appear to be an overwhelming task by promising yourself and your parents that you will move slowly. Parents will be much more comfortable if they are given a chance to digest new information at their own pace. Children need time, too, as it gives them the opportunity to adjust to a sudden role reversal. The best place to start looking for someone to help is close to home with your parents' current advisers. Their lawyer, accountant, banker, or broker may have a financial adviser to recommend.

The first step is to create an overall plan that incorporates cash flow needs as well as your parents' long-term goals. Other key considerations include your parents' tolerance for risk and their personal situation. Health, age, and the desire to provide for children, stepchildren, and grandchildren are important factors. Your parents' tax status, their investment sophistication, and the amount of personal involvement they want to shoulder are significant too. Your parents' adviser needs to understand and plan for the possibility that one or both parents may require specialized care at some point. Also, the adviser should use a top-to-bottom approach in making suggestions. Avoid advisers who just want to manage your parents' money according to a predetermined strategy or those who use a "back-of-the-envelope" approach, suggesting a portfolio design based on cursory discussions.

Your parents will require several types of specialized expertise that could include the following:

- An adviser who can perform a big-picture analysis and show your parents various expenditure alternatives, illustrating how long their money will last given alternative spending patterns and investment return assumptions
- An adviser who can factor the impact of Medicare and long-term care costs into your parents' overall financial picture
- An adviser who can help your parents determine what percentage of their portfolio should be invested in stocks, bonds, and cash. This may be the single most important financial decision an investor makes because studies show that more than 90 percent of investment return is determined by the percentage allocated to specific asset classes.
- An adviser who will help your parents choose a combination of investment styles (buying growth stocks versus stocks with low price-earnings ratios)
- An adviser who will select individual securities or mutual funds while providing on-going professional management services
- A legal adviser who can create a tax-efficient estate plan

Financial Planners

If your parents have $500,000 or less and/or prefer to work with just one adviser, then a financial planner may be your best choice. A financial planner is a professional who helps your parents define their objectives and coordinate various concerns. Financial planning is a complex process because planners try to evaluate all aspects of your parents' financial situation; so look for a planner who will give this process the diligent attention it requires. A good financial planner asks lots of questions and can be equated to a doctor who specializes in internal medicine. A planner is your parents' overall financial caregiver and coordinates their care with other professionals when the situation warrants it.

You should look for a planner whose clients are similar to your parents. If possible, seek out a planner who specializes in helping older individuals or is knowledgeable about the specific situations your parents are facing. Most planners offer an initial free consultation when both the planner and the client have an opportunity to size each other up. During the initial interview, check the planner's formal educational background, professional training and certification, years of experience and ongoing continuing education activities. If the planner promises quick riches, instant financial gain, or returns of more than 8 percent annually, be wary! Look for a planner who will provide your parent with a written itemized estimate.

Another important issue is to find out how the planner gets paid. The purported "good guys," those planners who depend only on fee income, usually have a higher hourly fee that typically makes them more expensive than advisers who sell products (insurance or mutual funds, for example) too. But consulting with fee-only advisers eliminates the obligation to buy financial products and the concern that the planner has a vested interest in information offered. However, fee-only planners do not offer implementation services, so your parents will need to add other service relationships. Avoid those planners who offer a free plan, as these plans are usually worth about what you paid for them—nothing. Planners who sell products may be able to charge a lower hourly fee and may eliminate the need to go elsewhere for ancillary advice. They do, however, earn a commission on any products they sell, so your parents need to be comfortable with that.

If you're interested in hiring a planner but don't have a referral from one of your parents' current advisers, check the list of resources featured later in this chapter. You may contact any of the professional associations listed there to obtain recommendations on local advisers. Also, from time to time many periodicals identify outstanding planners you may want to interview. Plan to pay between $1,500 and $4,000 for a comprehensive financial plan or an hourly fee ranging from $100 to $250. The fee of a planner who provides ongoing money management services for your parents typically is around 1 percent or more of the assets managed, but the exact fee usually depends on the size of the account.

I know that fees can be a showstopper for parents who grew up during the depression and remember when pocket change would buy an all-day movie ticket. So the idea of paying $100 plus an hour for something that your parents feel they can and should handle themselves requires some salesmanship on

What a Financial Planner Should Provide

• • • • •

A planner should provide an examination of your parents' personal finances that includes:

- Determination of cash flow requirements

- An accurate picture of assets and debts

- An evaluation of insurance coverage

- An examination of an overall investment strategy

- A projection of financial needs during retirement, including an assessment of long-term care requirements

- An analysis of how long their money will last

- An estate-planning review

- Identification of overlooked factors and other options that should be considered

- Description of problem areas

- Suggestions for improving their financial status

- Referrals to specialists if and when appropriate

- Products that make sense *only* within the context of their overall plan

- An opportunity for ongoing service

• • • • •

your part. I would advise telling your folks that spending a little money now can and will make a big difference. They will accomplish several goals: They will get all their paperwork organized and thus eliminate a potential burden on their children; they will get knowledgeable advice about their investments, which may be the key factor enabling them to maintain their current lifestyle; they will be informed about the most tax-effective ways for transferring their assets during their lifetime and at death; and they will learn how to handle their money so that they don't overspend or underspend their resources.

As an experienced financial planner, I can tell you that in 99 percent of cases, a plan pays for itself before the client walks out the door. And spending money on a planner is just smart business today because it's far too complex to try to go it on your own.

Investment Advisers

These are trained security analysts who select individual securities for clients based on a specific investment philosophy. The responsibility of these 8,000 nation-wide managers is to select superior investments that will provide clients the best return over time and make sell decisions when a security no longer offers the same investment potential. Advisers spend their days monitoring the world's markets, reviewing corporate financial statements, evaluating economic conditions, and performing specialized research. One appeal of using an adviser is that clients know exactly how their funds are being invested; they receive a statement each month detailing their portfolio. Continuity of management is also an appealing feature in a professional firm; if someone goes on vacation or has a long-term disability, other advisers are brought in to watch over your parents' money.

Independent advisory firms who employ security analysts manage money on behalf of private clients and institutions. Minimums start at $150,000 at the smaller firms and ratchet upward to a $1 million at the larger firms. Your challenge is to ferret out the good advisers from the bad, which is no easy task. For one thing, comparative information on investment advisers is difficult to decipher because advisers manage numerous accounts, each with its own mandate. Some clients want a portfolio that creates lots of current income; other clients want a portfolio that grows rapidly but doesn't provide any current income. A third group may focus on security of their principal, placing avoidance of market risk at the top of their investment wish list. Clients' differing objectives often make it difficult to determine, based on an adviser's track record, what he or she can and will do for your parents, who may have still another objective in mind.

In order to evaluate potential advisers, investors must conduct their own research and make projections based on the information provided by the adviser. But this can be a problem as there's no guarantee your parents' account will be managed in the same way or by the same analyst. Then there's always the problem of *survivorship bias*. Clients who feel they've received poor service (i.e., they were disappointed with the investment return) pull their account and leave the firm. But the clients who are receiving a satisfactory or, even better, a stellar return stick around, thus creating a statistical upward bias in investment return computations.

The best thing you can do to protect your parents is to ask the advisory firm if its results are prepared according to the Association for Investment Management and Research (AIMR) guidelines. These guidelines are designed to promote full reliability and disclosure; they provide a benchmark so you can compare the results of several firms on a uniform basis. Look for advisers who base their fees on the market value of the holdings so as your parents' account increases, so does the adviser's income and vice versa. But, ultimately, you'll just have to hope for the best, because there are never any guarantees in the wacky world of investments.

Your parents need to be comfortable with the firm's investment philosophy—also referred to as its money management style. *Style* is a fancy word for explaining how an advisory firm consistently makes its investment decisions. Some firms favor investing their clients' money in stocks issued by small firms that no one has ever heard of, thinking that this strategy will produce above-

For a free copy of Performance Presentation Standards published by the Association for Investment Management Research, write to:

PBD Inc.
1650 Bluegrass Lakes Parkway
Alpharetta, GA 30201

• • • • •

average returns. Other firms prefer to buy stocks in companies whose names are household words. If your parents want to use an adviser, they probably should have at least $1 million so they can spread their money around between at least two managers with different investment styles. For example, a value manager, whose style features buying stocks with low price-earnings ratios, may have a great year today and a terrible year tomorrow. The same goes for a manager who may favor growth stocks, yield plays, or foreign stocks and bonds; all of these managers' comparable returns vary from year to year.

So if your parents mix part of their portfolio with a value manager and the remainder with one who buys stocks issued by companies growing quickly, for example, they can add diversification to their portfolio. Diversification is highly prized by investors as it is a proven method for reducing investment risk and volatility while providing equal or greater overall investment return. For example, value managers earned less than zilch in 1985. But managers who in 1985 bought growth stocks issued by the smaller companies or S&P 500 stocks issued by the 500 largest U.S. companies returned over 30 percent for their investors. If you had invested all your money with a value manager that year, you would have been distraught. But I don't want to leave you with the wrong impression. Over time, all investment styles revert to the mean—that is, they provide about the same return over the long run—but can differ sharply over the short haul.

All of these considerations quickly create a decision process that can overwhelm the bravest investor. So that's where your parents' current advisers can provide considerable value. It's hoped that your parents' advisers can recommend an advisory firm they've worked with over the years that has produced excellent results for its clients in both up and down markets. Interview the people they recommend and then contact the professional organizations listed later in this chapter, and get some more names too. I would recommend interviewing at least five firms before making a decision. Costs are an important consideration as well because, as mentioned above, fees are typically a percentage of assets that can range from .075 percent for a large account to 1.5 percent for a small account.

Other Choices

Not surprisingly given the difficulty of hiring professional talent, a whole new industry has evolved to help potential clients locate suitable advisers. *Investment management consultants* will act as talent scouts in searching for just the right manager for your parents' unique requirements. *Brokerage firms and banks* now offer "wrap accounts," which provide clients with access to one-stop shopping for money managers that they can screen, hire, and monitor. Major *accounting firms* will also help you and your parents locate an adviser and for a fee will evaluate your personal situation and then recommend three managers for your parents to choose from. *Bank trust departments* will also manage your parents' money. If your parents are unable to locate a local adviser but are devotees of one of the larger *mutual fund families,* such as Fidelity or Vanguard, they may want to use the professional money management services offered by a mutual fund. The more you look around, the more you will discover that the choices are almost endless. All these choices have costs associated with them, though, so ask how much all this advice will cost before signing the dotted line.

Any of the advisers listed in Figure 8.1 will provide the requisite hand-holding that your parents are seeking. Ask about the process used to select an adviser and what ongoing information you will receive that details the activity

---

Figure 8.1

• • • • •

Providers of Financial Services

Services	Yourself or a broker	Brokerage firms that manage managers	Banks	Mutual fund companies that manage money for clients	Fee-based advisers
			Providers		
Buy individual stocks	X		X		X
Buy no-load funds	X		X	X	X
Buy load funds	X		X		X
Use common "trust" funds			X		X
Wrap accounts		X	X		X

in your account. All of these financial professionals should ask your parents to complete an extensive questionnaire that inquires about their investment return expectations, liquidity needs, and risk tolerance. In turn, your parents should request projections based on how the firm has performed compared with returns produced by both the overall stock market as well as by managers who use the same investment style.

The historical information showing how managers performed over time will indicate to your parents what kind of investment performance they can expect from the adviser in the future. In addition, your parents should insist that the adviser respond to changing economic conditions. If your parents are paying for services, they have the right to expect a dynamic portfolio, not one that stays static regardless of changing interest rates or the relative strength of the dollar. Most advisers also include tax documentation as part of their overall fee structure.

Why Hire Someone to Help?

At this point you may be asking yourself, why go to all this trouble when my brother is a trust officer and my sister an accountant, and I've bought a few mutual funds in my life too? Perhaps that's true. Perhaps your family is overflowing with qualified individuals who would gladly accept the responsibility of helping your parents manage their money. But first, stop and ask yourself if

Questions You Should Ask Your Advisers

• • • • •

- What is your minimum account size?

- What is the size of your average account?

- Do you base your fees on account size or per transaction, or do you charge a flat fee?

- What should I expect to pay in first-year fees?

- How do you make your investment decisions?

- Do you receive the same compensation regardless of the investments you recommend?

- Does your firm participate in sales contests?

- Who does your investment research?

- Do you sell any of your research to other investment professionals?

- How long have you been in business?

- What are the principals' professional background?

- What is the background of the individual who will be assigned my account?

- Who will be my regular contact person?

- How often will I receive an accounting?

- How often will I have a one-to-one meeting with my manager?

- Will my investment decisions be made by an individual or by a team of professionals?

- How have your results compared with industry averages?

- Are your results computed according to AIMR guidelines?

- How do you make personal investment decisions for your own account?

- Can you provide me with references?

- May I see a prototype report?

• • • • •

a responsible relative can really make objective suggestions. After all, and I can tell you this from personal experience, it's truly difficult to manage money for a family member. "Advisers" who have a kinship (or personal) relationship with the ones being advised tend to make different decisions than they do for others.

Second, recognize that the relative who is working hard on your parents' behalf faces a situation with very little emotional upside but a big downside. Everyone expects the relative to do a stellar job. But creating excellent investment returns is more difficult than it seems; the investment results of over one-half of all professionals are lower than the results obtained from an unmanaged

Questions You Should Ask Yourself

• • • • •

- Can I read the reports?

- How do I feel about paying the fees?

- Am I comfortable with the answers?

- Do I feel the firm has enough experience handling similar accounts?

- Do I like its investment approach?

- Do I feel its personnel are well trained, motivated, and personable?

- Do I feel that I will have enough personal access to my adviser?

- Am I comfortable with the references?

- Have I called the National Association of Securities Dealers disciplinary history hot line at 800-289-9999 to inquire about the adviser?

• • • • •

portfolio such as an index fund. What happens in the best-case scenario if the family money manager does a great job? Probably everyone will yawn and say, "Nice job, Charlie." But if Charlie does a terrible job, a family crisis will ensue and, let's face it, it's tough to fire a family member. So please think long and hard before you or another family member blithely agrees to manage your parents' financial affairs—it's a much more difficult task than it appears on the surface.

Insurance Advisers

An analysis of your parents' financial situation would not be complete without a review of their insurance coverage. If your parents have selected a financial planner as their adviser, he or she may be able to review their insurance coverage too. But it may be wise to get a second opinion from the agent who initially sold the policies. Insurance is a vital aspect of financial planning, and proper titling of insurance is crucial for reducing estate taxes. Equally significant is making sure that your parents have a type of coverage that most people don't think about—umbrella liability insurance. We live in a litigious society, so it's more likely today than ever before that an individual will be subjected to a lawsuit. If your parents are volunteer Scout leaders or sit on the board of directors for a nonprofit organization, they could be sued for wrongs allegedly committed by that organization. The list of potential law-suits they could face boggles the mind, and the more wealth they have accumulated, the more likely they will be sued.

Suggest to your parents they should purchase an umbrella liability policy just to be on the safe side. An umbrella policy provides additional coverage on top of the existing liability limits your parents already carry on their homeowners and automobile policy. Those underlying limits are tapped first if there is a claim. But if the claim goes beyond those basic limits, or the claim is not covered by either of those policies, the umbrella policy comes into play. Umbrella policies cover such suits as those alleging libel and slander, and they also pay defense costs even if a suit is groundless. Coverage starts at a $1 million and can be increased in million-dollar increments. Look for a policy with the broadest possible coverage. It's usually a good idea to coordinate your liability coverage on your car, house, and umbrella policy by purchasing all of the coverage from the same insurer.

Estate Planners

A less compelling, but nevertheless important, issue for some parents is the strategy they could implement to reduce their estate taxes. Since 1916 Congress has levied an estate tax on the transfer of assets at death to reduce the concentration of wealth. In the past, few individuals worried about paying estate taxes as the vast majority of estates were too small. According to the *New York Times* in a December 22, 1996, article entitled "For the Wealthy, Death Is More Certain than Taxes," in 1993, the most recent year for which data were available, only 1.5 percent of all estates were subject to estate taxes.

But all of that is about to change, and experts are looking at the prospect of a collective transfer of wealth ranging from $5 trillion to $10 trillion during the next decade. That's a lot of money, and given the spectacular size of many of the upcoming estates, there is bound to be a dramatic increase in the percentage of estates that will be subject to taxation. If your parents have a combined estate that exceeds $625,000 in 1998 (ratcheting up to $1 million in 2006), they should start thinking now about how they can reduce their estate taxes, which can take up to 55¢ of each dollar that is passed to the next generation.

It's true there is an unlimited marital deduction that allows all the money to be passed untaxed to the surviving spouse. But when the surviving spouse dies, the estate taxes can be so egregious that proper planning can save a family thousands and thousands of dollars in unnecessary estate taxes. For starters, by incorporating trusts into their planning, your parents can each take advantage of the individual exclusion. The proper use of trusts doubles the amount your parents can pass on free of estate taxes to subsequent generations.

Lifetime Planning

Gifting

One popular strategy is for parents to give away money during their lifetime. Naturally, gifting is only appropriate in situations where parents have other substantial assets that can provide them with exceptional financial security. Lifetime giving allows savvy parents and grandparents to save on estate taxes while providing them the opportunity to see their loved ones enjoy the

Resources

• • • • •

Licensed Independent Network of CPA Financial Planners (LINC)
800-737-2727
www.linpfp.com

Institute of Certified Financial Planners
800-282-7526
www.icfp.org

National Association of Personal Financial Advisors (NAPFA) (fee-only planners)
800-366-2732
www.napfa.org

International Association for Financial Planning (offers a free form for interviewing financial planners)
800-945-4237
www.iafp.org

CDA/Cadence (produces the Investment Advisor Performance Survey)
800-833-1394
www.cda.com

Money Manager Review (tracks 600+ financial advisers for $295 annually)
415-386-7111
www.managereview.com

Investment Management Consultants Association (will help you find a money manager)
303-770-3377
www.imca.org

• • • • •

money. An individual can give away $10,000 a year to anyone he or she chooses free from any gift tax, and a married couple can together give $20,000 away annually providing they sign a joint gift tax return. The money can be given directly to an individual or can be held in an irrevocable trust for later distribution. Providing the trust is properly drafted, the trust assets will qualify for the gift tax exclusion. If wealthy parents want to gift even more money tax-free, they can pay an unlimited amount for others' medical expenses or for tuition bills as long as the money is paid directly to the appropriate institution.

If your parents have lots of extra money, they may want to consider giving away their $625,000 one-time exemption while they are still alive. If they can part with the money now, they can not only remove that amount from their taxable estate but can remove the growth of that money as well. As an example, let's say Harry, a well-to-do executive, gives his son, Fred, his estate tax exemption amount of $625,000 today. If Harry's gift grows by a 7 percent after-tax amount annually, the original largesse will be worth $1.25 million ten years later when Harry dies. If Harry had waited until his death, only $625,000 would have escaped taxation instead of the $1.25 million.

Family Limited Partnerships

These partnerships, FLPs, are a nifty new way for moving money from the older to the younger generation. Most parents are worried that if they give away large amounts of money during their lifetime, they themselves could run out of funds. Most aging parents don't want to lose control over their funds either because, as do most people, they like to be in charge. They also worry about the impact of gifting too much money too soon to their children. A family limited partnership can reduce many of these concerns and has the added advantage of consolidating all the family's assets in one place.

In a limited partnership arrangement, the general partners (the parents) keep control over the assets and the cash those assets generate, even though they have gifted the assets to their children, who are the limited partners. The limited partners can't make investment or management decisions so the value of their shares, according to a 1993 IRS ruling, can be discounted for gift tax purposes. The discounting results from a tax law fluke decreeing that these minority interests lack marketability, thus making them less valuable in the open market. The discounting factor allows the parents to give away even more than $10,000 annually or more than $625,000 in a once-in-a lifetime gift. Setting up

Their Stories

• • • • •

Sam Walton, founder of the famed retail chain Wal-Mart, was a firm believer in estate planning. Back in 1953, even before Wal-Mart was a twinkle in his eye, Sam established a family partnership to hold his business interests. By the time Sam died in 1992, the Walton family fortune was worth $25.3 billion, but it's widely believed that Sam completely escaped the estate tax bullet. At the time of his death Sam owned just 10 percent of the partnership. Apparently, Sam left his interest to his wife for life, the interest to be donated to charity at her death. Since spousal transfers at death are not taxed, his wife paid no taxes, and if her interest is bequeathed to charity, her interest will not be taxed either. Sam did pay some tax on the assets he gave to his children, but it was a fraction of the amount that ordinarily would have been imposed at his death, especially given the huge increase in the value of the Wal-Mart chain over the years. Sam said, "The best way to reduce paying estate taxes is to give your assets away before they appreciate." And you thought that Sam Walton was just another guy who enjoyed driving a pickup. He was not only a retailing genius but was also extraordinarily savvy about preserving his hard-earned wealth.

• • • • •

a family limited partnership is complex and expensive, so it's only suited for those families with substantial assets—over $2 million. Also, because tax laws change, seek out an adviser with extensive experience in this area.

Charitable Remainder Trust (CRT) and Charitable Remainder Unitrust (CRUT)

CRTs and CRUTs allow donors to set up trusts they fund during their life. At the time donations are made, the donors can take an immediate tax deduction for the value of the remainder interest, which is established according to strict IRS guidelines. Then at death, the trust assets pass directly to the designated charity. The appeal of this strategy is twofold. First, donors receive a stream of income from the trust during their lifetime. With a CRT, donors receive a fixed amount each year. With a unitrust, the trust assets are turned over to a professional manager who assumes the responsibility for managing the initial donation. But there's no fixed distribution amount, so donors assume all the investment risk.

This strategy works especially well for individuals who need more current income and own assets that pay little or no income or have appreciated significantly since the donor acquired the asset. For example, let's say that your mom owns a vacant lot in Arizona she purchased in 1969; the lot has appreciated significantly from its original price of $100,000 to its current value of $2 million. While this is a nice problem for Mom to have, it also creates a dilemma. An empty lot produces no current income; thus this asset is not appropriate for Mom, who needs money to pay her bills. She could cash out the investment, but the amount she would owe in capital gains taxes would be staggering.

A CRUT, however, offers a solution for Mom's problem. By implementing a CRUT, Mom could donate the land to her alma mater and take an income tax deduction at today's inflated Sun Belt property values based on an IRS table. When all's said and done, Mom accomplishes the following: (1) She avoids paying the capital gains tax on her profits because she donated the property to a tax-exempt institution; (2) she gets a big current income tax deduction for her charitable donation; (3) the school replaces Mom's empty lot with monthly income for her; and (4) Mom is fulfilling a lifelong dream by supporting her alma mater.

Life Insurance Trusts

Life insurance trusts ensure that the proceeds of your parents' life insurance policy are kept out of their estate. Let's say that Dad buys a million-dollar life insurance policy on his life to provide money for estate taxes levied on the family business and to create a college fund for his five grandchildren. If Dad owns the policy, it is included in his estate and is subject to estate taxes. If his estate is large, the government will take 55 percent of the million dollars, leaving only $450,000, which eliminates any potential funds for the grandchildren.

But if Dad sets up a properly drafted irrevocable life insurance trust to hold the policy, and he gifts the money to pay the premium to the trust each year, the entire proceeds will escape estate taxes because the trust, not Dad, owns the policy. Naturally, stringent rules must be followed, which prevents Dad from having any control over the life insurance policy. The trust must own all incidents of ownership, including the right to change beneficiaries, borrow against the policy, or turn in the policy for its cash value. The insured—in this case, Dad—is cut off from those rights and that in turn allows the beneficiaries to receive the money free from estate taxes.

Personal Residence Trusts

These devices allow homeowners to place their residence in an irrevocable trust for a specific number of years. During the term of the trust, your parents continue to enjoy their home as usual. At the end of the term, the house is gifted to a beneficiary. The beauty of this arrangement is that it is possible to discount the value of the home at the time of the gift, and, according to IRS rules, the longer the term of the trust, the deeper the discount. Thus, it may be possible for your parents to keep their home for a long time while still minimizing gift and/or estate taxes. Another possibility is that your parents may want to place their vacation home in a personal residence trust.

Private Annuities

Private annuities are different from those we commonly associate with retirement planning because a commercial insurance company is not involved. Rather, a private annuity is a legal agreement between individuals and is often used when property is transferred between parents and children. This type of arrangement can be structured so that parents still retain control over an asset while the asset is legally removed from their estate. In return, the child makes periodic payments to the parents.

Testamentary Planning

The most basic strategy for estate planning for married couples is to make sure that each partner retains the individual $625,000 exemption. This problem can be solved simply by setting up two trusts (one should be a marital deduction and the other a credit shelter trust) to hold the couple's assets. The procedure has been a standard estate-planning technique for over 20 years.

With today's fractured families, it's getting more and more common for older couples to be in their second or even third marriage with all the resultant problems from such entanglements. A device called a *qualified terminal interest property trust* (QTIP) may smooth out some problems of the "I don't want my money going to *your* children" variety.

Your father, for example, can ensure that whatever funds are left at the end of his current spouse's life will be left to his biological children by leaving the maximum exemption amount (currently $625,000) in a credit shelter trust, which will pay income to his current spouse during her lifetime. At your stepparent's death, the proceeds would go to you and your siblings. The rest of the assets could fund a QTIP that distributes income to his current spouse, but your father can control who will receive the balance of the trust upon his spouse's death. A QTIP trust lets a wealthy individual minimize estate tax burdens while providing for a spouse and ensuring that the remaining funds are passed to the beneficiaries he designates.

A final strategy to consider is a *generation-skipping trust* (GST), which allows money to pass to the third generation (grandchildren) without additional estate taxes. Here's how it works. Grandpa has an estate of $5 million. If he wants to use his personal exemption, he can fund a trust while he's living; otherwise, when he dies the estate is taxed at the marginal rate and distributed according to his wishes. However, he has an ace up his sleeve as he has set up a GST for $1 million (the current maximum allowable amount). He has already paid tax on his estate, but the money in the GST can be passed directly to his grandchildren without getting taxed a second time at his daughter's death. The daughter is able to obtain income from the trust if she likes and perhaps a bit extra from the principal if she needs it, but the principal need not be included in her taxable estate when she dies.

All the estate-planning ideas described above will work for the right people under the right circumstances. But remember that some of these tax-savings devices are a bit like those little straw cylinders that look so innocuous until you stick your fingers inside and can't extricate them. These estate-planning ideas are easy to set up but very difficult to dismantle. So proceed carefully before you encourage your parents to sign on the dotted line.

What to Do If Your Parents Have Money

• • • • •

- Talk to your parents about their finances.

- Don't assume they know how to manage their wealth wisely.

- Ask to meet with their advisers annually.

- If they don't have professional help, find help for them.

- If they still refuse to seek professional help after months of cajoling, insist that at a minimum they simplify their financial life so you would at least be able to manage their affairs in an emergency.

- Continue to expose your parents to the complexities of today's financial markets.

- Insist they read this book.

• • • • •

CHAPTER 9

Managing Health Care Costs

"The system [Medicare] has produced a new disease . . . Insurance Dermatitis . . . an allergy of sorts which results from direct contact with forms that cause people to break out in a rash, put off surgery, walk around with broken legs, and consult *Readers Digest* instead of going to the doctor."

—Humorist Erma Bombeck

It's old news that in addition to the unbelievable expense of health care today, figuring out the newfangled approaches for service delivery is daunting. But it is a revelation for adult children trying to cope with managed care constraints and increased employee health care costs to learn that their aging parents face many of these same problems. Many adult children think that once their oldest parent reaches 65, their parents' medical plight is over. It's commonly thought by those under 65 that the elderly are 100 percent covered. But first each parent has to meet the age-65 requirement: Mom qualifies only when she reaches 65 and Dad qualifies only when he reaches 65.

It's even more discouraging to learn that many aging parents have to spend a significant percentage—an average of around 15 percent of net income—paying health care bills even though 99 percent of all older Americans are covered by the federal health insurance program Medicare. Then, too, Congress has recently authorized many new types of delivery systems for Medicare, so now your parents also have the dubious distinction of trying to figure out the best service payment options, ranging from Medicare HMOs to Medicare medical savings accounts.

If your parents spend 15¢ of every after-tax dollar on medical care, then health care costs start to take on a whole new level of importance. But it's not just the raw amount your parents spend that counts. The challenge is to allocate those dollars so they create the greatest amount of good. You can aid your parents and yourself, too, by learning more about their choices. Careful decision making is very important but difficult given all the complexities inherent in health care payment systems for the elderly. Much of the dilemma is created by the need to make intelligent choices among assorted possibilities that offer different levels of coverage and cost. But if you can fathom the various alternatives, you can go a long way toward helping your parents spend their health care dollars wisely.

Understanding the system will eliminate the danger of your parents being underinsured while simultaneously avoiding the needless cost of being over-insured. In addition, this exercise will create more peace of mind as all of us worry how our parents will pay health care bills, especially when we have only a vague notion of how much coverage their insurance actually provides. This chapter explores the federal, state, and private health insurance programs for seniors.

Medicare

Medicare, the federal health insurance program for Americans 65 and over, is the first line of defense. Unlike some other programs, Medicare is not based on federally defined income and asset limitations, at least not yet. As a result, the program provides equal coverage for all seniors regardless of their financial situation. Your parents are, or will be, automatically covered by Medicare when they turn 65 if they are receiving Social Security retirement benefits. However, parents who are still employed and not yet collecting Social Security benefits must apply for benefits by contacting their local Social Security Administration office. It's best to apply at least three months before turning 65 so that potential delays are eliminated. The special rules that apply to parents who continue to work after 65 and are entitled to receive employer-sponsored medical insurance should be carefully scrutinized.

Enrollment is free for Part A coverage of Medicare if your parents qualify for Social Security retirement benefits. However, if your parents are among the small minority of Americans who are ineligible for Medicare because they never contributed to the Social Security system or they have too few quarters of work coverage to qualify, they can opt to enroll by paying the monthly premium. The monthly hospital insurance premium was $309 in 1998 for those who had fewer than 30 quarters of Social Security work credits or $170 each month if they had between 30 and 39 quarters of covered work. Enrolling is usually a good idea as Medicare eligibility is not predicated on an individual's health status. Eligibility questions may be answered by calling the Social Security Administration at 800-772-1213.

That's the good news. The bad news is that the coverage was never designed, even back in 1965 when it was instituted, to provide broad coverage. Rather, it was always intended to be a partial safety net offering excellent coverage for acute care and so-so coverage for other health problems. Medicare does not cover most preventive health care procedures nor self-administered medications, such as prescription or over-the-counter drugs. It also features a set of complex rules requiring beneficiaries to pay premiums, deductibles, and coinsurance that even the Health Care Financing Administration (HCFA), which oversees Medicare, admits is "hard to understand." Health insurance benefits are always quirky, but Medicare, with its two distinct programs—one for inpatient care (Part A) and the other for outpatient care (Part B) and each with its own set of rules—is especially troublesome until you understand its procedures.

The difficult part is that if your parents get seriously ill or develop a debilitating condition requiring daily help, their Medicare coverage has more holes than Swiss cheese. Unfortunately, those holes are in places where you would least expect them, making the coverage unpredictable. The items not covered by Medicare are so significant that the American Association of Retired Persons (AARP) claims that Medicare now pays for less than half of the total health care of older persons. Thus, it's crucial to understand those items that Medicare does *not* cover as well as those it does.

Medicare Basics

Medicare is comprised of two parts: Part A, the hospital coverage, is financed by ongoing Social Security payroll taxes; Part B, which covers physicians' bills and outpatient treatments, is financed by user premiums automatically deducted from the recipients' Social Security retirement payments ($43.80 in 1998). Part B coverage is augmented with contributions from general federal tax revenues. User premiums fund about 25 percent of the costs and the federal government makes up the balance. Recent legislative changes require that Part B premiums paid by recipients must fund at least 25 percent of the costs, so you can expect that your parents' premiums will continue to rise as medical costs increase. But the good news is that Part B premiums may be deductible for federal income tax purposes.

Your parents can refuse Part B coverage but will be assessed a premium penalty of 10 percent for each year of nonparticipation unless they were covered during that period by a corporate plan. If Dad refuses Part B when he's 65, has no other coverage, and then wants to institute coverage when he's 70, the premium will be 50 percent higher than it would have been if he had opted to purchase the coverage when he was 65. If you want to learn the fine points of Medicare, pick up a free copy of the government publication *Your Medicare Handbook* from your local Social Security office; it is also available by mail or phone from a Social Security or Medicare office or can be downloaded directly from HCFA's Web site at www.hcfa.gov.

Medicare Part A. Part A provides comprehensive coverage if your parents are hospitalized providing the facility is Medicare approved. Coverage for nonparticipating hospitals (i.e., nonapproved facilities) is not assured. After a per-event deductible of $764 (the 1998 amount), Medicare pays almost all costs for a semiprivate room for the first 60 days. After that, the daily copayment is $191 a day for days 61 through 90, which comes directly out of recipients' pockets if they have no coverage other than Medicare. After a stay exceeding 90 days, recipients must dip into their reserve days. They have 60 nonrenewable reserve days, which means that these days of extra coverage cannot be tapped again. The copayment is $382 a day for reserve days 91 through 150; after 150 days, all Medicare coverage for that benefit period ceases.

Medicare Part A offers limited coverage for skilled nursing care. Days 1 through 20 are covered in full providing that the patient was hospitalized first for 3 days within the last 30 days and the skilled nursing care is providing continuing care for the same problem. This rule creates problems for many families as only one-half of all nursing home admissions are preceded by a hospital stay. A doctor must certify that the patient's condition requires daily skilled nursing or rehabilitation services. In other words, in order to qualify, your parent must have an acute illness. For days 21 through 100, the copayment is $95 a day. Medicare Part A nursing home coverage ceases after 100 days. Coverage for rehabilitation programs is subject to the same limitations but stops when the patient is no longer improving. Medicare provides no coverage for frail individuals who aren't sick but require daily assistance with such routine activities as dressing or eating. Figure 9.1 is a summary of Part A provisions.

Medicare Part B. Part B claims are administered by 32 separate carriers, each managing a specific geographic region. Medicare Part B fees, which are billed by physicians and outpatient clinics, are subject to a $100 annual

Figure 9.1

· · · · ·
1998 Medicare Part A Guidelines

Services	Benefit Period*	Medicare Responsibility	Patient Responsibility
Hospitalization: Semiprivate room, hospital services, and supplies	First 60 days	All but $764	$764
	61st through 90th day	All but $191 a day	$191 a day
	91st through 150th day	All but $368 a day	$382 a day and must use the once-in-a-lifetime non-renewable 60 reserve days
Nursing Home: Semiprivate room services and supplies for patients who have required prior hospitalization	First 20 days	100% of approved amount	
	Additional 80 days	All but $95 a day	$95 a day
	Beyond 100 days	Nothing	All costs

*Benefit period starts when the patient is admitted to the hospital and ends after he or she has been discharged for 60 continuous days.

one-time deductible, and most charges require a 20 percent copayment from the recipient. But the amount that your parents will actually pay for doctors' fees are based on the following three factors:

1. *The value Medicare assigns a specific service.* This number is referred to as the "approved" amount. If the doctor charges $225 for a service but Medicare determines that the service is only worth $130, Medicare will determine its reimbursement based on the approved amount of $130, not on the actual charge of $225.

2. *Whether the doctor is a "participating" or "nonparticipating" physician.* A participating physician agrees to accept the approved amount as payment in full and only bills the patient directly for the 20 percent copayment. Thus, in the above example, a participating physician agrees to accept the $130 as payment in full, billing Medicare for 80 percent, or $104, and collecting $26 directly from the patient. In most cases the fee of a nonparticipating physician is limited to 115 percent of the approved amount. Thus, in the above example, the doctor could charge $149.50 and would receive $104.00 from Medicare and $45.50 from the patient. Doctors must complete the Part B Medicare forms whether they participate or not.

   If a doctor is nonparticipating, the patient will have to pay the doctor's bill on a front-end basis and wait to receive reimbursement from Medicare for the $104. You can try to convince a nonparticipating doctor to "participate" in your parent's situation. It's estimated that between 25 and 50 percent of all doctors participate. You can obtain a directory of participating physicians directly from HCFA at no charge. But remember there is no law mandating that doctors have to treat Medicare patients.

3. *Where your parents live.* Some states have imposed even more stringent restrictions on the amount doctors can charge. Some states don't allow nonparticipating doctors to exceed the approved amount, while other states base doctors' charges on a sliding scale up to 115 percent of the approved amount.

Be aware that charges for other items—for example, ambulance services or durable equipment such as hospital beds—are not limited. Thus, if a provider charges $200 for a brace and the approved amount for that item is $100,

Medicare pays 80 percent of the approved amount, or $80, and the patient is responsible for the remaining $120. The only way to know if a provider accepts the approved amount, whether the provider sells durable equipment or is a medical doctor, is to ask. To find out what suppliers of medical goods and services are allowed to charge in your parents' state, check with the toll-free state insurance department's hot line for the details.

Home health care benefits, the fastest growing component of eldercare, are very restricted. The current limit is for 21 days of continuous part-time daily care up to 35 hours a week and limited intermittent care. Your parent must be homebound, care must be ordered by a physician, and a doctor must review the plan of care every two months. There is no provision for 24-hour care. Medicare does cover periodic skilled nursing care, in-home physical or speech therapists, some medical supplies, and rehabilitation equipment. The services must be provided by a Medicare-certified supplier. Figure 9.2 summarizes Medicare Part B provisions.

Figure 9.2 • • • • • 1998 Medicare Part B Guidelines

Services	Benefit	Medicare Pays	Patient Pays
Doctor bills	Treatment	80% of approved charge	$100 deductible plus 20% of approved charge
Home health care	Approved services	100% of services	Nothing
Durable equipment, e.g., wheelchairs, etc.	Approved services	80% of approved charge	Remainder of the cost
Outpatient treatment	Approved services	80% of approved charge	Outpatient services are not subject to the limiting charge. Patient responsible for 20% of what the hospital charges, not 20% of the approved amount

Minimizing costs. All doctors and qualified labs must accept assignment for diagnostic clinical laboratory tests. Your parents can minimize other Part B costs if they seek out providers who are willing to accept assignment—that is, they will accept Medicare's approved amount as payment in full. This leaves your parent responsible only for the 20 percent copayment (if they have other coverage, they may not have to pay anything). So before your parents purchase a piece of equipment, hire an ambulance, or engage a doctor, they should check to ensure that the provider accepts assignment. Some retiree plans don't cover all providers, so remind your parents that it's their responsibility to ask if the provider accepts Medicare assignment before they blithely agree to a medical device or medical treatment.

Another concern is managing the paperwork. If the provider does not accept assignment, your parent will be billed for the whole amount immediately. After the claim is processed, your parent will receive a check from Medicare for 80 percent of the approved amount. Your parent will need to keep copies of everything submitted and may want to create a tracking system to ensure he or she has been reimbursed by Medicare. For complicated illnesses or medical problems, the task of staying on top of medical bills can be daunting. Help *is* available if you or your parent becomes inundated by paperwork. The first

Prescription Drug Coverage

• • • • •

Prescription drug costs are an important and growing concern for the elderly. Some states offer pharmaceutical assistance programs, so check with your parents' state insurance counseling hot line to inquire about relief plans for drug costs that may be available to your parents. Also, many employer-sponsored programs provide drug coverage and about 20 percent of the elderly purchase Medigap policies that offer prescription coverage, write Vitt & Siegenthaler.

• • • • •

When a Doctor Agrees to Participate

• • • • •

Your dad goes to the emergency room with an irregular heartbeat. The participating emergency room doctor, who works for a private group, submits the following bill to Medicare:

	Charge	Medicare's Approved Amount
Emergency room visit	$270.00	$136.00
Electrocardiogram	52.00	12.00
Totals	$352.00	$148.00
Total Medicare approved	$148.00	
Medicare pays ($148 × 80%)	118.40	
Your parent owes ($148 × 20%)	$29.60	

In this instance, where the doctor agrees to accept assignment, your dad is responsible for paying the doctor just $30, or if he has other coverage such as a Medigap policy or retiree coverage, the insurance may cover the balance.

• • • • •

Medicare Gaps (as of 1998)

• • • • •

- Hospital deductible for each benefit period ($764)

- Hospital copayments after 61 through 90 days ($191 per day)

- Hospital copayment for reserve days 91 through 150 ($382 per day)

- Skilled nursing facility for days 21 through 100 ($95 per day)

- All hospital costs after 150 days

- Copayments for doctors, ambulances, supplies, and equipment (20%)

- Costs that exceed the approved amount

- Custodial care

- Long-term nursing home care

- Private duty nurses

- Routine care

- Self-administered drugs

- Glasses and hearing aids

- Dental care

- Most chiropractic services

- Items not considered medically necessary

- First three pints of blood

- Home-delivered meals

- Care received outside the United States

• • • • •

When a Supplier Is Nonparticipating

• • • • •

Your mom requires a brace to help her get back on her feet. The company selling the brace is nonparticipating, which means that Mom has to "front-end" the bill, which she does in full. The company submits the bill to Medicare, which in turn sends Mom the following statement:

	Charge	Medicare-Approved Amount
Brace rental	$189.00	$100.46
Total Medicare-approved	$100.46	
Medicare pays (100.46 × .8)	80.37	
Attached is a check for:	$ 80.37	

The cost of buying or renting durable equipment, unlike doctors' bills, is not subject to any Medicare-imposed limiting charges. Your mom will get a check for $80.37, which represents 80 percent of the Medicare-approved amount, leaving Mom on the hook for almost $109. If the supplier had been willing to accept assignment, it would have agreed to accept the Medicare-approved amount as full payment, leaving Mom responsible for about $20, the 20 percent copayment. The difference can be significant when a supplier does not accept assignment.

• • • • •

place to start is with the intermediary who sent the form and whose toll-free phone number will be listed on the report.

Senior centers often set aside a few hours each week to assist individuals with Medicare paperwork. Social Security offices should be able to help too. Or find help by calling AARP's Medicare/Medicaid assistance program, which is available in 33 states. To locate a volunteer in your area, call AARP at 202-434-2277. Each state insurance office offers free counseling for individuals who are struggling with paperwork, entitlement questions, or both. You may locate the service by contacting your local Area Agency on Aging or by checking the back of *Your Medicare Handbook.* Trained counselors will provide hands-on help with forms and some even teach recipients a system for tracking their charges.

Not surprisingly, a new profession has evolved to assist people who are overwhelmed with health care claims. Other firms not only will help with paperwork but will investigate for overcharges. The firm keeps half of what they recover and remits the remainder to your parent. Check your local yellow pages under health claims service to locate professionals in your area. Or you may want to contact the National Organization of Claims Assistance Professionals at 630-963-3500, which can refer you to local professionals who handle health care claims paperwork. Beware, however, before you hire someone to assist you that this is a new, unregulated, unlicensed service so proceed with care.

Health Care Delivery Options

The major advantage of the popular fee-for-service system is that your parents are free to select any doctor or medical supplier. However, under the traditional system, Medicare only pays a set percentage of some expenses and the patient must shoulder costs for all prescription medications and most preventive care plus the deductibles, copayments, and charges that exceed the approved amount. An increasingly popular alternative chosen by 4.4 million of the 38 million Medicare beneficiaries is a health maintenance organization (HMO), available to anyone who qualifies for Medicare. HMO membership avoids many traditional expenses making medical costs more predictable.

HMO participants must select their primary care physician from a limited group. They continue to pay the Medicare Part B premium and may pay the HMO an additional monthly premium plus a small copayment for each service. In addition to eliminating much troublesome paperwork, an important cost-savings feature of HMOs is that participants don't need to purchase a Medigap policy, which has become increasingly expensive. But if your parents have a retiree plan, encourage them to keep it in place until they are sure they are satisfied with their HMO.

Newly enacted legislation offers additional health care payment alternatives. It is too early as of this writing to know exactly how these new options will evolve but they include *private fee-for-service plans.* These private plans may pay doctors much higher fees than Medicare's approved amounts and don't reward doctors for limiting services. The fee for membership is in addition to the Part B amount. *Private contracting* allows seniors to pay their own way for a physician who is not willing to accept the current limitation of 115 percent of the approved amount. *Medical savings accounts* offer coverage through a combination of a high-deductible insurance policy and a tax-free savings account for routine expenses. The new law also authorizes additional managed care programs such as *preferred provider organizations* (PPOs), which have a select group of doctors but also allows using outside providers for an extra fee, and *provider-sponsored organizations,* which will be formed by doctors and hospitals to service Medicare recipients.

So which is best, a managed care approach such as an HMO or the traditional fee-for-service plan? If your parents' funds are limited, an HMO usually includes more medical services for the same amount of money. Many HMOs provide benefits that Medicare does not cover, including preventive care, prescription drugs, dental care, hearing aids, and eyeglasses. Also, an HMO usually allows an unlimited number of visits per month, especially important for parents requiring constant skilled medical care.

A significant downside, though, is that HMOs limit your choice of doctors and may limit access to specialists. Another problem is obtaining covered health care away from home. For parents who have two homes or travel frequently, an HMO may not be the best choice. Ultimately, the best health care option for your parents depends on the benefits offered under each plan; the doctors' qualifications and their location; and your parents' financial situation, health, and, perhaps most important, personal preferences.

The Medicare appeals process. What can you or your parents do if you feel that Medicare has been unfair? Perhaps coverage has been denied for what seems to be a routine claim or a parent was forced out of the hospital much too soon. Other common problems include nursing home reimbursements and coverage for home health care costs. Most adult children feel frustrated and helpless in these instances but there is hope: Medicare provides an appeals process clearly outlined on its claim forms. Very few Medicare recipients, less than 5 percent, ever appeal, but the success rate for those who do complain is surprisingly high. Statistics differ, but according to government reports, somewhere between 50 and 75 percent of all appealed claims are overturned because many denials simply result from insufficient documentation or other paperwork snafus.

If your doctor accepts assignment, the problem of getting a claim paid lands in the doctor's lap. Your parents have to worry about payment only on their medical bills with a front-end payment. The appeals process has four aspects that move you further up the system. The first step, a Medicare review, is fairly simple; you can communicate your problem in writing. More than 63 percent of Part B Medicare reviews are successful. The "Explanation of Medicare Benefits" (EOMB), or "Summary Notice," shows if the physician's fee exceeded the limiting charge; if so, you should contact the doctor directly. If the problem is not with a doctor—the claim was denied, for example—and you want to keep the process simple, mark "Please Review" on the top of the EOMB and return the form, keeping a copy for your files.

You can strengthen your request for a review with additional information furnished by your health care provider documenting the necessity of your parent's treatment, so it's wise to keep medical bills on file for a few years. Claim denials often result from routine claims that are not properly processed or claims for nontraditional treatments. Territorial variations are also a factor; local processors have some discretion, so the same claims may be paid in one jurisdiction but denied in another.

If the initial review is unsuccessful, a patient has the right to know the basis for the denial. The patient can go to the next level by requesting a fair hearing, providing the claim is for $100 or more. This process involves meeting with a Medicare hearing officer, who applies Medicare policies and guidelines; in these cases the reversal rate is 60 percent. If these measures are not successful, the patient can then demand an administrative hearing as long as the contested Part B claim is for $500 or more. At this level, the proceedings are similar to a regular civil suit, including sworn testimony. When all else fails, claims for over $1,000 can be taken to a U.S. district court, where an attorney is required. The main issue is medical necessity and whether the treatment is regularly covered by Medicare. The potential benefits are well worth the aggravation, but try to get some outside advice from a Senior Center representative or an elder law attorney first—especially if a substantial sum is involved. AARP also has a Medicare Assistance Program in some states that may be able to guide you. Note that your parent's medical provider is not allowed to demand payment for services until the appeals process has been completed. So hold on to the checkbook till then.

HMOs are purported to be a paperless system, but they have their own set of problems usually caused by a patient who doesn't understand the underlying rules. A common issue for HMO participants is failing to get permission from the primary care doctor before consulting a specialist. Then, as a result, the HMO will deny the claim. But as with Medicare, HMOs by law must offer an appeals process. HMOs are required to provide written notice if a service, such as access to a specialist, is denied, and the notice must also provide information on the appeals process. As of April 1997, HMOs also must offer a 72-hour expedited review process for situations in which the patient is critically ill and a determination may literally be a matter of life and death. Complaining about an HMO actually may be easier than a Medicare appeal because HMOs are regulated by state departments of insurance and thus you may actually be able to talk to the same person every time you call. Also, states are required by the federal government to offer free counseling for individualized help.

Medigap Insurance

Medigap insurance policies, sold by private insurance companies, are specifically designed to help pay health care costs that are either not covered or are not fully covered by Medicare, thereby resulting in gaps in coverage and hence the name Medigap. Some seniors are entitled to continued coverage from their former employer, but coverage for retired employees is usually not under a Medigap policy and, unlike a Medigap policy, is not designed to coordinate with Medicare. A retiree policy may offer equal or even better coverage than a standard policy, however, especially for prescription drugs. If your parents are not entitled to employee coverage and choose traditional Medicare fee-for-service insurance, they need to be concerned about the gaps in coverage. They can augment their traditional Medicare coverage with a Medigap policy that protects seniors from the coverage gaps, which are mostly in Part B, by paying Medicare deductibles and copayments and extending benefit periods.

These policies are so popular that older Americans spend literally billions of dollars on these policies. Fortunately, since 1992 federal law limits insurers to offering a lineup of ten standard plans designated by letters from A to J. A is the most basic plan and provides Part A coinsurance for days 61 through 90, one-time reserve for days 91 through 150, coverage for 365 additional days after Part A benefits end; it also pays the Part B 20 percent per-occurrence coinsurance. Plan J provides the most comprehensive coverage, including benefits for at-home recovery and self-administered prescriptions. The best part of Medigap insurance is that there are few restriction on doctors, access to specialists or hospitals, procedures, or tests as long as the service is covered by Medicare and the provider is Medicare approved.

The most important distinctions between the plans, as seen in Figure 9.3, are the coverage for prescription drugs and balance billing. Policy J offers coverage up to $3,000 a year for prescription drugs after a $250 deductible. Coverage for balance billing, the amount your parent is required to pay over the approved amount, is another option. If a doctor doesn't accept assignment or you think your parent will require durable medical equipment, which is an item like a hospital bed that will not be used up quickly, then you should look into

Figure 9.3 • • • • • Standardized Medigap Policies

Benefits	Plans									
	A	B	C	D	E	F	G	H	I	J
Basic	X	X	X	X	X	X	X	X	X	X
Hospital deductible	X	X	X	X	X	X	X	X	X	X
Nursing home copayment			X	X	X	X	X	X	X	X
Part B deductible ($100)			X			X				X
Excess Part B charges						100%	80%		100%	100%
Foreign travel emergency			X	X	X	X	X	X	X	X
At-home recovery				X			X		X	X
Self-administered drugs								$1,250	$1,250	$3,000

the balance billing feature offered in policies F, G, I, and J. Your parent may end up with some coverage he or she doesn't need or really want, but supplemental policies can't be customized to suit individual preferences.

Shopping for a Medigap policy is a breeze compared with choosing other insurance as it's relatively simple to determine the coverage and then compare prices. Another good feature is that Medigap policies must be guaranteed to be renewable and can be canceled only for nonpayment. The best time to purchase Medigap insurance is within the first six months after your parent enrolls in Medicare. During that period, your parent has the right to purchase a Medigap policy regardless of prior health problems—pricing discrimination is forbidden. Also, the new law signed in August 1997 allows former policyholders to reinstate their Medigap coverage policy at the same rate within the first 12 months if they opted for an HMO, became dissatisfied, and want to return to the traditional Medicare fee-for-service program.

Shop around for the best price and service. Studies by the United Seniors Health Cooperative show that premiums for the same plan can vary by as much as 100 percent. *Kiplinger's Personal Finance Magazine,* in its January 1998 issue, noted that annual costs ranged from $544 in Florida for an A policy to $1,812 depending on the insurer. Look for a company that allows you to switch plans once you have enrolled. Be on guard for limits for coverage on preexisting health conditions and the company rating. Insurance company rating services such as A. M. Best (212-439-2200), Standard & Poor's (212-208-1527), and Moody's (212-553-0377) can be purchased directly or are available at the public library. You also might want to ask the company to provide its premium schedules or outlines of coverage, a report detailing premium increase history. If the company won't produce the report, be wary. Some insurers offer crossover billing, which automatically coordinates Medicare and Medigap coverage with the suppliers and can be a lifesaver if your parents have numerous claims.

Medicaid

Medicare combined with a Medigap policy or a Medicare HMO will cover most routine and acute health care needs. But many parents need some type of daily assistance, especially after 75. Most families strive to keep their elderly in their own home as long as possible. But in some circumstances, especially when the parent has a mental disorder such as Alzheimer's disease, institutionalized care may be the only rational alternative. Finding good care is difficult but paying for a long-term nursing-home stay or long-term home health care services can be more difficult and in some instances all but impossible. Depending on the region of the country, the cost of nursing home care ranges from $30,000 to $60,000 annually with a national average of $40,000 a year.

As a result, Medicaid, the means-tested program for low-income Americans, pays for almost half of all long-term care in the United States. Medicaid is jointly funded by the federal (55 percent) and state government (45 percent) and administered by each state within broad federal guidelines. States have considerable latitude; thus, no two statewide Medicaid programs are alike. The first place to start understanding the features of a state-specific Medicaid program is to obtain literature from that state.

General guidelines in most states are similar. Individuals must be impoverished in order to qualify. A single individual may have exempt assets such as a home, a car worth no more than $4,500, some household possessions, and $2,000 in liquid assets. Married couples are allowed to keep the same items except that the value of their car is not limited to $4,500 and liquid assets may total $3,000. However, in the case of nursing home care or home care for the elderly, specific guidelines are designed to protect the noninstitutionalized spouse. The "community spouse," the spouse who remains in the family home, is allowed to retain some monthly income. Usually, the monthly income exemption equals 150 percent of the poverty line, or about $1,200, plus in most states an additional housing allowance. The exempt amount may be even higher in some states if the income is paid directly to the community spouse in his or her name alone. The community spouse may also retain half of the couple's assets up to a maximum of $80,000 depending on state guidelines.

No one wants to be poor, but some seniors deliberately impoverish themselves so they qualify for Medicaid's nursing-home and home health care benefits. Congress, which has been aggressively trying to balance the budget, has no sense of humor about these attempts. It has moved to make it difficult, if not impossible, to collect Medicaid benefits if seniors deliberately divest themselves of assets. Congress has instituted stiff "look-back" rules covering asset transfers for less-than-fair-value to third parties such as children. So if Mom offers to sell you the family business for one dollar so she can qualify for Medicaid, when the business would fetch $1 million in the open market, there could be a problem.

If assets are transferred outright to a third party, then the look-back period is three years. If your parent set up a trust to hold assets, a transfer must have taken place at least five years before in order to qualify for Medicaid. The formula is complicated, but if a parent transfers funds and then enters a nursing home, the parent may still be responsible for the monthly bills based on when the transfer was made and how much money was transferred. The law has also been rewritten to make Medicaid trusts currently impractical for most people.

Granny Goes to Jail

In 1996 Congress passed the Kassebaum-Kennedy law, which included a section that the pundits entitle the *Granny Goes to Jail Law*. This provision criminalized the transfer of assets in order for a senior to qualify for Medicaid. Where the original law focused on penalizing the senior transferring the assets, the new provision—an amendment signed into law August 5, 1997—makes it a crime to "for a fee counsel or assist an individual to make certain asset transfers."

The legality of this provision is being hotly debated because it seems that lawyers and other advisers now commit a crime when they advise their clients of actions that themselves are not crimes. The issue probably will end up being settled by the Supreme Court. But even if the 1997 amendment is declared unconstitutional, the handwriting is on the wall. The federal government now mandates that individual states create a Medicaid recovery program. Each state is required by federal law to sue the estates of Medicaid recipients who have received payment for certain types of care during their lifetime. Even if Mom or Dad sets up a trust or gives away money within the acceptable time frames, the state can still lay claim to the estate and obtain the funds postmortem. Somehow, I don't think that you will be amused if you have to sell the family business to pay the government back for nursing-home bills incurred during your parents' lifetime.

The upshot of all this is that Congress, either with this provision or with one that surely will replace it, is determined to make people with the means pay for their own long-term care. Being able to pay for one's own care has distinct advantages, however. It's true that Medicaid does pay for half of the nursing-home care in the United States, but the amount it pays per bed is generally less than the cost of the care provided. Unfortunately, patients with funds end up subsidizing those without funds. Many nursing homes refuse to accept Medicaid patients so that locating care can be a problem. In addition, a family has no control over which facility is selected because Medicaid directs patients to the first available bed.

Long-Term Care Insurance

Buying long-term care insurance is becoming a more attractive notion given such recent events as the introduction of tax-qualified long-term care insurance products. Starting in 1997, the premiums for long-term care insurance may now be added to your parents' (and yours too) medical expenses for tax purposes. That means that any expenses above the 7.5 percent of adjusted gross income (AGI) may be deductible for taxpayers who itemize. The total amount you or your parents can deduct is limited by age; those younger than 40 can deduct only $200 for premiums, but that amount increases to $2,500 for those over 71. Even if the premium deductions don't help, the benefits are not considered taxable income, which is the single most important feature of the new tax-exempt policies as benefits from older policies may be taxable.

Long-term care policies themselves have improved over the years and are a much better deal for the consumer; benefits have increased while premiums have decreased. Another newly introduced feature allows a policy owner to use the benefits for home care, adult day care, assisted living, or other community-based programs in addition to a conventional nursing home. But even with recent legislation and policy improvements, should your parents consider purchasing a long-term care policy?

If your parents' joint assets are less than $100,000, not including their home, then it probably makes no sense to purchase a long-term care policy because they probably can't afford the premium and Medicaid may pay for care given the present eligibility rules. If your parents have substantial assets that would allow them to pay for the cost of long-term care out of current income, they are not likely candidates for long-term care insurance. Because they have the financial wherewithal to pay for care without becoming impoverished, it's not advisable to spend money protecting themselves from an unknown, but probably affordable, cost. On the other hand, those whose assets range from $100,000 to $750,000 may want to consider buying long-term care insurance.

But you want to avoid the problem of your parents paying so much for long-term care insurance that they limit their retirement lifestyle. A cost-savings strategy is to take out a policy with an extensive waiting period, which transfers some of the risk to the policyholder and reduces the premium to an amount your parents may be able to handle without financial strain. Another approach to keeping premiums low if your parents' assets are meager is to purchase a policy with limited coverage—say three years—as only one in four of the 43 percent of all seniors who actually enter a nursing home will spend more than one year there and only 1 in 11 who enter a nursing home will spend five years living there. Buying a policy does entail costs in the form of an annual premium, but the distinct advantage is that the cost of providing long-term care is predictable.

The harder problem is selecting the policy. The best arrangement is to work with a knowledgeable agent whose work is mainly focused on long-term care insurance. Unfortunately, Congress has not created model long-term care policies as it has with Medigap policies, so the permutations and combinations are endless. Over 120 companies, including American Travelers, Bankers Life and Casualty, CNA, and John Hancock, offer policies and each company has several options to chose from. You may want to start by contacting the Health Insurance Counseling Program in your parents' state department of insurance to get the names of companies licensed to sell policies in their state. The following is a list of issues you will want to consider:

- What is the definition of disability?
- Are there restrictions or exclusions?
- Is the policy renewable?
- Are there paid-up provisions?
- Under what circumstances can the company increase the premium?
- Who can provide reimbursed care?
- Will the policy provide for custodial care?
- What is the lifetime maximum benefit?
- Is there an inflation rider?
- How long is the elimination period?
- Are the premiums deductible?
- How is the company rated?
- What is the annual cost?

Caring for a Frail Parent at Home

We have taken a look at techniques for managing health care costs. But another issue often arises for adult children at some point: What should they do when Mom or Dad can't be left alone? Sometimes parents need short-term skilled care as hospitals are sending patients home earlier and sicker. But in other instances, your parents may require long-term care. Mom isn't sick but may be frail, forgetful, or depressed. Other seniors may suffer from chronic debilitating conditions that make it difficult for them to manage without some type of outside help. So there you are, either next door or a thousand miles away, trying to come up with a solution. The issue may be compounded by family dynamics. One sibling has a ready solution, while another is convinced his approach is better. These types of problems can sometimes be solved by obtaining more information. Your first mission is to investigate the type of resources available in your parent's community. You'll also want to consider the following issues:

- Can community resources such as adult day care be used?
- If not, how much home care is required (e.g., daily, 24-hour, or intermittent)?
- If you decide to hire a helper, should you use an agency or hire privately?
- What qualifications does the helper need?
- Who can supervise the helper?
- Who will be responsible for the costs: Medicare, Medicaid, another federal or state agency, Medigap insurance, the VA, long-term care insurance, or the parent or other family members?

Community resources for seniors may include protective services for adults unable to manage their affairs, adult day care, senior centers, meal delivery, home health care services, homemakers, "friendly" visitors, and alarm devices that elderly people can activate if there's a problem. Your first stop for finding what's available is the local Area Agency on Aging (AAA) hot line, which will be listed in the blue pages of the local phone book or in the yellow pages under "Senior Citizens." The World Wide Web is a gold mine of information for adult children, too (read *Helpful Free Publications/Web Sites*). AAA may be able to suggest a local organization that has a trained social worker who can develop a care program specifically for your parent at no cost. Other ideas include contacting your employer to see if it sponsors an elder care counseling program for employees.

If you can't find Area Agency on Aging number, contact the Eldercare Locator hot line at 800-677-1116. This federally funded hot line is another important source and provides detailed information about 4,800 local programs for seniors identified by zip code. If you live in an area with sparse services, creativity may be required. For example, you may want to contract with a local restaurant to provide meals if your parents' community doesn't offer a meals-on-wheels program. Chances are that the help you arrange will come from several sources, including a patchwork of community, government, and private-pay arrangements.

Hiring a helper yourself differs from contracting with a home-health agency. The major advantage of hiring privately is control. You and your parent control who enters your parent's home and when. Agencies sometimes change workers daily or weekly or severely limit their activities. Because agencies need to cover overhead and make a profit, agency workers are usually more expensive. You can expect to save about 30 percent or more from agency fees if you hire directly. But finding qualified home care workers may be a challenge, especially if you're trying to do it from a distance. Hiring someone yourself is an impractical solution, if you feel your parents will require home care services for a long time, perhaps indefinitely, and there is no close friend or family member available locally to monitor the employee's work.

Some communities offer registries of home health care workers but are not required to screen the applicants, so you or your parents are responsible for conducting background checks. You can also locate applicants by advertising in the local paper, in church bulletins, or at local colleges that train nurses or physical therapists. You might also consult the local United Way agency, the Family Service of America agency, or your parents' clergy or rabbi. You need to be very clear on the type of work required, qualifications, hours, and compensation. A job description that includes a list of responsibilities, hours, work rules, compensation, vacations and benefits (if any), and evaluation criteria will help mitigate future misunderstandings. The job description can also serve as a focus of the interview.

Have the applicant complete a written job application and check carefully to determine the applicant's background, work history, educational qualifications, and references. Look for aides who are licensed practical nurses (LPNs) or have received a state health-aid certification. Ask if the aide is bonded and make sure you contact *all* the references. Look for a steady work history, solid references, and be prepared to pay a minimum of $8 an hour. According to *Business Week* magazine, the total cost for a live-in caregiver averaged about $50,000 annually in 1997. You need to be cautious because home health care workers aren't subject to the same ongoing scrutiny as other employees. You can do the groundwork yourself regarding prior employment or educational achievement, but if you feel uncomfortable checking further into an individual's background, companies listed in the yellow pages under "Investigators" will conduct background checks on your behalf.

The investigation company will charge about $150 and can obtain a variety of information: the candidate's driving record, court records for prior arrests or incarceration, educational credentials, Social Security number validation, driving records, or any workers' compensation claims. You'll need to obtain the candidate's permission first, however, before the investigation company can proceed. In addition, the amount of information that can be obtained about a prospective employee is limited in many states. This effort may seem like overkill but it's estimated that in Florida, for example, 25 percent of home health care workers have a criminal background, according to Helen Susik.

A serious drawback to hiring directly is the need to comply with ongoing tax rules and to avert legal complications. You must make certain that the individual you hire is a citizen or has an authentic work card. In addition, you must withhold federal, state, and Social Security taxes. You must also be concerned about state unemployment taxes and workers' compensation laws. Order IRS Publication 926, *Household Employer's Tax Guide,* which outlines federal tax rules. You need to be aware of applicable state and federal labor, health, and safety laws, so you should also contact the department of labor in the state where your parents live to learn about its state-specific requirements.

Better yet, hire a local accountant to worry about all this stuff. The peace of mind is well worth the costs. A local accountant should be able to tell you about the state's workers' compensation coverage or can refer you to a competent adviser to help you obtain the coverage you need. It's also a good idea to contact your parents' homeowners insurance agent. You'll probably want to increase your parents' liability coverage and/or consider purchasing umbrella liability insurance to protect your parents against any claims made by the worker while in your parents' employment. A private company, Paychex (800-884-

2425) will handle much of the paperwork for a weekly fee of about $9 per employee. And, finally, you might want to check with the family lawyer to make sure that you haven't forgotten anything and then consult with a local labor lawyer to ensure you are taking all the necessary steps to protect yourself and your parents from unnecessary legal exposure if you hire a home health care worker privately.

If the thought of this overwhelms you but you don't want to work with an agency or there isn't one in your parents' area, you may want to consider hiring a geriatric care manager to assist you, especially if you are a long-distance child unfamiliar with local resources. Geriatric care managers usually are social workers, gerontologists, or registered nurses with advanced degrees and can connect you with the resources that your parents need. The major advantage of using a manager is that he or she is knowledgeable about local offerings of the multifaceted services that may be required to care for a frail parent. It's usually an overwhelming task for adult children unfamiliar with the diverse world of eldercare to step in and locate the appropriate services or personnel. Care managers may be available from a local social service agency for a small fee and are very familiar with not-for-profit and public resources.

Private-practice managers are more expensive, charging from $200 to $350 for an initial evaluation and $50 to $125 an hour for follow-up work depending on both the locale and the manager's work experience and training. They are knowledgeable about a whole range of services, including access to public as well as private resources. If you want to explore the private care manager route, contact the professional association, National Association of Professional Geriatric Care Managers at 602-881-8008. You can obtain a copy of its national directory for $35. Look for a manager who is certified by this professional organization and licensed to practice in your parents' state. Your manager should have a good working knowledge of local services and financial payment mechanisms, and should be able to provide solid references.

Another avenue for locating a local professional is to contact the local United Way, hospital social workers, family service agencies, or area colleges that offer gerontology certification programs. Care managers are especially helpful in situations where family members live far away or disagree about the best solution. "Attempting to understand complicated eligibility requirements and locating the most suitable services for an elderly family member can create stress and conflict within families," write Vitt and Siegenthaler. A good care manager can identify which services your parent needs, can help hire home workers, coordinate medical, legal, and financial matters, monitor the situation, and offer emotional support for everyone concerned. In addition, geriatric care managers can be especially effective when long-standing family differences are a problem.

Managers, according to Vitt and Siegenthaler,

- identify problems and the need for specific services;
- create a service plan;
- hire and monitor ongoing service providers;
- review financial, legal, and medical arrangements;
- act as a liaison to long-distance family members;
- assist with moving an older person to a facility that provides required services; and
- offer emotional support.

Home health care agencies are listed in the phone book, or you can find one by contacting the Elder Care Locator hot line. Look for an agency that is both Medicare accredited and Medicare certified. To find if your parents' state is one of those with a licensing program, call the state department of insurance. It may be by trial and error that you find the agency that meets your parents' needs. It is very important when you interview an agency to inquire about its training and supervision, which varies substantially from agency to agency. You should plan to pay about $15 to $20 an hour for custodial services and up to $60 an hour for skilled care.

Look for a provider that offers to develop a written plan for your review, that has been in business for at least three years, and that can provide references from satisfied families. The Health Care Financing Administration (HCFA) inspects certified home health care agencies and prepares a Medicare Survey Report on each agency available from each state's department of insurance. And each state must operate a toll-free home health care telephone hot line and an investigative unit to provide information about, and receive complaints regarding, certified agencies.

Other questions you should ask a home health care agency are the following:

- How long have you been serving the community?
- How do you recruit and train your employees?

- Do they meet the federal training requirement for at least 75 hours of classroom and practical training?
- What is the minimum number of hours of employment required?
- Does the agency create a written care plan outlining the specific tasks to be carried out by each caregiver?
- What will be the cost for basic services?
- What will be the cost for additional services?
- Are your employees bonded and covered by workers' compensation?
- Will your agency assume full liability for all problems?
- Do you conduct security checks before you hire?
- Do you provide 24-hour care?
- How do you handle emergencies?
- Will there be ongoing supervision and, if so, who will supervise the worker and how often will the supervisor visit?
- Will I receive a written bill outlining a detailed list of charges?
- Can you provide me with a list of references?

I realize that learning about all these senior health care issues is both depressing and overwhelming. It's not just a simple matter requiring merely a sense of duty and some diligence. But I would tell you from personal experi-

Helpful Free Publications/Web Sites

• • • • •

AARP 202-434-2277
www.aarp.org
Medicare: What It Covers—What It Doesn't
Knowing Your Rights : Medicare Protections for Hospital Patients
When Your Medicare Bill Doesn't Seem Right: How to Appeal Medicare Part B

Health Care Financing Administration
www.hfca.gov or www.medicare.gov
Your Medicare Handbook
Medicare and Other Health Benefits: Who Pays First?
199X Guide to Health Insurance for People with Medicare

Social Security Administration 800-638-6833
www.ssa.gov
199X Guide to Health Insurance for People with Medicare
Medicare and Managed Care Plans

National Association of Insurance Commissioners
120 West 12th Street, # 1100
Kansas City, MO 64105
www.naic.org
A Shoppers Guide to Long-Term Care Insurance

Health Insurance Association of America
555 13th Street, NW, #600
Washington, DC 20004
www.hiaa.org
Guide to Long-Term Care Insurance
Long-Term Care Insurance: An Employer's Guide

National Association for Home Care
228 Seventh Street, SE
Washington, DC 20003
www.nahc.org
How to Choose a Home Care Provider: A Consumer's Guide

Administration on Aging
www.aoa.dhhs.gov

• • • • •

ence that you don't want to be blind-sided by this information either. I have a file about a foot thick containing a family member's Medicare statements resulting from illness and other woes. If these forms arrive when you are in a state of shock to begin with, I can attest to the fact that that's a very tough time to start learning about your parents' health insurance. So do yourself a favor and start talking to your parents about their health care coverage well before a crisis hits.

Medical Insurance Checklist

- Financial literacy studies show that most adult children are clueless about Medicare. This comes as no surprise as few of us can understand our own ever-changing medical coverage let alone understand yet another program.
- This chapter should provide you enough information to begin the process of looking at your parents' coverage and determining if it's adequate.
- If you require more information, check with a knowledgeable professional, such as an insurance agent who specializes in various medical policies including Medigap and long-term care; an elder law attorney; a social worker; a hospital discharge planner; or a geriatric care manager. Insurance for your parents is far too complex to try to go it alone.

Figure

9.4

• • • • •
Putting It All Together: A Comparative Analysis

	Current cost for last 12 months	Amount you would have spent if you had purchased a Medigap policy or joined an HMO[1]	Differences
Medicare Part A: Premium	$_____	$_____	$_____
Medicare Part B: Premium	_____	_____	_____
Medigap policy	_____	_____	_____
Retiree insurance premium	_____	_____	_____
HMO dues	_____	_____	_____
Uncovered preventive care	_____	_____	_____
Out-of-pocket expenses for prescriptions	_____	_____	_____
Other out-of-pocket costs[2]	_____	_____	_____
Deductibles paid	_____	_____	_____
Coinsurance paid	_____	_____	_____
Balance billing amounts due	_____	_____	_____
Other	_____	_____	_____
Total Owed	$_____	$_____	$_____

[1]Your parents' medical costs are probably as low as they can go if they already belong to an HMO, but you might want to go through this exercise anyway. For others, add all the costs incurred. Then compare coverage and costs for Medicare alone with the cost of adding a Medigap policy (see www.quotesmith.com for examples) or a Medicare HMO.

[2]These include dental costs, eye glasses, and hearing aids.

CHAPTER 10

Questions and Answers

"If a man will begin with certainties, he shall end in doubts;
but if he will be content to begin with doubts, he shall end
with certainties."

—Francis Bacon, 1605

We've reviewed the major legal, financial, and emotional aspects of improving the lives of our aging parents. But specific eldercare concerns vary enormously from one situation to another. To help you deal with your own situation, I've gathered additional information about common dilemmas presented in a question-and-answer format.

Getting Started

I'd like to start getting more involved in my parents' lives, but after 30 years of independent living, I'm not sure where to start. What simple beginning steps can I take which would be helpful to my parents?

1. Buy your parents a prepaid phone card so they can call you, other family members, or friends when they feel like sharing an important moment.
2. Call the local Area Agency on Aging to determine what services are available in your parents' locale.
3. If your parents enjoy animals, help them acquire a pet and all the requisite paraphernalia.
4. Make a big fuss over Mother's Day, Father's Day, your parents' birthdays, and even Arbor Day.

5. Discuss Medicare gaps with them so they understand how the system works.

6. Help them determine if they qualify for federal health care benefits from the Veterans Administration (VA) or coverage through the Qualified Medicare Beneficiary (QMB) program.

7. Assist them in evaluating the pros and cons of health care coverage from a private source such as a corporate retiree plan or a Medigap policy.

8. Call once a week.

9. Encourage them to move their assets into an account that combines checking, savings, brokerage, a debit card, and automatic bill-paying services. A combined statement makes it much easier for your parents to keep a watchful eye on their personal finances.

10. Help them review their Medicare claim forms to ensure they have been properly reimbursed.

11. Help them list title designations for all their assets because improper ownership designations can create unintended consequences.

12. Contact the local community college, YMCA, YWCA, or park district to inquire about classes that may be of interest to your parents.

13. Donate a pint of blood in the name of a parent anticipating surgery.

14. Help them complete the organizer contained in this book.

15. Ask the Elderhostel organization to put your parents on its mailing list. Over 250,000 people participate in Elderhostel programs each year. Maybe your parents would like to join in on the fun.

16. Buy them a National Parks Golden Passport ($10) that is available from the U.S. Parks Department and provides people 62 and over, as well as their passengers, free lifetime entrance to all the national parks.

17. For parents struggling with compiling tax returns, contact either AARP or the IRS to determine how they can get free tax-preparation assistance.

18. Help them evaluate their potential for increasing their income. Could they work; increase investment, trust, or annuity income; rent out a house that sits idle for parts of the year; or even rent out a single room in their home in return for household assistance or additional income?

19. Determine if a reverse mortgage would be appropriate for them.

20. Tell them that you love them.

Your Eldercare Team

I'm sure my parents will need some type of assistance in the future. This isn't an immediate concern, but I worry and feel unprepared to cope with the different aspects of aging. To whom can I turn for help?

Elder law attorney. An attorney who specializes in the legal aspects of entitlement programs, competency issues, and the rights of the elderly.

Estate attorney. An attorney who specializes in intergenerational or charitable asset transfers.

Friendly visitor. A volunteer who visits the elderly to provide companionship and support.

Geriatric care manager. An experienced professional with an advanced degree in health care or social services who devises treatment plans for the elderly.

Geriatric physician. A medical doctor who specializes in physical problems caused by aging.

Geriatric social worker. A licensed professional who helps seniors and/or their family make informed eldercare decisions.

Health insurance counseling and assistance program. Insurance counseling funded by the federal government but offered by individual states. Counselors answer questions about Medicare, Medicare HMOs, Medigap insurance, Medicaid, QMB, and long-term care insurance options.

Home health aide. A trained and certified individual who cares for the elderly and the terminally ill. The aide usually provides assistance to a skilled nurse and helps with medication and personal care activities. In some instances the services of a home health aide will be covered by Medicare.

Home healthcare agency. Usually a for-profit organization that specializes in offering at-home skilled nursing services, physical therapy, and home health aide services.

Homemaker services. Individuals who assist the elderly with personal care and household duties, enabling them to remain living independently in their home.

Hospital discharge planners. Social workers employed in a hospital setting who can help families arrange for ongoing home care for elderly or chronically ill patients.

Meals-on-wheels. Program that provides home-delivered meals to the disabled and elderly.

Nutritionist. A professional who assists individuals with special dietary needs.

Therapist. A trained individual who provides occupational, physical, or speech therapy.

Visiting nurse. The Visiting Nurse Association offers trained nurses who make home visits. Their services may be available under either Medicare's home health care coverage or Medicaid.

The Eldercare Locator at 800-677-1116 or your local Area Agency on Aging is a good source for identifying community-based services. Family Service of America 800-221-2681 or the National Family Caregivers Association 800-896-3650 may also be helpful. Call Eldercare America at 301-593-1621 if you're considering contacting a private organization to learn where you can attend one of its informational workshops.

Employee Assistance Programs

My parents need my help, but with a full-time job and two teenagers I have so little time to figure out the best options. Where can I turn for the help that I need?

According to a recent survey compiled by Hewitt Associates, "Eldercare programs are now being offered by nearly one-third of employers, an increase of 17 percent over the number of employers offering eldercare assistance in 1991." The most common eldercare service is a resource and referral program offered by about 80 percent of the companies who provide eldercare assistance. Flextime is offered by about 66 percent of all employers and is considered by many employees to be the best eldercare benefit currently available. About 25 percent of the companies offering eldercare assistance also offer employees the opportunity to purchase long-term care insurance, and many of these insurance programs allow employees to cover both themselves and their parents, according to Hewitt.

Experts note that eldercare has become the pioneering employee benefit of the 1990s but is evolving slowly just as child care benefits did some 15 years ago. One of the driving forces is eldercare demands hitting high-level management people where it hurts—on their appointment calendars and ultimately their company's bottom line—and thus explaining why many companies have taken significant steps to reduce the pressures of eldercare on their employees.

Corporate resource hot lines are usually manned by an outside firm that provides individualized recommendations. This is crucial as eldercare options differ dramatically from one community to the next, leaving the rookie caregiver in a quandary over where to turn for help. A referral service can help an employee locate diverse resources ranging from home health aide providers to transportation services and elder law attorneys. A study by the American Business Collaboration for Quality Dependent Care, a corporate consortium, has determined that each call to a hot line saves an individual employee about 17 hours of personal research.

Other corporate eldercare programs distribute general information to employees about various eldercare issues. Some companies offer printed materials and others workshops, seminars, and support groups led by outside professionals who specialize in eldercare issues. In order of availability, hot lines are followed by eldercare seminars, support groups, corporate-sponsored long-term care insurance, and case management services.

According to *Working Woman* magazine, the future of corporate-sponsored eldercare programs will be in the employee's backyard. More and more companies are funding community-based programs that provide assistance to those elderly who wish to remain independent. Companies are discovering that it is more effective to donate money to ongoing programs than attempt to reinvent the eldercare wheel. IBM was an early leader in this initiative and has contributed to the local development of an eldercare infrastructure serving both its employees and the community at large. The eldercare movement has also been actively supported by AT&T, which has provided millions of dollars to seed community eldercare programs, according to Vitt and Siegenthaler.

Quick Tips for Long-Distance Children

My parents live far away and I'm increasingly concerned about their situation. What can I do now that would enable me to be more effective in the future?

1. Get to know your parents' friends, advisers, neighbors, and religious leaders at their place of worship.
2. If you have never met your parents' primary physician, ask if you could stop in for a five-minute visit next time you're in town.

3. Learn where your parents go and what they do with their time. Go on a typical outing with them to become more acquainted with their daily habits.

4. Talk with them about their wishes if they can no longer live independently.

5. On the next trip home, help them complete the organizer offered in this book. It's imperative that long-distance children have a reliable, but centralized, source for locating the information they will surely need.

6. Find out where they keep the check book, their bank statements, their tax returns, and other information that would help you manage their routine bills.

7. Ask the bank that holds their mortgage, their health and life insurance carriers, and their utility provider to send you duplicates of non-payment notices.

8. If your parents don't have a durable power of attorney, ask them to set up a small joint account with a close family member or friend who could pay routine bills in the event of an emergency.

9. Ask your parents to introduce you to the mysteries of their personal filing system.

10. Have them save a copy of their old yellow pages books that you can take home for reference. When you are trying to locate services, you'd be surprised how helpful something simple like yellow pages can be.

Medical Care Fraud

My parents require several types of medical care from rehabilitation to a cardiac surgeon. I am concerned about locating qualified medical personnel and protecting them against medical abuse.

The American Board of Medical Specialties (800-776-2378) has a hot line where you can determine if a specialist is certified with an accredited board. If you are seeking a qualified general practitioner, the American Board of Internal Medicine (202-289-1700) provides referrals to board-certified internists. The American Academy of Family Practice (800-274-2278) can make referrals to a board-certified family practice physician.

Unfortunately, the elderly are far too often given only cursory medical care. The *Journal of the American Medical Association (JAMA)* has reported that up to 25 percent of the elderly have received inappropriate prescriptions. Always get a second opinion, and if your parents need a referral, call the Medicare hotline at 800-638-6833 for suggestions. If a parent is hospitalized, the hospital may offer a patient advocate who can help out. The advocate can mediate complaints and usually is knowledgeable about your parents' care options, including the right to question the hospital's discharge decision. It's really important for your parents to insist on being heard.

The elderly are at risk for many types of abuse, but the most prevalent are in the area of consumer fraud. Both the federal government and state governments have enacted significant legislation that protects all consumers and can be used to protect the elderly, who are at greater risk for exploitation than most consumers. Specific problem areas include these:

- Durable medical equipment manufacturers of such items as walkers and electric beds who misrepresent the benefits of their products and advertise them as "miracle" cures for conditions that conventional medical science is unable to treat
- Misleading hearing-aid advertising claiming benefits that can't be provided or suggesting that Medicare pays for hearing aids (Medicare typically covers a hearing test but not the cost of the medical device itself.)
- Door-to-door sales, which are covered by a three-day cooling-off period mandated by an FTC rule that sellers must let buyers know *in writing* that buyers have the right to cancel purchases within three days if an item costs more than $25. Don't let your parents be the target of unscrupulous schemes designed to dupe them out of their life savings.

Coping with a Troubled Family

My relationship with my parents is strained, making our discussions about their financial and legal affairs all the more difficult. What can you suggest for dealing with situations such as mine?

Given the nature of your relationship with your parents, you may want to use the softer, backdoor approach. Thus, you may want to start the process by offering to help them pay their routine bills, open their mail, or help organize their files. It's a small step but one that will help both you and your parents get a better handle on their affairs. Also encourage them to consolidate their affairs if their assets are spread across numerous accounts. If grandchildren are of age, suggest that the younger generation becomes involved because grandparents are usually more receptive to grandchildren.

Challenges differ depending on specific circumstances. Much of the time our parents hear what they want to hear. They may also be resistant to change, but sometimes adult children, given the dynamics of the situation, just can't be effective, no matter how hard they try. There are, however, other resources to investigate—public or private agencies in your community that are better equipped to cope with the problems than you are. And many parents are more receptive to outside intervention than to suggestions made by family members. Some of the assistance an outside agency can provide include:

- Helping parents who are having trouble adjusting to retirement
- Counseling a family that is experiencing considerable intergenerational problems
- Helping seniors who are trying to decide if they should move into a life-care community or need health care assistance
- Pleading the case of hospitalized seniors regarding bills and/or treatment procedures
- Helping to arrange the help of financial planners, insurance agents, or elder law attorneys who specialize in advising the elderly

Damned If I Do, Damned If I Don't

My parents are forever telling me how difficult it is to cope given their physical and mental limitations. But when I try to provide workable suggestions, they just ignore me. What do they want from me anyway?

It's distressing, but you must accept the idea that you can't solve all of your parents' problems as much as you'd like to. You have to set your own limits by telling yourself that a predicament created by bad planning or by ill health often creates a set of circumstances that an adult child is ill equipped to handle. An adult child can't be expected to replace a wide range of interests, pleasures, and relationships that a parent has lost. In addition, sometimes our parents' problems are intractable, creating situations that their children just can't change or solve. Everything in life could have been done better. Don't dwell on could of or should of; deal with the current reality the best you can.

In this specific case, about the only solution is to listen to your parents complain and understand that they are just trying to vent their feelings but aren't looking to you for solutions.

When to Retain an Attorney

My parents and I are in the process of getting their legal mechanisms squared away. We don't want to waste money on needless attorney's fees, but we don't want to be penny-wise and pound-foolish either. When is it appropriate to hire an attorney?

Hire a knowledgeable attorney to review your parents' documents and to suggest other techniques that may be applicable in their situation. You and your parents don't want to be frantically seeking professional advice when it's too late to take corrective action. Most government programs for the elderly offer an appeals process if coverage is denied for major claims. Given the complex nature of these programs, you should consider hiring legal counsel if the amount of money in question is considerable. And certainly always consult with your parents' attorney in the event of a crisis.

Legal Terms

My parents and I trying to get all their legal mechanisms in place, and we're working with an elder law attorney to draft the documents. But the attorney keeps using terms that confuse us, and my parents become upset after our meetings as they don't understand what the attorney is talking about. Can you help us?

The best advice is to *ask* the attorney what the phrases or words mean that you and your parents don't understand. Your parents or you are paying! But these definitions may help.

Advance directive. A legal instrument that expresses an individual's health care preferences in the event of a serious illness or incapacity. A living will and a power of attorney for health care are considered advance directives.

Do Not Resuscitate (DNR). An order signed by the attending physician with permission from the patient or the patient's agent that instructs medical workers not to revive a patient whose heart stops. Most DNRs only apply to institutional settings such as hospitals or nursing homes. But some states now allow DNRs to apply in noninstitutional settings as well, such as patients' homes.

Durable power of attorney. A legal instrument that gives an agent authority as stipulated in the document to make certain decisions on behalf of the signer until the document is revoked. The instrument remains in force from the day it is signed until revoked and continues to be valid even if the signer becomes mentally incompetent.

Durable power of attorney for health care. A legal document that names an agent to make health care decisions on behalf of the signer if the signer is unable to make his or her own decisions.

Durable power of attorney for property. A legal document that names an agent to make decisions on behalf of the signer in regard to the items noted in the document. The principal, the individual who signs the document, may execute a limited power of attorney that is limited to the time period covered, or the principal may execute a general power of attorney that extends into the future without any time limits.

Guardianship. A legal process whereby an authorized individual or institution is appointed to oversee an incompetent person's personal or legal affairs. Guardianship regulations vary greatly between states, so do consult with a local law school or bar association to learn more about the specific rules applicable to the state where your parents or other family members live.

Living will. A legal document that outlines the signer's wishes regarding care guidelines in the event of a terminal illness. Physicians risk liability if they ignore the provisions of a living will, but often physicians are not aware of a patient's wishes, or the wishes are not expressed clearly enough. Physicians who object to advance directives as a matter of conscience can refuse to honor it, but federal law mandates that if a hospital or physician refuses to carry out a patient's wishes, the patient may be transferred to another hospital.

Protective services. Programs found in almost every state to assist individuals who need help with managing their financial and personal business affairs. Individuals can seek out the services or they can be imposed through an incompetency hearing.

Representative payee. An individual, public agency, nonprofit organization, or bank that is empowered to receive and administer individuals' Social Security benefits when beneficiaries aren't able to act in their own best interest.

Springing power of attorney. A durable power of attorney effective only in the event that a principal becomes disabled.

Surrogate decision making. Refers to the codificaiton of common practice by some states that empowers certain individuals, usually in order of priority, to make decisions for an incompetent patient who has neither a living will nor a health care agent. Check with Choice in Dying or with a local attorney to ascertain the laws in your parents' state of residence if they refuse to sign an advance directive.

Trust. A legal entity created by an owner who places his or her property into the trust, legally transferring title to a trustee for the benefit of designated beneficiaries.

Roth IRA

My parents' retirement income is less than $35,000 annually but I'm wondering if switching to a Roth IRA is in their best interest. Should they convert their current IRA into a Roth IRA?

Roth IRAs are a good choice for younger Americans because the funds can be withdrawn after age 59½ tax-free. But it's questionable whether a Roth would be appropriate in this situation. Your parents' income is modest and they would reduce the size of their IRA when they switch as the entire balance becomes taxable income. The Roth may be attractive for individuals with a high net worth who don't need to spend their IRA funds, for the money continues to compound; the minimum distribution rules that apply at age 70½ don't apply to Roth IRAs. Also, those individuals with a high net worth may benefit from paying the income tax on the funds now, thereby lowering estate taxes. The World Wide Web has numerous sites offering interactive IRA conversion calculators. These are helpful tools for making an informed choice, but, in general, a Roth IRA is a more appropriate retirement planning tool for you than it is for your parents.

Social Security

My parents qualify to receive Social Security retirement benefits soon. I find it very difficult to understand exactly how the Social Security system works. Can you give me a quick overview?

Approximately 69 percent of Social Security tax dollars collected are used to pay for benefits to dependents of deceased workers and to retirees and their dependents. The Medicare trust fund takes another 19 percent and the remaining 12 percent is paid out in disability claims. Call 800-772-1213 or visit Web site www.ssa.gov and ask for a *Request for Earnings and Benefit Estimate Statement.* This report from the Social Security Administration will provide your parents with their earnings history along with estimates of retirement, disability, and death benefits. It's a good idea to order this information periodically yourself to ensure that you have been properly credited with all your earnings.

The amount of your parents' benefits will be based on the number of acquired work credits and the amount of money earned during their lifetime. Each three-month period they have worked at a job covered by Social Security entitles them to receive one work credit. Work credits don't have to be obtained sequentially; once you earn a credit it stays on your record. Most workers require 40 credits or ten years of work to qualify for full benefits.

Your benefit amount is based on your averaged earnings. The higher the average, the greater the benefit up to a maximum amount. Your parents can take early retirement at 62 and will receive a benefit that is about 20 percent less than if they had waited until 65. The normal retirement age is now 65 and will gradually increase to 67 starting in 2003. Generally, if your parents enjoy an average life expectancy, the total amount of their retirement benefits will be the same regardless of whether they start drawing their benefits at 62 or at 65. On the other hand, people who retire after 65 receive an increased benefit depending on how long they wait to claim their Social Security benefits.

Benefits are designed to increase annually based on the cost-of-living index. About 20 percent of all Social Security recipients have to pay tax on their benefits, but at the other end of the wage spectrum, the federal government offers benefits for the low-income elderly that are sometimes supplemented by individual states. The supplemental security income (SSI) program was established in 1972 to provide public aid in the form of a monthly income to the low-income aged who qualify. Contact your local Social Security office to determine if your parents are entitled to receive benefits; it's thought that as many as 1.5 million eligible low-income elderly never even apply.

Medicare

My parents qualify to receive Medicare benefits soon. I find it very difficult to understand how Medicare works. Can you give me a quick overview?

The defining issue of the 1990s has been health care. Unlike many younger Americans, at least seniors are covered by a medical plan. The federal program, Medicare, was established in 1965 and is comprised of two parts: one for inpatient coverage (Part A) and one for doctor bills, home health care, durable equipment, and other services (Part B). Enrollment for Part A is automatic for anyone who is entitled to receive Social Security retirement benefits; others may enroll by paying the monthly premium. Part B is 75 percent funded by the federal government and 25 percent by user premiums, which currently cost about $45 monthly. The premiums are usually automatically deducted from your parents' monthly Social Security check. This program is administered by the Health Care Financing Administration (HCFA).

You won't have to deal with Part A inpatient coverage very much as the benefits are paid directly to the provider unless you owe money for deductibles or copayments. Part B is another story, though, as you receive a claim form detailing the payments for each treatment. When your parents use Part B benefits, they must pay a $100 annual deductible and thereafter a 20 percent copayment for most services. Your parents are also responsible for all permissible charges in excess of Medicare's approved amount and for all charges for services and supplies that are not covered by Medicare.

To keep your costs in hand, look for providers that agree to directly participate in the Medicare reimbursement system; medical suppliers that participate agree to accept the approved amount. This means they accept what Medicare provides as payment in full, leaving your parent responsible for just the 20 percent copayment. You can obtain a free directory of participating providers from your local Medicare office.

Physicians are limited by law to charge only 115 percent of Medicare's approved amount; companies that sell medical supplies or provide ambulance services are not subject to charge limitations. Physicians or suppliers are required by law to bill Medicare directly within one year for their services. If you've paid a supplier, then the Medicare reimbursement will be sent to you directly. If you disagree with a Medicare claim decision, you have the right to appeal; your Part B form explains how to handle the problem. Most people who do appeal are successful in getting the problem resolved to their satisfaction.

Enrollment in Medicare HMOs usually removes you from the paperwork loop as claims are handled directly between the HMO and Medicare. In addition, instead of paying the deductibles and coinsurance amounts, your costs are usually limited to a monthly premium and a small service copayment. For more information about managed care plans, request a copy of the leaflet *Medicare and Managed Care Plans* from Social Security Administration office or call 800-638-6833 to request a copy.

Medicare Forms

My parents have asked me to help them decipher the paperwork they receive from Medicare. I find these forms so difficult to understand. I'm wondering where I can find some help.

Check Figure 10.1 for copies of the two forms currently used by most claims handlers. Keep these close at hand to refer to the explanations should the need arise.

Medicare Language

These Medicare forms would be easier to understand if I understood the specialized language. What do all these confusing terms really mean?

Actual charge. The amount billed by the medical provider.

Approved amount. The amount that Medicare feels a covered service is worth and pays.

Assignment. Acceptance by a physician or other medical supplier of Medicare's approved amount as payment in full.

Benefit period. The time that begins when a Medicare recipient enters the hospital and ends when he or she has been out of the hospital or other facility for 60 consecutive days. There is no limit on the number of benefit periods a beneficiary is entitled to receive, but there is a limit on the number of days Medicare will cover during each benefit period.

Coinsurance. The portion of the Medicare-approved amount that the beneficiary must pay, which is usually 20 percent under the covered Part B Medicare-approved services.

Deductible. The amount a beneficiary must pay first before Medicare starts kicking in. Part A services are subject to a per-event deductible, whereas Part B services have an annual deductible of $100.

Excess charge. The difference between Medicare's approved amount and the amount billed to the recipient.

Limiting charge. The maximum amount a supplier may bill for a given service if the physician or supplier does not accept assignment. The limiting charge

Figure

10.1

• • • • •

Explanation of Medicare Benefits

U.S. DEPARTMENT OF HEALTH AND HUMAN SERVICES/HEALTH CARE FINANCING ADMINISTRATION

1.

MEDICARE BENEFIT NOTICE

2.

DATE 3.

HEALTH INSURANCE CLAIM NUMBER
4.

←

Always use this number
when writing about your claim

THIS IS NOT A BILL

This notice shows what benefits were used by you and the covered services not paid by Medicare for the period shown in item 1. See other side of this form for additional information which may apply to your claim.

1 SERVICES FURNISHED BY	DATE(S)	BENEFITS USED
5.	6.	7.

2 PAYMENT STATUS
8.
9.
10.

If you have any questions
about this record, call
or write ▶

TELEPHONE NUMBER

FORM HCFA-1533 (12-96)

Explanation of the Medicare Benefit Notice

1. Shows Medicare has processed a claim under your Part A Hospital Insurance.

2. Shows your name and address. Always check for accuracy. Report corrections or changes as soon as possible to your health care provider and the Medicare office.

3. Shows the date your claim was processed.

4. Shows your Medicare number.

5. Shows the name and address of the hospital or skilled nursing facility that provided your services.

6. Shows the date(s) you were an inpatient of the hospital or skilled nursing facility.

7. Shows the amount and type of benefit days that you used.

8. Shows the amount for which you are responsible.

9. Shows an informational message about Medicare as secondary payer. If you have other insurance which should pay before Medicare, please let us know. We do not need to know about your supplemental (Medigap) policy.

10. Shows the name, address and telephone number of the intermediary who processed your claim.

Empire Medicare Services

P.O. Box 4846, Syracuse, New York 13221-4846

Telephone: 800-442-8430   Nassau/Suffolk (516) 244-5100

1.   YOUR RECORD OF PART B MEDICARE BENEFITS USED

IN A HOSPITAL · SKILLED NURSING FACILITY · HOME HEALTH AGENCY · PHYSICAL THERAPY PROVIDER
OR COMPREHENSIVE OUTPATIENT REHABILITATION FACILITY SERVICES

THIS IS NOT A BILL

2.

	DATE
	3.

YOUR MEDICARE NUMBER
HEALTH INSURANCE CLAIM NUMBER

4.

ALWAYS USE THIS NUMBER WHEN WRITING ABOUT YOUR CLAIM

OUR RECORDS SHOW YOU RECEIVED SERVICES FROM	PROVIDER NAME, ADDRESS AND STATE	DATE OF FIRST SERVICE
	6.	**7a.**
DOCUMENT CONTROL NUMBER		DATE OF LAST SERVICE
5.		**7b.**

TYPE OF SERVICE	BILLED CHARGES	REMARKS
8.	**9.**	**10.**

A. TOTAL BILLED CHARGES →	**11.**	
B. $ **12.** CASH DEDUCTIBLE (PART B DEDUCTIBLE APPLIED)		$ **13.** OF YOUR DEDUCTIBLE IS NOW MET
C. $ **14.** BLOOD DEDUCTIBLE (NOT TO BE APPLIED AGAINST CASH DEDUCTIBLE)		
D. $ **15.** COINSURANCE, 20% OF (A MINUS SUM OF B + C		
E. $ **16.** YOUR TOTAL RESPONSIBILITY 1.	**17.**	**18.** 2. AMOUNT YOU PAID PROVIDER
DO NOT SEND CHECKS FOR DEDUCTIBLE TO MEDICARE		**19.** 3. AMOUNT YOU OWE PROVIDER
F.		**20.** 4. AMOUNT OWED YOU (REFUND ENCLOSED)
G.		
H. BALANCE OF BILLED CHARGES	**21.**	YOU ARE NOT RESPONSIBLE FOR PAYMENT OF THE BALANCE OF THE BILLED CHARGES.

SMC 14 (12-90)

22.

Explanation of Your Record of Part B Medicare Benefits Used

1. Shows Medicare has processed a claim under your Part B Medical Insurance.

2. Shows your name and address. Always check for accuracy. Report corrections or changes as soon as possible to your health care provider and the Medicare office.

3. Shows the date your claim was processed or, if it is a duplicate copy, the date the duplicate copy was requested.

4. Shows your Medicare number.

5. Shows the unique number assigned to your claim by Medicare when your claim was processed.

6. Shows the name and address of the hospital or other provider (ESRD or Rehabilitation facility or Part B Skilled Nursing Facility) that provided your services. In some cases, you may not have been to the hospital shown. Your doctor may have referred tests performed in his or her office to the facility for processing.

7a,b. Shows the date(s) service received. If there was only one date billed, that date will be shown in both boxes.
   If there were several dates of service within a period, the start and end dates for the billing period will be shown. Some facilities bill for a month at a time. In this case, the first and last date of the month will be shown even if you did not receive services on those days.

8. Shows the service(s) provided. A patient may receive many services during a hospital visit. Only a limited number can be listed on the form. Therefore, some are grouped as "other". "Other" may include such items as ambulatory surgical care, operating room services, recovery room services and radiology services. For a more detailed explanation you can contact the Medicare office listed on your form.

9. Shows a breakdown of the charges billed to Medicare for your services. Exception—"Other" See #8 for explanation.

10. Shows informational messages. For example, if your services were diagnostic laboratory, there will be a message explaining that no deductible or coinsurance is applied to those services.

11. Shows the total charges billed to Medicare by the provider.

12. Shows the unmet portion of your yearly Part B deductible which is being applied to the charges on this claim.

13. Shows how much of your $100 Part B deductible has been met for the current calendar year. It includes any deductible applied to this claim.

14. In New York State, the American Red Cross replaces blood.

15. Shows 20% of the total billed charges subject to coinsurance.

16,17. Shows the amount for which you are responsible.

18. Shows any amount you may have paid the provider.

19. Shows the amount you owe to the provider. This amount may be paid by Medicaid or a supplemental insurer.

20. Shows any amount that is owed to you by Medicare. You will also receive a check for this amount.

21. Shows the amount considered covered by the Medicare payment.

22. Shows if your claim has been sent to a supplemental insurer for further review.

is 15 percent above the fee schedule allowed for participating physicians. Medical equipment and ambulance services are not subject to a limiting charge.

Medicaid. A federally sponsored state-run program for very low income individuals. Medicaid pays for 100 percent of all medical and nursing home expenses.

Medicare carrier. An insurance company that processes Part B claims. Carriers differ according to geographic location; their area as well as their names and addresses are spelled out in the back of *Your Medicare Handbook.*

Medicare hospital insurance. Part A coverage that helps pay for medically necessary inpatient care.

Medicare intermediary. An insurance company that processes Part A claims for inpatient care. Beneficiaries have little contact with intermediaries, which deal directly with institutions, but you will hear from your parent's intermediary if your parent owes a deductible or a copayment for care.

Medicare medical insurance. Part B insurance that pays for medically necessary doctors' services, medical supplies, and other outpatient treatments.

Participating physician or *supplier.* A medical provider that agrees to accept assignment on all Medicare claims.

Qualified Medicare beneficiary (QMB). A low-income individual who does not meet Medicaid guidelines but is entitled to receive assistance from Medicaid with Part A deductibles and Part B monthly premiums and copayments.

Medigap Insurance

My parents are about to retire and have asked me about Medigap insurance. I thought that my parents would be fully covered for all medical services when they reached 65, but I guess that's not true. How should we go about looking for additional health insurance to supplement Medicare?

Medicare does not pay the full cost of health care for the elderly. There are four basic ways to solve this problem:

1. Having corporate retiree coverage
2. Becoming a qualified Medicare beneficiary (QMB)
3. Buying Medigap insurance
4. Joining a Medicare HMO or other alternative payment system

First find out if your parents are eligible for retiree coverage or meet the income and asset limitations required by the QMB program, which is administered by the state Medicaid office. If your parents don't qualify for either of these programs, the next thing you may want to do is call the toll-free insurance-counseling hot line provided by your parents' state department of insurance.

The phone number is available from the Area Agency on Aging or from the World Wide Web at www.medicareinfo.com. Trained counselors can help you with specific questions and can also advise you about who offers Medigap insurance in your parents' state. You may also want to consult with United Seniors Health Cooperative (USHC) (www.usch-online.org) or buy your parents a subscription to the USHC newsletter, which will keep them abreast of the ever changing health care insurance landscape.

It's best to act quickly. The first six months after a parent is 65 and enrolled in Part B, he or she has the right to purchase the Medigap policy of choice regardless of any health problems. During this time your parent can't be denied coverage or suffer price discrimination as a result of health status. After that window has passed, the insurer has the right to rate the policy based on prior health history. And in most states, companies can base their decisions on medical underwriting, which gives them the right to deny coverage if they choose. Your parent also wants to understand how companies calculate the premium. Ask if premiums will increase with age, health status, or number of claims submitted.

Medigap insurance, which is limited to a choice of ten standardized plans, is specifically designed to supplement Medicare coverage. Medigap policies are characterized by letter designations ranging from A to J. A offers the most basic coverage and J the most comprehensive. Because the companies are offering the same services, they are limited to competing on service, reliability, and price. Remember that prices vary widely. In its recent survey, Weiss Ratings Inc. discovered that even in the same area the cost for the same policy ranged from $544 to $1,984 annually. Weiss sells customized comparisons of Medigap policies for $49 (800-289-9222) or consult Quotesmith at www.quotesmith.com where you can do your own research.

Basic coverage includes hospital copayments and extends the benefit period. It also pays the 20 percent coinsurance for medical expenses required by Medicare Part B recipients and the 50 percent copayment for mental health services plus the first three pints of blood yearly that Medicare doesn't cover. After that, the other policies offer additional "bells and whistles," such as the Part A hospital deductible, nursing-home copayment, Medicare Part B annual deductible, foreign travel emergency treatment, at-home recovery (maximum annual benefit $1,600), Medicare Part B excess charges, preventive screening, and outpatient prescription drugs. If your parent requires expensive prescriptions, buy the J policy as it pays 50 percent of prescription costs up to $3,000 annually after a $250 deductible is met. If your parent is vulnerable to balance billing or bills that exceed the approved amount, select G as it also provides for Part B excess charges and includes at-home recovery costs.

Get an outline of coverage that insurers are required by law to provide. Check carefully for exclusions on the basis of preexisting conditions and go slowly if you change carriers. Your parents have 30 days to cancel a policy and receive a full refund of all premiums paid if they change their minds.

Medicaid

My parents have depleted most of their assets and depend on me to pro- vide much of their support. I need to learn more about Medicaid as they need full-time nursing home care. Could you provide me with a quick overview?

Medicaid was established in 1965 and is a medical care program for low- income individuals that is jointly administered by each state and the federal government. It is a means-tested program available only to those individuals who can meet stringent income and asset limitations. Basically, you really have to be broke to qualify to receive Medicaid. Eligibility is complex and is based on state, not federal, regulations; thus, requirements vary significantly depend- ing on the jurisdiction. Coverage is automatically extended to people who are in the Aid to Dependent Children program and usually to those who receive supplemental security income (SSI), but some states have enacted statutes that make it more difficult to qualify for Medicaid than for SSI. But the good news is that if your parent does qualify for Medicaid, unlike the Medicare program almost all medical services plus ancillary costs, such as transportation assis- tance, will be covered.

Section 1924 of the Social Security Act protects against the impoverish- ment of a married person resulting from his or her spouse entering a nursing home. Federal law protects the "community spouse" from having to liquidate all assets to cover nursing-home bills. The protected amount varies by state, but generally the community spouse is allowed to keep around $80,000 in liq- uid assets such as cash or stocks (but it can go as low as $15,000 in some states) and about $2,000 of monthly income depending on specific circumstances.

Certain assets are exempt and are thus not included in Medicaid eligibil- ity computations. Exempt assets for a married couple include the marital home, regardless of its value, while the community spouse continues to reside in the home. Other exempt assets for a married couple, one of whom needs nursing home care, are an automobile and all household goods and personal effects required for daily living. If your mother is single, however, her home may not be considered an exempt asset if it's established that she will never be able to return home. The value of her car is limited to $2,500 and personal effects are capped at $2,000.

If your mother wants to protect her home, any of the following transfers are permissible: The home may be conveyed to a child who is disabled and under age 21, to a brother or sister who has some ownership interest in the home and was living with your mother for a period of at least one year immediately before she entered the nursing home, or to a caretaker son or daughter who lived with her for at least two years immediately before she entered a nursing home.

The federal government has clamped down on families seeking to give away assets to qualify for Medicaid. But there are still a few permissible strategies worth considering. The best method for protecting assets without getting into trouble is to convert nonexempt assets into exempt assets. For example, your parents have a big mortgage but also have money in the bank that would count against them. If they use their savings to pay off the mortgage, they will successfully have converted a countable asset into an exempt asset. If their mortgage is fully paid, they could use the funds to purchase a larger house or to make improvements to their existing home. Your parents could also buy a new car with their countable savings. Or, in some instances, your parents could purchase an annuity. Some desperate seniors take the extreme measure of getting divorced. An uncontested divorce awards the community spouse the house and all the nonexempt property, thereby impoverishing the institutionalized spouse and enabling him or her to qualify for Medicaid. But always get advice before you proceed as these techniques are coming under increasing scrutiny.

Middle Income Americans

My parents are among the majority of older Americans who are too wealthy to qualify for most aid programs but are far too poor to live a life that incorporates travel and expensive hobbies. I wish there is more that I could do to help them.

Let's start by looking at what younger seniors (60 through 75) can do to enhance their cash flow.

- It may be a serious mistake for your parents to consider early retirement, especially if they are eligible for a corporate pension. Corporate plans typically reduce their distributions by 6 percent for each year of early retirement.
- Make sure that a parent doesn't take a life-only distribution on his or her corporate pension as it puts the remaining spouse at substantial risk of having an impoverished old age.
- After-retirement work may be appropriate depending on the circumstances. Your parents can receive earned income up to Social Security limitations and still receive their full Social Security benefits. This income can be helpful by eliminating the need to dip into savings, by providing for long-desired travel, or by funding a Roth IRA to enhance later cash flow.
- Help your parents prepare a postretirement budget, including an analysis of the cost of living in a new community if they are considering relocation. Far too often, retirees try to "make do" when they could "make out" with additional preplanning.
- Seniors pay too much income tax. Write for *Protecting Older Americans Against Overpayment of Income Taxes* to ensure that your parents claim every legitimate deduction. Contact the Special Committee on Aging, U.S. Senate, Washington, DC 20510 for a copy.

Seniors over 75 may want to consider a reverse mortgage or use assets hidden in a life insurance policy to create additional cash flow. It would also be a wise idea to help them see if they qualify for additional income through SSI or the QMB program, which helps with Medicare premiums, deductibles, and copayments.

Resources

Books

Barnett, Terry James. *Living Wills and More.* New York: John Wiley, 1992.

Brody, Elaine M. *Women in the Middle: Their Parent Care Years.* New York: Springer, 1990.

Cohen, Stephen Z. *The Other Generation Gap: The Middle-Aged and Their Aging Parents.* New York: Dodd Mead, 1988.

Commerce Clearing House. *What Every Senior Citizen Ought to Know.* Chicago: Commerce Clearing House, 1993.

Cutler, Neal E., Davis Gregg, and M. Powell Lawton. *Aging, Money, and Life Satisfaction.* New York: Springer, 1992.

Daly, Eugene J. *Thy Will Be Done: A Guide to Wills, Taxation, and Estate Planning for Older Persons.* Amherst, NY: Prometheus Books, 1994.

Downing, Neil. *Maximize Your IRA.* Chicago: Dearborn Financial Publishing, 1997.

Downs, Hugh. *Fifty to Forever.* Nashville: Thomas Nelson, 1994.

Edinberg, Mark A. *Talking with Your Aging Parents.* Boston: Shambhala, 1987.

Eisenberg, Richard, ed. *The Money Book of Personal Finance.* New York: Warner Books, 1996.

Estes, Carroll L., and James H. Swan. *The Long-Term Care Crisis: Elders Trapped in the No-Care Zone.* Newbury Park, NJ: Sage Publications, 1993.

Evans, Eve, and Alan Fox. *Tax Heaven or Hell.* Houston: Vacation Publications, 1996.

Fadia, Vijay. *Protect Your Assets from the Catastrophic Costs of Nursing Home Care.* Torrance, CA: Homestead Publishing, 1994.

Feldesman, Walter. *Dictionary of Eldercare Terminology.* Washington, DC: United Seniors Health Cooperative, 1997.

Ernst and Young. *Ernst & Young's Total Financial Planner.* New York: John Wiley, 1996.

Fisher, Roger, and Danny Ertel. *Getting Ready to Negotiate: The Getting to Yes Workbook.* New York: Penguin Books, 1995.

Fisher, Roger, and William Ury. *Getting to Yes: Negotiation Agreement without Giving In.* 2d ed. New York: Houghton Mifflin, 1991.

Greenberg, Vivian E. *Children of a Certain Age: Adults and Their Aging Parents.* New York: Lexington Books, 1993.

Goetz, Jason. *Long-Term Care.* Chicago: Dearborn Financial Publishing, 1997.

Gruber, Joan M. *Your Money: It's a Family Affair.* Dallas: Odenwald Books, 1996.

Hallman, Victor G., and Jerry S. Rosenbloom. *Personal Financial Planning.* New York: McGraw-Hill, 1993

Heath, Angela. *A Survival Guide for Far Away Caregivers.* San Luis Obispo, CA: America Source Books, 1995.

Hughes, Theodore E. *J. K. Lasser's Consumer Guide to Protecting and Preserving Everything You Own.* New York: Macmillian, 1996.

Liber, Phyllis, Gloria Murphy, and Annette Meikur Schwartz. *Stop Treating Me Like a Child, But First, Can You Lend Me Some Money?* Secaucus, NJ: Carol Publishing, 1995.

Logan, John, and Glenna D. Spitz. *Family Ties: Enduring Relations Between Parents and Their Grown Children.* Philadelphia: Temple University Press, 1996.

McLean, Andrew James. *How to Retire on the House.* Chicago: Contemporary Books, 1990.

Morris, Virginia. *How to Care for Aging Parents.* New York: Workmen Publishing, 1996.

Moskowitz, Francine, and Robert Moskowitz. *Parenting Your Aging Parents.* Woodland Hills, CA: Key Publications, 1992.

National Institute on Aging. *Resource Directory for Older People.* Gaithersburg, MD: National Institute on Aging, 1996.

Regan, John J., and Michael Gilfx. *Tax, Estate and Financial Planning for the Elderly: Forms and Practice.* New York: Matthew Bender, 1996.

Rusk, Tom, M.D. *The Power of Ethical Persuasion: From Conflict to Partnership at Work and in Private Life.* New York: Viking Press, 1993.

Rolick, Karen Ann. *Living Trusts and Simple Ways to Avoid Probate: With Forms.* Naperville, IL: Sourcebooks, 1998.

Savageau, David. *Retirement Places Rated.* New York: Macmillan Travel, 1995.

Schaffzin, Nicholas Reed. *Don't Be a Chump!: Negotiating Skills You Need.* New York: Random House, 1995.

Schlesinger, Sanford J. and Barbara J. Scheiner. *Planning for the Elderly or Incapacitated Client.* Chicago: Commerce Clearing House, 1993.

Scholen, Ken. *Home-Made Money: Consumer's Guide to Home Equity Conversion.* Washington, DC: American Association of Retired Persons, 1996.

Scholen, Ken. *Your New Retirement Nest Egg: A Consumer Guide to the New Reverse Mortgages.* Apple Valley, MN: NCHEC Press, 1996.

Schomp, Virginia. *The Aging Parent Handbook.* New York: Harper Paperbacks, 1997.

Shane, Darlene V. *Finances after 50: Financial Planning for the Rest of Your Life.* New York: Harper Perennial Library, 1993.

Sheehy, Gail. *New Passages: Mapping Your Life Across Time.* New York: Random House, 1995.

Skala, Ken. *American Guidance for Seniors. . . . And Their Caregivers.* Falls Church, VA: Key Communications, 1997.

Solomon, David, Elyse Salend, and Anna Nolen Rahman. *A Consumer's Guide to Aging.* Baltimore: Johns Hopkins University Press, 1992.

Strauss, Peter J. and Nancy M. Lederman. *The Elder Law Handbook: A Legal and Financial Guide for Caregivers and Senior.* New York: Facts on File, 1996.

Susik, Helen. *Hiring Home Caregivers: The Family Guide to In-Home Eldercare.* San Luis Obispo, CA: Impact Publications, 1995.

Swartz, Melvin Jay. *Retire without Fear: Your Guide to Financial Security.* Chicago: Dearborn Financial Publishing, 1994.

Ury, William. *Getting Past No: Negotiating Your Way from Confrontation to Co-operation.* New York: Bantam Books, 1993.

Vitt, Lois, Ph.D., and Jurg Siegenthaler, Ph.D. *Encyclopedia of Financial Gerontology.* Westport, CT: Greenwood Press, 1996.

Westhem, Andrew D., and Donald Jay Korn. *Protecting What's Yours: How to Safeguard Your Assets and Maintain Your Personal Wealth.* New York: Carol Communications, 1995

Newspapers, Magazine, and Journal Articles; Studies; Monographs; Booklets; and Newsletters

American Association of Retired Persons. *AARP Publications & A/V Programs.* Washington, DC: 1998.

American Association of Retired Persons. *Look Before You Leap: A Guide to Early Retirement Incentive Programs,* 1994.

Asinof, Lynn. "Putting Your Finances in Order Also May Mean Putting Your Folks in Order as Well." Personal Finance Section, *Wall Street Journal,* Internet ed. (December 1, 1997).

"Beyond Medicare: New Choices in Health Insurance," *New York Times* Internet ed. (August 10, 1997).

Boyd, Malcolm. "The Top Ten." *Modern Maturity* (March–April 1998): 72.

"Budget Bill Medicare Clauses Offer New Options and Fears." *The Wall Street Journal,* Internet ed. (August 13, 1997).

Capell, Kerry. "Your Parents are Ailing. Now What?" *Business Week* (April 15, 1996): 116.

Clements, Jonathan. "Retired and Running Low on Savings? Here Are Some Ideas to Bridge the Gap." *The Wall Street Journal* (May 6, 1997): C1.

————. "Keeping Finances Simple Isn't Easy but These 22 Strategies Should Help." *The Wall Street Journal* (June 3, 1997): C1.

Chambers, Nancy. "Where to Turn for Help." *Working Woman* (June 1995): 49.

Chen, David. "Caring for Aged Parents." *New York Times* (April 18, 1997), p. B5.

Cutler, Neal E. Ph.D. "Where Do You Look for Help?" 48 *Journal of the American Society of CLU & ChFC* (1994): 38–41.

Cutler, Neal E. Ph.D. "Financial Literacy 2000." *Journal of the American Society of CLU & ChFC* (July 1996).

Deloitte & Touche. "New Year's Resolutions to Organize Personal Finances." *CPA Journal* (March 1997): 12.

Equitable Foundation. *Aging Parents and Common Sense* (New York: Equitable Foundation, 1994).

Fidelity Investments. *Perspective* (Financial Management Issue, Spring 1998).

"For the Wealthy, Death Is More Certain Than Taxes," *The New York Times* Internet ed. (Dec. 22, 1996).

Furchgott, Roy. "Rescuing a Relative Who Won't Accept Help: A Personal Effort That Took a Turn Off Course." *New York Times* (August 10, 1997), p. F1.

Gladstone, Jodi. "Services and Support for Seniors." *Arizona Daily Star and Tucson Citizen* Supplement (February 20, 1998), pp. 49–50.

Gordon, Derek. "Is Retirement Number Crunching Making You Feel Old Already? Our Sites Will Do the Work for You." *Money* (July 1997), p. 39.

Health Care Financing Administration. *Your Medicare Handbook 1998* (Washington, DC: GPO, 1997).

Hewitt Associates. *Work and Family Benefits Provided by Major U.S. Employers in 1996: Based on Practices of 1,050 Employees.* (Lincolnshire, IL: Hewitt Associates, 1997).

"How to Live to Be 100." *Newsweek* (June 30, 1997), pp. 56–67.

Juhl, Marian H. "A Tatoo in Time." *Newsweek* (October 13, 1997).

Katt, Peter. "Coordinating Estate Planning and Life Insurance." *AAII Journal* (April 1995).

———. "Gift Planning and the Use of Life Insurance." *AAII Journal* (August 1997).

Kuhn, Susan. "Dealing with Your Parents' Finances." *Fortune* (September 30, 1996), pp. 274–75.

Metropolitan Life Insurance Company. *The MetLife Study of Employer Costs for Working Caregivers* (Bethesda, MD: National Alliance for Caregiving, 1997).

National Alliance for Caregiving and American Association of Retired Persons. *Family Caregiving in the United States* (June 1997).

National Association of Insurance Commissioners and the Health Care Financing Administration. *1998 Guide to Health Insurance for People With Medicare* (1997).

National Retirement Income Policy Committee. *National Retirement Income Research Papers: Income Replacement in Retirement* (American Society of Pension Actuaries, 1994).

National Public Radio. "Inheritances by Adult Children," *All Things Considered* (May 12, 1997).

Phoenix Home Life Corporation. *1997 Phoenix Fiscal Fitness Survey.* www.phl.com.

Rogers, Doug. "Retirement Needs Underestimated, Poll Finds." *Investor's Business Daily* (February 24, 1997), p. B3.

Roha, Ronaleen. "Medigap: One Size Doesn't Fit All." *Kiplinger Online* (January, 1998).

"Reverse Mortgages." *Consumer Reports* (July 1995) Internet ed.

Schellenbarger, Sue. "More Family Members Are Working Together to Care for Elders." *The Wall Street Journal* (July 23, 1997), p. B1.

Stettner, Morey. "Pennies from Heaven." *Worth* (July/August, 1996): 114.

Topolnicki, Denise M. "How to Care for Aging Parents Without Going Broke." *Money* (May 1996): 128.

U.S. Department of the Treasury. *Household Employer's Tax Guides,* Publication #926 (Washington, DC: GPO, 1997).

U.S. Department of the Treasury, Internal Revenue Service. *Your Federal Income Tax* (Publication 17) (Washington, DC: GPO, 1997).

Wagner, Donna, Ph.D. *Comparative Analysis of Caregiver Data for Caregivers to the Elderly 1987 and 1997* (Bethesda, MD: National Alliance for Caregiving, 1997).

Warren, Larkin. "Survival Lessons: A Writer Passes Along the Emotional Insights Gained While Caring for Her Ailing Mother." *Working Woman* (June 1995): 46.

Willis, Clint. "Mind over Money." *Working Woman* (February 1995): 30.

———. "When to Talk about Money." *Working Woman* (June 1995): 42.

"Why Having a Living Will Is Not Enough." *Kiplinger Online* (Nov. 1997).

Index